D0852681

One Report

One Report

Integrated Reporting for a Sustainable Strategy

Robert G. Eccles
Michael P. Krzus

John Wiley & Sons, Inc.

Published by John Wiley & Sons, Inc., Hoboken, New Jersey.
Published simultaneously in Canada.

For general information on our other products and services, or for technical support, please contact our Customer Care Department within the United States at (800) 762-2974, outside the United States at (317) 572-3993 or via fax at (317) 572-4002.

Wiley also publishes its books in a variety of electronic formats. Some content that appears in print may not be available in electronic books. For more information about Wiley products, visit our Web site at www.wiley.com.

Library of Congress Cataloging-in-Publication Data

Eccles, Robert G.
One report : integrated reporting for a sustainable strategy / Robert G. Eccles, Michael P. Krzus.
p. cm.
Includes bibliographical references and index.
ISBN 978-0-470-58751-5 (cloth)
1. Corporation reports. 2. Social responsibility of business. 3. Sustainability.
I. Krzus, Michael P. II. Title.
HG4028.B2E23 2010
658.1–dc22

2009046297

Printed in the United States of America.

10 9 8 7 6 5 4 3 2 1

Contents

Foreword

It was many years ago I first heard the optimistic adage "you do well by doing good." Back then, advocates of so-called Corporate Social Responsibility were trying to make a business case for good corporate behavior. Few were persuaded.

The main reason for lack of success in winning support for the "being good," is that the adage was not true. Many companies did well by being bad. Creative accounting, unfair labor practices, corporate secrecy, monopolistic behaviors, externalizing costs, and shady environmental behaviors could help beef up the bottom line. Not to mention that corporate executives themselves could "do well" by paying astronomical bonuses, even while their companies were struggling.

But today all this is changing.

The collapse of the financial system and the global economic crisis of 2009 were a wake-up call to the world. It's become clear that business can't succeed in a world that is failing. We need to rethink and rebuild many of the organizations and institutions of the past around a new set of principles and behaviors.

In fact, the crisis and its aftereffects represent more than a recession. It is a punctuation point in history. Arguably many of the pillars of economic and social life have come to the end of their life cycle. The financial services industry, for example, needs more than a fresh infusion of capital or some new regulations; it needs a whole new operating model. Our transportation system, based on the internal combustion engine, is changing the earth's climate. There is no challenge more important than creating a green energy grid and a reindustrialization of the planet for sustainability. The American auto industry, once the epitome of the industrial economy, has collapsed. As companies in other sectors cut their costs to stay alive, many began to see that hunkering down, while necessary, was insufficient for success. From manufacturing to retail, smart managers have begun to initiate long-overdue changes to their structures and strategies. There is a growing appreciation that "conventional wisdom" isn't going to cut it for success in this century. We need to reinvent our institutions.

At the same time, an old force with new power is rising in business, one that has far-reaching implications for most everyone. Nascent for half a century, this force has quietly gained momentum through the last decade and is now triggering profound changes across the corporate world. Evidence suggests firms that embrace this force and harness its power will thrive. Those who ignore or oppose it will suffer.

The force is *transparency*.

Globalization, instant communications, organized civil society—and now a crisis in trust, have changed the rules of the game. Firms are being held to complex and changing sets of standards—from unrelenting webs of "stakeholders" who pass judgment on corporate behavior—to regulations, new and old, that govern and often complicate everyday activities. In an ultra-transparent world of instant communications, every step and misstep is subject to scrutiny. And every company with a brand or reputation to protect is vulnerable.

Customers can evaluate the worth of products and services at levels not possible before. Employees share formerly secret information about corporate strategy, management, and challenges. To collaborate effectively, companies and their business partners have no choice but to share intimate knowledge with one another. Powerful institutional investors today own or manage most wealth, and they are developing X-ray vision. Finally, in a world of instant communications, whistleblowers, inquisitive media, and Googling, citizens, NGOs, and communities routinely put firms under the microscope.

I've produced a few "studies in bad timing" in my life. One stellar example was a book I co-authored with the brilliant business strategist David Ticoll: *The Naked Corporation: How the Age of Transparency Will Revolutionize Business.* As people researching how technology changes things, we became interested in how the Internet would change the use and communication of information. We defined transparency as "access to pertinent information by stakeholders." By "pertinent," we meant information that can help if you have it and hurt if you don't.

It's been almost a decade since the book hit the streets. We argued that the corporation is becoming naked, and as a result will have no choice but to rethink values and behaviors—for the better. Our tag line was "You're going to be naked, so you'd better be buff!" Reviewers either loved the book or hated it. Sales were modest. My deepest regret, in hindsight, was that clearly the book was not read and heeded by the leaders of our financial services industries. Lacking "fitness," they brought down the industry and with it the global economy.

To paraphrase Victor Hugo, there is nothing so powerful as an idea whose time has come—again. To build trusting relationships and succeed in a transparent economy, growing numbers of firms in all parts of the globe are being forced to behave more responsibly than ever. Disgraced banks represent the old model—a dying breed. Business integrity is on the rise, not just for legal or purely ethical reasons but because it makes economic sense. Companies need to do good—act with integrity—not just to secure a healthy business environment, but for their own sustainability and competitive advantage. Firms that exhibit ethical values, openness, and candor have discovered that they can be more competitive and more profitable. Institutional investors who practice these behaviors will be more sustainable themselves and NGOs that do the same will increase their impact on the causes they care about.

Further, today's winners increasingly undress for success. Our research suggests that open corporations perform better. Transparency is a new form of power, which pays off when harnessed. Rather than to be feared, transparency is becoming central to business success. Rather than be stripped unwillingly, smart firms are choosing to be open. Over time, what we call open enterprises—firms that operate with candor, integrity, and engagement—are most likely to survive and thrive. And any bank executives who think they can return to the old ways are mistaken. In the new business environment firms *will* do well by doing good.

Which is why I'm so excited about the publication of *One Report*.

"How can anyone be excited about corporate reporting," you might ask?

Fair enough—in the past, the typical annual report was a pretty bland and limited way of communicating with shareholders and other stakeholders. It was historical, focusing on the past. It was a static document, produced on paper and prohibiting the reader from further exploration or analysis. It dealt primarily with financial information. While essential, financial data alone did not convey a comprehensive picture of corporate health. It was opaque—often the more detailed data, the more difficult it was to understand. There was little nonfinancial information necessary to provide a clear view on current performance and enable more accurate predictions regarding future prospects. It was separate from the company's "Corporate Social Responsibility" or "Sustainability" report, relegating these documents to minor status and preventing the integration of information about critical topics such as risk. Because the report was paper, it was an island—not linked to other pertinent data and information that might help a stakeholder understand the company or an executive manage it more effectively.

Measuring and reporting nonfinancial information has become important for reasons other than valuation. Because of the huge changes happening in the global economy and every industry, and the challenges of rebuilding society for the 21st century, nonfinancial aspects of performance have implications beyond boards, auditors, audit committees, and investors. It's time to acknowledge that firms do have stakeholders, who have a legitimate, important, and overall healthy interest in the breadth, veracity, and integrity of corporate performance and behavior. Thus, directors and managers find themselves in a vastly more complex environment, increasingly accountable to and influenced by multiple stakeholders and pressured from all sides for better reporting on corporate health and behavior.

As a result, boards of directors are facing rising expectations in corporate reporting, but many directors feel they lack effective tools to deliver. Directors are spending more time and are asking more questions. Managers are all but exhausted trying to provide relevant information in a form directors and others can digest. Everyone is working harder, but it's not clear that we're any wiser for their efforts.

The bottom line is that shareholders, board members, regulators, employees, customers, journalists, and other stakeholders have had a very limited view of the corporation. The irresistible force of transparency has met the immovable object of an outdated and even dangerous model of reporting. Exhibit A? The world could not foresee the impending collapse of the financial services industry.

It's time for a change in reporting. It's time for "One Report," as defined by Eccles and Krzus. We need a comprehensive, networked, real-time, living-and-breathing system that, through integrated reporting, provides a single version of the truth to all concerned parties, inside and out. When viewed in this context, rethinking reporting is not a bore—it is at the very heart of the success and survival of companies and even our economy.

The good news is that the digital revolution has matured to the point where this is possible. Dubbed the Web 2.0, the Internet has evolved from a network of Web sites that enable organizations to simply present information. It is now a computing platform in its own right. Elements of a computer—and elements of a computer program—can be spread out across the Internet and seamlessly combined as necessary. The Internet is becoming a giant computer that everyone can program—providing a global infrastructure for creativity, participation, sharing, and self-organization.

When all companies share a global computer with all stakeholders, there is new world of possibilities for positive transparency and engagement while at the same time appropriately protecting intellectual property, legitimate corporate secrets, and the privacy of individuals.

I can say with confidence that there are no two better people in the world to lay out the future of reporting than Bob Eccles and Mike Krzus. Over the years, I have been inspired by their vision and tireless attempts to bring about better transparency, corporate governance, and business performance through better reporting. It is in part because of their leadership that the reporting landscape is changing, not just in theory but in practice. As you will read, there are a number of powerful examples of companies doing exactly what Eccles and Krzus have been advocating for years.

If you want your company to succeed and be trusted, you should read this book. If you are a person with integrity, the book will be music to your ears. If you want to live a principled life of consequence, please read this book and act on its recommendations for how integrated reporting can be adopted as broadly and rapidly as possible.

For the expanding global economy and our shrinking and increasingly fragile planet, the stakes are very high that we get this right.

DON TAPSCOTT

Don Tapscott is the co-author of 13 books about technology in business and society, most recently Grown Up Digital: How the Net Generation Is Changing Your World. *His upcoming book (with Anthony D. Williams) is working titled* Rebuilding the World. *He is Chairman of the think tank nGenera Insight.*

Acknowledgments

In writing this book, we were fortunate to have the support of four extremely capable research associates. This book could not have been written without Susan Thyne, a full-time research associate at the Harvard Business School. We are deeply grateful to her for her hard work and good humor throughout an intense project. Susan did most of the key library research and is one of the toughest and most capable editors we have ever met. Every single chapter bears the stamp of her rigorous mind and insistence on clear exposition. She also made important substantive contributions to Chapter 5. Kyle Armbrester also provided extremely valuable input through online research and his knowledge of the Internet, doing this on his own time while holding down a full-time job as a freelance IT strategy consultant and project leader at The Exeter Group. In particular, we could not have written Chapter 7 without him, but he helped in many other ways as well. Akiko Kanno of Harvard Business School's Japan Research Center was instrumental in writing the Ricoh example and served as an effective bridge between two cultures while having to do extra translations as well. Dilyana Karadzhova was extremely helpful just when we needed an extra pair of hands by jumping in toward the end, even as she was starting her senior year at

Harvard College, and teaming up effectively with Kyle on Chapter 7. Finally, we want to thank our editor at Wiley, Tim Burgard, for his assistance and encouragement—and required good humor at times—during the intense period of writing this book.

The content of this book was heavily influenced by what for us turned out to be two important meetings. The first was at Saint James's Palace on September 11, 2009, and is described more fully in Chapter 1. As a result of this meeting, we were forced to sharpen our ideas, and the first and last chapters were dramatically changed. That said, we bear sole responsibility for their content and the book as a whole. This meeting also increased our sense of urgency about the need for integrated reporting and gave us some needed energy to finish the book upon our return to Boston. Attending this meeting were Roger Adams, Wim Bartels, Trevor Bowden, Paul Druckman, John Elkington, Jessica Fries, Deborah Gilshan, Alan Knight, Claudia Kruse, Ernst Ligteringen, Alan McGill, Sir Mark Moody Stuart, Pavan Sukhdev, John Swannick, Mike Wallace, and Will Webster, all of whom we want to thank again for taking time out of their busy lives.

The second key meeting was held on August 6, 2009, at the Harvard Business School and we want to thank Marcy Murninghan for getting it organized. Chapter 7 would not exist without this meeting, because it was here that we finally broke through our own "paper paradigm" and realized that the Internet is at the core of integrated reporting. Attending this meeting were Bill Baue, Steve Lydenberg, Caroline Rees, Allen White, and Stone Wiske. We thank them as well for taking the time to help us see the light here.

Like all books, this one went through many drafts, and we benefited from the insights and constructive criticism of a number of people who read earlier drafts of chapters, sometimes several times. Our thanks here go to Peter DeSimone, Sean Gilbert, Bob Herz, Bob Kaplan, Ernst Ligteringen, Marcy Murninghan, Karen Myers, Bob Pozen, Jeff Williams, Mike Willis, and Joe Zhou.

In doing the research for this book, we conducted a large number of interviews. In many cases, these resulted in content for the book, reflected in the quotes it contains. We want to thank all of these people and the organizations they represent for sharing their ideas and making ours better: Mikako Awano, V. Balakrishnan, Mike Barry, Scott Bolick, Helmut Bossert, Luiz Fernando de Araujo Brandao, Matt Christensen, Eric Cohen, Srikant Datar, Jean-Philippe Desmartin, Harris Diamond, Andrea Doane, Philippa Gibson Eccles, James Engell, James Farrar, Marc Fox, Ralf Frank, Michael Fuerst, Leslie Gaines-Ross, Emilio Galli Zugaro, Sean Gilbert, Lois Guthrie, Rodolfo Guttilla, Ivan Herman, Paul Hodgson, Beth Holzman, Carsten Ingerslev, Frank Janssen, Helle Bank Jorgensen, Bob Kaplan, Rakesh Khurana, Michael Kimbrough, Mervyn King, Steve Lewis, Shiro Kondo, Ernst Ligteringen, Jay Lorsch, Mindy Lubber, Christoph Lueneburger, Steve Lydenberg, Bob Massie, Brendan May, Bill McAndrews, James McCarthy, Gunnar Miller, Zenji Miura, Rachael Morgan, John Moran, Mary Morris, Hibachi Moriyama, Filipe Moura, Dorje Mundle, Shima Nakao, Rusty Nelligan, Bob Pozen, Curtis Ravenel, Nick Ridehalgh, Carlos Alberto de Oliveira Roxo, Kiyoshi Sakai, Rick Samans, Thomas Scheiwiller, Volker Seidl, Anne Simpson, Susanne Stormer, Francis Sullivan, Tatsuo Tani, Gary Turkel, Shehei Ura, Klaas van den Berg, Eric von Hippel, Sarah Weber, Allen White, Jon Williams, Mike Willis, Lisa Woll, and Joe Zhou.

The Harvard Business School was an important source of intellectual, moral, and financial support. Robert Eccles would like to thank Dean Jay Light, Senior Associate Dean and Director of Research Srikant Datar, Organizational Behavior Unit Head David Thomas, and Senior Associate Dean for Planning and University Affairs Peter Tufano. In addition, Professors Bharat Anand, Michel Anteby, Lynda Applegate, Joe Badaracco, Julie Battilana, Mike Beer, Roy Chua, Tom DeLong, Alnoor Ebrahim, Amy Edmondson, Tom Eisenmann, Nabil El-Hage, Robin Ely, Ben Esty, Jack Gabarro, Heidi Gardner, Dave Garvin, Ray Gilmartin, Boris Groysberg, Ranjay Gulati, Jan Hammond, Paul Healy, Rebecca Henderson, Linda Hill, Marco Iansiti, Bob Kaplan, Rob Kaplan, Carl Kester, Rakesh Khurana, Rajiv Lal, Paul Lawrence, Deishin Lee, Dutch Leonard, Jay Lorsch, Josh Margolis, Chris Marquis, Warren McFarlan, Kathleen McGinn, Bob Merton, Das Narayandas, Tsedal Neeley, Nitin Nohria, Felix Oberholzer-Gee, Lynn Paine, Krishna Palepu, Andre Perold, Leslie Perlow, Jeff Polzer, Bob Pozen, John Quelch, Kash Rangan, Forest Reinhardt, Clayton Rose, Rick Ruback,

Bill Sahlman, Jim Sebenius, Sandra Sucher, David Thomas, Mike Toffel, Norm Wasserman, Julie Wulff, and David Yoffie have all been wonderful colleagues, and he is delighted to be back with them again.

Two accounting firms also provided important financial and intellectual support. PricewaterhouseCoopers (PwC) has been a leader in improving corporate reporting for many years, and Robert Eccles has had the privilege of working with a number of people there, including some as co-authors on previous books. A number of PwC partners and employees were extremely helpful in writing this book. We couldn't possibly list all of the people at PwC who, in the past and the present, contributed to the ideas in the book, but here we want to acknowledge Eric Cohen, Fred Cohen, Sam DiPiazza, Miles Everson, William Gee, Fred Gertsen, Craig Hamer, Joe Herron, Helle Bank Jorgensen, Arco ten Klooster, Fritz Litjens, Gary Meltzer, Bob Moritz, Rusty Nelligan, Tim Padgett, David Phillips, Malcolm Preston, Bob Rees, Nick Ridehalgh, Thomas Scheiwiller, Alison Thomas, Klaas van den Berg, Jon Williams, Mike Willis, and Nora Wu. Mr. Eccles would also like to personally thank Juan Pujadas for many interesting conversations and for his support and friendship for many years.

Michael Krzus would like to thank his partners and colleagues at Grant Thornton for supporting his work on many initiatives to improve business reporting. In particular, he wants to acknowledge the support of Ed Nusbaum, Stephen Chipman, and Trent Gazzaway during the months spent researching and writing this book. A thank you is also extended to Bridgette Hodges, Gina Kim, Kristen Malinconico, and Susan Jones for their assistance with Chapters 2 and 3. Michael Krzus is especially grateful to Mike Starr for giving him the opportunity and freedom to try to help shape the future of the accounting profession.

Many organizations, listed in Appendix A, contributed to this book. We would like to single out the Global Reporting Initiative, including its founders Bob Massie and Allen White, and current staff including Teresa Fogelberg, Sean Gilbert, Ernst Ligteringen, Leontien Plugge, Randy Thym, Mike Wallace, and Joris Wiemer for help and insights through the book writing process.

Many others helped us with this book, and here we want to thank Eric Baggesen, Viraal Basari, Doug Bannerman, Martin Bennett,

Rob Berridge, Laura Berry, Daniel Beunza, Edward Bickham, Susan Blesener, Mike Blumstein, Sheila Bonini, Mark Bromley, Barbara Evans, Frank Curtiss, Judith Czelusniak, Driek Desmet, Robin Edme, Fabrizio Ferraro, Hendrick Garz, Richard Gaul, Robin Giampa, Sara Greene, Antony Henshaw, Bozena Jankowska, Lars Göran Johansson, Anne Kelly, Ellen Kennedy, Matt Kiernan, Peter Knight, Bala Krishnamoorthy, Cary Krosinki, Judy Kuszewski, Lance Lau, Peter Laurent, Christian Lawrence, Rick Love, Ray Madden, Bill McGrew, Tor Mesoy, Bob Monks, Sophia Munoz, Herman Mulder, Jane Nelson, Mohandas Pai, Simon Propper, Anjali Raina, Gargi Ray, David Russell, James Salo, Eliott Saltzman, Judy Sandford, Roland Schatz, Torsten Schuessler, Tim Smith, Peggy Smyth, Richard Spencer, John Stantial, Dan Summerfield, Raj Thamotheram, Folkert van der Molen, Paul Vitello, Claudia Volk, Mark Wade, Lara Warner, Liv Watson, Toby Webb, Richard Wells, Hugh Wheelan, Mike Wing, and David Wood.

Finally, and most importantly, we want to thank our wives, Anne Laurin Eccles and Marilyn Mueller Krzus, for their love, patience, and support while we wrote this book. It has been an intense experience in which we were often mentally absent even when physically present. But now that the book is done, we look forward to spending more time with them and talking about something other than *One Report*.

Introduction

In September 2009, the time of this writing, the financial market crisis of late 2008 appears to be receding—perhaps too quickly for some important lessons to be learned—although it also appears that the economic recovery will take a much longer time. In an important speech on financial reform, President Barack Obama said, "Unfortunately, there are some in the financial industry who are misreading this moment. Instead of learning the lessons of Lehman and the crisis from which we are recovering, they are choosing to ignore them. They do so not just at their own peril, but at our nation's."[1] At this same time, the 2009 United Nations Climate Conference, to be held in Copenhagen, is less than three months away, and the general consensus is that this crisis is much bigger than the financial crisis and failure to address it soon will have more than cyclical consequences. Some believe it is already too late and that future generations will bear the cost of our inaction. Again quoting President Obama, "Few challenges facing America—and the world—are more urgent than combating climate change. The science is beyond dispute and the facts are clear."[2] On September 16, 2009, a global group of 181 investment institutions representing assets of $13 trillion

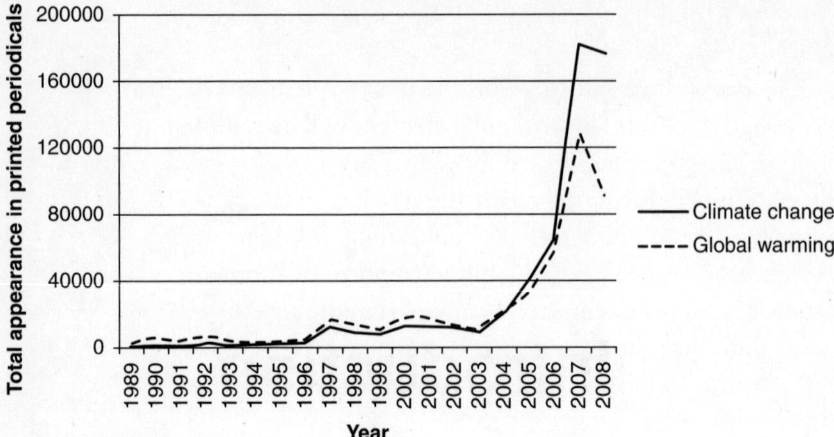

Exhibit I.1 Increasing Use of the Terms *Climate Change* and *Global Warming*, 1989–2008*

*We produced all of our "Increasing Use of the Term" figures using the Dow Jones Factiva database to measure the frequency with which the terms in question were used in all of the publications included in the database.

issued a statement in support of the Copenhagen meeting and stated that "private capital is essential to achieving the transformation to a low-carbon economy" and observed that "climate risks and opportunities may have significant financial implications for individual companies and may therefore affect the performance of investment portfolios."[3]

Evidence of the growing public concern about *climate change* and *global warming* is shown in Exhibit I.1. The graphical lines based on simple word counts in a database of news publications show that the mention of these two terms increased exponentially in 2004. James J. McCarthy, professor at Harvard University and former Intergovernmental Panel on Climate Change working group co-chair, noted, "in 2000, the science matured, and it became clear that in a warmer world there will be climate impact on all continents. There are vulnerabilities everywhere, and there will be losers in every country and every region."[4] As the consensus in the scientific community spread into society at large, awareness about climate change started to increase; the slope increased dramatically in 2004, the year of the U.S. presidential election, in which this was a prominent issue. The curve steepened again in 2006, when Al Gore's film *An Inconvenient Truth* came out, as did *The Stern Review on the*

Economics of Climate Change, a 700-page report released on October 30, 2006.[5]

It seems clear that the world is at a crossroads in dealing with these crises and that some fundamental changes will be required to shift course in a meaningful way. The underlying motivation for this book is our belief that more integrated reporting is a key part of the solution. Today, more and more companies are publishing voluntary "Corporate Social Responsibility" or "Sustainability" reports to supplement their annual reports, which contain the financial statements that every listed company must file. In most cases, there is very little linkage between the information published in these separate reports. To have a real impact, these separate reports need to be integrated with each other, thereby demonstrating that the company has a sustainable strategy based on a commitment to corporate social responsibility that is contributing to a sustainable society that takes into account the needs of all stakeholders, of which shareholders are one type. If attention to environmental, social, and governance (ESG) performance is integrated into basic business processes, then what is the logic for producing separate financial and nonfinancial reports?

The reverse logic also holds. One mechanism for creating sustainable strategies for a sustainable society is for companies to commit to more integrated external reporting. As they work to do this, they will locate any gaps in embedding sustainability into the company's strategy and operations and will be motivated to correct the situation. Climate change, limitations on the availability of water in various forms, diminishing natural resources of many kinds, the need to provide economically viable and meaningful jobs for billions of people, the importance of making the best use of human capital in a knowledge economy, the operational and reputational risk faced by the world's largest companies in a multistakeholder society, and the elusive goal of providing proper corporate governance to companies on which shareholders and all other stakeholders depend all mean that an excessive focus on short-term financial performance must be replaced by a longer-term view which recognizes that a sustainable company depends upon its contribution to a sustainable society. The central message of this book is that more integrated reporting of financial, environmental, social, and governance performance is essential.

We refer to this more integrated reporting as *One Report*. This term comes from the fact that a few innovative companies in different countries and industries all over the world have explicitly declared that they are now producing one integrated report. Most of them have only been doing so for the past year or two. We believe we are at a turning point, and that the number will increase very quickly. We also hope that this book will accelerate the trend.

A single document, One Report, is the result of more integrated reporting, which can only happen if sustainability is embedded in a company's strategy. It is the most effective way of demonstrating internal integration, and it is also a discipline for ensuring that integration exists. Integrated external reporting is impossible without integrated internal management. One Report is both a tool and a symbolic representation of a company's commitment to sustainability.

It is also much more than that. It is about moving from a periodic static document to ongoing reporting about the company's financial and nonfinancial successes and failures. This shift enables dialogue and engagement that involves listening as well as talking. Dialogue and engagement are vastly enabled by the Internet, today's Web 2.0 tools and technologies, and tomorrow's Web 3.0—the "semantic Web." One Report is about a collective conversation between companies acting as corporate citizens; analysts and investors; standards setters and regulators; and civil society, as represented by NGOs (nongovernmental organizations), associations of many kinds, and individual citizens. Through integrated reporting, we hope that the bright line sometimes drawn between shareholders and other stakeholders will blur, and that *all* stakeholders will adopt a more holistic perspective. One Report alone cannot make this happen, but we believe it can play a catalytic role.

One Report is about greater transparency; thus, we should be transparent about our intentions. The authors are actors in, as well as analysts of, the corporate reporting scene today. Eccles's interest in this topic goes back to the late 1980s, directly after getting tenure at the Harvard Business School and beginning a research program on improving corporate reporting. Since then he has been involved in a number of private and public initiatives to make this happen. Krzus's involvement goes back to his appointment as Executive Director of the American Institute of Certified Public Accountants Special Committee on Enhanced Business Reporting in December 2002.

In writing this book, one thing that has become painfully clear to us is the ambiguity of language. We could have not written this book without using terms such as *corporate social responsibility*, *ESG metrics*, *intangible assets*, *intellectual capital*, *key performance indicators*, *nonfinancial information*, *stakeholders*, *sustainable development*, *sustainability*, and *civil society*. We are aware that these terms mean different things to different people and that, in some cases, the terms themselves may be disagreeable to some readers. We are not trying to resolve this linguistic dispute. All we can and will do is be explicit about our own definitions of these words.

Another disclaimer is in order. This book is about the contribution integrated reporting can make to sustainable company strategies that contribute to a sustainable society. Here we will be discussing companies that are practicing One Report to show that it can be and is being done, and why and how. Much of our information comes from public sources. In some cases, we have had the privilege of talking to people at the companies themselves; this includes some companies that are not doing One Report, but that are doing things in the spirit of integrated reporting and stakeholder dialogue and engagement. We are deeply grateful to all of these individuals and their companies for their contribution to this book.

At the same time, the inclusion of any company in this book is not an endorsement of the businesses they are in, the strategies they are pursuing, or the degree to which sustainability is embedded into their operations. We simply do not have the necessary data or expertise to make this judgment. We are also very aware that every single company in this book has its detractors. The extent to which each of these companies is engaged with its stakeholders to address these issues varies, but such engagement is a critical aspect of One Report. Finally, we obviously have no idea what the future bears for any of the companies discussed here. Some may prosper for decades. Some may fail in the near future for reasons we cannot foresee. Should this happen, there certainly will and should be a debate about the quality of their external reporting, including the strengths and weaknesses of their One Report.

In writing this book, we have had a number of conversations with individuals and organizations who are committed to improving corporate reporting and, specifically, to emphasizing more integrated reporting. This includes academics, analysts and investors, executives, regulators and standards setters, and members of civil society, such as NGOs and associations of various kinds. Out of these conversations have come various initiatives, such as the one described in Chapter 1, that we hope will move this agenda forward. There are also important initiatives taking place in which we have no part at this time but may in the future. Seen in this context, our book is a means to an end, not an end in itself. One Report by itself will not ensure that companies have sustainable strategies that contribute to a sustainable society, but we strongly believe that it can play an important role.

Here we make a personal commitment to provide our own support to the rapid and broad adoption of high-quality integrated reporting. At the encouragement of governmental representatives from nine countries, we are creating the Web site www.integratedreporting.org. It will be a platform on which dialogue, engagement, sharing, and learning can take place. We invite companies and governments to provide information on what they are doing and links to their Web sites, including their One Reports, so that we can learn from each other. We invite all members of every company's integrated reporting community of stakeholders to comment on these efforts and make suggestions for improvements. We invite everyone to provide ideas, reflections, suggestions for readings, sources of information, frameworks, and Web-based applications of many kinds, including those for developing a better understanding about the relationship between financial and nonfinancial performance. We will be actively engaged on this Web site and happy to talk in more old-fashioned ways as well.

We have tried to make this book a reasonably comprehensive treatment of the topic without becoming excessively long. It is organized into eight chapters. Chapter 1 explains further what we mean by One Report and gives two good examples of companies that are practicing it: the Danish pharmaceutical company Novo Nordisk and the Brazilian cosmetics and fragrances company Natura. Chapter 2 looks at a U.S. company, United Technologies Corporation, that issued One Report for the first time in 2008 and describes this report in the context of the history of 50 years of corporate reporting at the company. Chapter 3 reviews the state of financial reporting today; Chapter 4 does the same for nonfinancial reporting. The reader who is familiar with these subjects can skim or skip these chapters. Chapter 5 provides the foundation argument for integrated reporting in the context of the convergence of corporate social responsibility, sustainable development, and competitive advantage. In Chapter 6, we make the case for One Report by explaining why it is in a company's best interest to practice more integrated reporting, providing evidence for why we think this is a trend about to take off, and addressing objections that can be made to One Report. As already noted, although One Report as a paper document is symbolically important, true integrated reporting is about much more than this. It involves leveraging the Internet and Web 2.0 tools and technologies to provide integrated reporting on a more continuous basis and to engage in dialogue and engagement with all stakeholders. We explain this in Chapter 7. In Chapter 8, we present the elements of an action plan for rapid and broad adoption of integrated reporting in the interest of ensuring a sustainable society. All of us have a stake in this. All of us have a stake in integrated reporting and One Report.

Notes

1. "Text of Obama's Speech on Financial Reform," *New York Times Online*, September 14, 2009. www.nytimes.com/2009/09/15/business/15obamatext.html, accessed September 2009.
2. Revkin, Andrew C. "Obama: Climate Plan Firm Amid Economic Woes," November 18, 2008, post on blog "Dot Earth, *New York Times*," http://dotearth.blogs.nytimes.com/2008/11/18/obama-climate-message-amid-economic-woes/, accessed September 2009.
3. "2009 Investor Statement on the Urgent Need for a Global Agreement on Climate Change," www.ceres.org/Document.Doc?id=495, accessed September 2009.
4. James McCarthy, interview with Robert Eccles and Susan Thyne, August 5, 2009.
5. HM Treasury. "Publication of the Stern Review on the Economics of Climate Change," October 20, 2006, press release, www.hm-treasury.gov.uk/press_stern_06.htm, accessed October 2009.

Chapter 1

What Is One Report?

On September 11, 2009, the authors participated in a meeting at St. James's Palace in London to discuss how best to achieve the integration of financial and nonfinancial reporting and to provide the authors with some comments on the ideas expressed in this book. The meeting brought together organizations with a range of different perspectives, including investors, standards setters, companies, accounting bodies, UN representatives, and members of civil society.[1] One output of this meeting was the agreement that an appropriate international body should initiate a process with the organizations that have the relevant expertise and recognition in the area of transparency, accounting, and reporting internationally to consider the development of an integrated sustainability and financial reporting framework as a critical step toward realizing a sustainable economy. It was agreed that now is the time to have the same level of coordinated international response as occurred with the financial crisis to the environmental crisis, which poses a far higher level of systemic risk to the global economy. Many G-20 leaders have recognized the threats posed to our society and prosperity by climate change, depletion of finite natural resources, and related issues and are starting to take action.

Current financial and sustainability reporting systems do not provide the necessary information to address these environmental or societal challenges. Bringing together those organizations that have responsibility for financial accounting and reporting with those that are widely recognized as leaders in nonfinancial accounting and reporting would make possible the establishment of the process, the governance structure and the guidelines under which an appropriate framework could be developed.

The Meaning of One Report

At the St. James's Palace meeting, there was a robust discussion about the idea and meaning of One Report, including the challenges in implementing integrated reporting at the company level and in gaining broad adoption for it at the public policy level. We were challenged to explain exactly what is meant by the term *One Report*. In its simplest terms, One Report means producing a single report that combines the financial and narrative information found in a company's annual report with the nonfinancial (such as on environmental, social, and governance issues) and narrative information found in a company's "Corporate Social Responsibility" or "Sustainability" report. But the integration of financial and nonfinancial reporting is about much more than simply issuing a combined paper document. It involves using the Internet to provide integrated reporting in ways that cannot be done on paper, such as through analytical tools that enable the user to do his or her own analysis of financial and nonfinancial information. It also involves providing information that is of particular interest to different stakeholders.

One Report doesn't mean *Only* One Report. It simply means that there should be one report that integrates the company's key financial and nonfinancial information. It by no means precludes the company from providing other information in many different ways that are targeted to specific users. Rather, One Report provides a conceptual platform that is supplemented by the technology platform of the company's Web site, from which much more detailed data can and should be provided to meet the information needs of a company's many stakeholders. Thus,

One Report has two meanings. The first and most narrow meaning is a single document, either in paper or perhaps electronically provided as a PDF file. The narrow meaning of One Report should not be lightly dismissed. It is a way of communicating to all stakeholders that the company is taking a holistic view of their interests, both as they complement each other and as they compete against each other. This broader stakeholder view, discussed in more detail in Chapter 5, is variously called "corporate social responsibility," "sustainability," and "corporate citizenship."[2]

The second and broader meaning is reporting financial and nonfinancial information in such a way that shows their impact on each other. Here companies can leverage the capabilities of the Internet and its Web 2.0 tools and technologies. Clearly, the degree of integration can vary enormously, so One Report is not simply the decision to provide such a report but also a journey in which a company commits to a path of continuous improvement in the degree of integration in its external reporting. The Danish biotechnology company Novozymes is the first company we are aware of to produce One Report, starting in 2002, and the company also makes effective use of the Internet to provide more detailed information than what is in its integrated annual report.[3]

Novo Nordisk: An Early Adopter of One Report

A good example of One Report, illustrating both its broad and narrow meanings, can be found in the Danish healthcare company Novo Nordisk, a world leader in diabetes care. Its *Annual Report 2008: Financial, social and environmental performance* is the company's fifth year of providing "one, inclusive document" and is a representation of its efforts to "drive integration of the financial and non-financial perspectives to business and [the ways it] seeks to reflect this in the approach to reporting."[4] This relatively long history of integrated reporting (the evolution of its corporate reporting is profiled in Exhibit 1.1) makes Novo Nordisk one of the earliest adopters of One Report, and its robust supplemental Web site explains the benefit of integrated information: "in combining the accounts for the company's financial and non-financial assets, the objective is to enhance stakeholders' evaluation of the company."[5]

Exhibit 1.1 Evolution of Corporate Reporting at Novo Nordisk

Year	Report Title	GRI Adherence Level	Assurance Provider	Annual Report
1995	Environmental Report 1995	—	SustainAbility	Online
1996	Environmental Report 1996	—	SustainAbility	Online
1997	Environment & Bioethics Report 1997	—	SustainAbility	Online
1998	Environment & Bioethics Report 1998	—	Deloitte & Touche	Online
1999	Environmental & Social Report 1999	—	Deloitte & Touche	
2000	The Novo Group Environmental and Social Report 2000 *Values in a global context*	1999 Guidelines	Deloitte & Touche	
2001	Reporting on the triple bottom line 2001 *Dealing with dilemmas*	1999 Guidelines	Deloitte & Touche	PDF/Online
2002	Sustainability Report 2002	G2: In Accordance (GRI-checked)	Deloitte & Touche	PDF/Online
2003	Sustainability Report 2003 *What does being there mean to you?*	G2: In Accordance (GRI-checked)	Deloitte	PDF/Online
2004	Annual Report 2004 *Can diabetes really be defeated?*	G2: In Accordance (GRI-checked)	PricewaterhouseCoopers	PDF/Online
2005	Annual Report 2005 *How Novo Nordisk is changing diabetes*	G2: In Accordance (GRI-checked)	PricewaterhouseCoopers	PDF/Online
2006	Annual Report 2006 *Action defines leadership*	G2: In Accordance (GRI-checked)	PricewaterhouseCoopers	PDF/Online
2007	Annual Report 2007 *United to change diabetes*	G3: A+ Self-declared	PricewaterhouseCoopers	PDF/Online
2008	Annual Report 2008 *Our focus is our strength*	G3: A+ Self-declared	PricewaterhouseCoopers	PDF/Online

SOURCE: Novo Nordisk, "Novo Nordisk Reporting History," http://annualreport2008.novonordisk.com/images/how-we-are-accountable/PDF/history.pdf, accessed September 2009.

In presenting integrated information, Novo Nordisk not only establishes the connection between its sustainable business practices (grounded in the Triple Bottom Line approach[6]) and its financial performance, but also connects the reporting of financial and nonfinancial data by the stringency of approach. Financial reporting is heavily regulated, and the company's reporting is based on International Financial Reporting Standards (IFRS). While standards for nonfinancial reporting are not yet widely established, due in part to the voluntary nature of reporting, Novo Nordisk reports its data using the Global Reporting Initiative's (GRI) G3 Sustainability Reporting Guidelines (explained more fully in Chapter 4). In clearly expressing its use of these guidelines, Novo Nordisk projects its commitment to being a company with sustainability in mind.

Furthermore, the company's required audit of its annual report was conducted by PricewaterhouseCoopers (PwC), which also provided assurance on its reported nonfinancial performance.[7] The audit of the annual report is primarily focused on financial information but also includes some nonfinancial information; the assurance, although not required, is focused on the nonfinancial reporting.

An important issue in determining what information should be reported, both financial and nonfinancial, is materiality. For the former, this is variously defined in terms of conceptual frameworks developed by the Financial Accounting Standards Board (FASB), the International Accounting Standards Board (IASB), and various regulatory agencies in different countries, such as the Securities and Exchange Commission (SEC) in the United States. No clear consensus definition exists for what is "material" financial information.

Similarly, no such consensus exists for nonfinancial information. Novo Nordisk uses the materiality criteria in AccountAbility's AA1000 Assurance Standard, the purpose of which "is to help assess, attest and strengthen the credibility and quality of an organisation's sustainability reporting and the underlying processes, systems and competences... Novo Nordisk's external assurance providers were requested to assure whether the non-financial performance included was to be considered material."[8]

Despite having an integrated annual report, Novo Nordisk recognized the need of some users to gain a more nuanced view of the company. To that end, the Web site for the report "caters to those stakeholders who take a particular interest in specific topics, providing additional background and data, particularly in relation to sustainability issues."[9] The site allows users to create their own customized version of the annual report by selecting particular chapters in whatever order they want them, is easy to navigate, and has an index to ease searching. Linked from this Web site is Novo Nordisk's corporate site, the company's more expansive online presence, where users can access more in-depth information about sustainability practices, get contact information for specific company officers for direct engagement, and play interactive games that illustrate the challenges Novo Nordisk faces in making tough decisions that involve trade-offs among its different stakeholders.

The way Novo Nordisk is handling its external reporting to shareholders and other stakeholders nicely illustrates the concept of One Report. The company provides a single paper document that contains information on both financial and nonfinancial performance with outside audit and assurance opinions. It also provides a great deal of supplemental information on its Web site, illustrating that One Report isn't *Only* One Report; it is a foundation from which additional information can be provided on an ongoing basis. One Report and the Internet both contribute to the broader process of dialogue and engagement with all of the company's stakeholders. One Report is a single report, but it is also about ongoing *reporting*. It is as much about listening as talking and emphasizes the creation of a collective conversation among the company and its stakeholders. Finally, One Report is based on a philosophy of continuing to improve a company's reporting practices. Despite the substantial progress made at Novo Nordisk, Susanne Stormer, Vice President of Global Triple Bottom Line Management, explained, "Novo Nordisk is focused on continuous improvement in the integration of its reporting. In particular, there will be greater alignment between the processes for financial and nonfinancial data, with increased rigor in the internal controls for nonfinancial data."[10]

Rhetoric and Design in Natura's 2008 Annual Report

The central role of the Internet in integrated reporting, illustrated by Novo Nordisk, does not lessen the importance of the paper annual report produced by the company. This document is a physical representation that symbolizes how the company sees itself and how it wants to be seen in the world. These documents can range from short and simple reports, largely based on tables of financial information, to ponderous tomes. They can be required regulatory filings with a cover on the front or something produced with thought and care.

The Brazilian cosmetics, fragrances, and personal hygiene company Natura is a good example of a company that sees value in a carefully crafted annual One Report. At the same time, it sees this report as simply one piece of its overall approach to integrated reporting, described in the section titled "Natura." The 2008 annual report is a slim 91-page four-color publication that makes effective use of photographs, diagrams, and graphics. The company clearly sees the report as an important way of presenting its purpose ("Our Reason for Being is to create and sell products and services that promote well-being/being well"[11]) and view of the role of business in society.

Implicit in the report is the effective use of rhetoric, "the art or the discipline that deals with the use of discourse, either spoken or written, to inform or persuade or motivate an audience, whether that audience is made up of one person or a group of persons."[12] The opening paragraphs in the "Message from Management" provide the context for the rest of the report:

> The wind has aroused a great hope in the international community, which has shown a growing concern with climate change, social inequalities, and planetary challenges. In this summary, we see the backdrop of what we have been experiencing in the world, especially last year.
>
> We at Natura see the crisis as perhaps representing—through a turn toward sustainability—the beginning of a profound change in the process of civilization, a new cycle, a slow and inexorable reversal of the threats to the future of the Earth.[13]

These paragraphs are a good example of the rhetorical devices of *pathos* and *ethos*. Citing Aristotle, Edward Corbett and Robert Connors outline three ways in which people are persuaded: "(1) by the appeal to their reason (*logos*); (2) by the appeal to their emotions (*pathos*); (3) by the appeal of our personality or character (*ethos*)."[14] Natura uses all three of these throughout its annual report.

Employing *logos* in discussing their strategy and management, Natura states that it has

> . . . good reason to believe that we are on the right track. The Brazilian cosmetics, fragrances and personal hygiene industry experienced another year of growth in 2008, expanding 16.3% in the target market or 9.3% in real terms up until October, according to partial data from the Brazilian Personal Hygiene Industry Association.[15]

This reasoning explains why its future prospects are promising; it is well-positioned in a growing market, and thus is a good investment for shareholders.

An example of *pathos* is its Vision:

> Because of its corporate behavior, the quality of the relationships it establishes and the quality of its products and services, Natura will be an international brand, identified with the community of people who are committed to building a better world, based on better relationships among themselves, with others, with nature of which they are part, with the whole.[16]

Here the company is appealing for support from "the community of people who are committed to building a better world" and thus tapping into the emotion of caring.

Finally, *ethos* is found in the company's stated beliefs, in which it describes its values and view of the role of business in society in poetic style, shown in Exhibit 1.2. Through words like peace, solidarity, truth, diversity, and beauty, Natura is seeking to persuade the reader of its worth as a "living organism" that is trying to "contribute to the evolution of society" and because "everything is interdependent," the company deserves the support of society in return.

Persuasion can also be achieved through design. Natura's annual report demonstrates the benefits of a physical, thoughtfully designed document that obviously has the reader in mind. Textual and numerical information are presented with a minimalist appeal, representative of Natura's position as a company whose products are made with

Exhibit 1.2 Natura's Beliefs

Life is a chain of relationships.

Nothing in the universe exists alone.
Everything is interdependent.

We believe that valuing relationships
is the foundation of an enormous human
revolution in the search for peace,
solidarity, and life in all of its manifestations.

Continuously striving for improvement
develops individuals, organizations,
and society.

Commitment to the truth is the route
to perfecting the quality of relationships.

The greater the diversity, the greater the
wealth and vitality of the whole system.

The search for beauty, which is the
genuine aspiration of every human
being, must be free of preconceived
ideas and manipulation.

The company, a living organism, is a
dynamic set of relationships. Its value
and longevity are connected to its
ability to contribute to the evolution
of society.

SOURCE: Natura, *Annual Report 2008*, p. 2.

simple, natural ingredients. The company includes both photographic imagery and abstractive, illustrative designs, making this an excellent example of how One Report can incorporate aesthetic and practical considerations—for example, the front cover shows a close-up, nearly abstracted product glass bottle of pouring water, accompanied by an illustrated scroll pattern in the lower right corner. The water motif continues as the cover folds out to reveal a two-page black and white spread of a pond and lily pads, juxtaposed to a colorful photograph of a woman holding a Natura product underneath flowing water. The back cover complements this imagery with another close-up photograph of flowing water. The notion of transparency, embodied in images of water, is mirrored by the visuals contained throughout the report. Cartoon-like drawings are used to simplify and illustrate key concepts, such as the stages of the "Natura Value Chain" and the main components of its strategy and management.

However, these whimsical design elements are paired with more concrete imagery that captures the eco-consciousness and honesty of Natura's reporting. The report's subtle yet vibrant color palette—from minty green to golden beige and violet—is reminiscent of traditional earth tones and again connects the contents with Natura's ingredients and concern for its environmental impact. Of course, Natura includes lucid, attractive photographs of its own products, presented either straight-on or artistically adorned, such as the shot of several glass bottles hanging from ribbons; both types reinforce Natura's focus on beauty and aesthetics. Other images, such as one close-up shot of Brazil nuts and another of buriti, an Amazonian fruit, capture the essence and literal foundation of the company's products. Yet photographs of employees and individuals actually making and using these products ground and humanize the company's message: Beauty is part of every person. There is a full-page photograph of children bathing with Natura products, and a casual shot of the management team against a background of water and trees accompanies its opening letter. Elsewhere, two individuals in lab suits and goggles give each other high-fives, and two more goggled employees appear several pages later. This use of repetitive imagery strengthens the cohesiveness of Natura's One Report philosophy that sustainability is embedded in the business operations and the company has an impact on all the people it touches.[17]

As Natura shows, One Report is a document as well as using technology to facilitate dialogue and engagement with all stakeholders. Both involve numbers, words, and images. One Report makes use of many different media formats to present a holistic view of the company to all of its stakeholders.

Natura

Founded in 1969, Natura, a Brazilian cosmetics company, began to focus its ties to its name—the Portuguese word related to nature—in the early 1990s by strengthening its relationship with the company's thousands of consultants who sold the products. Natura's three major shareholders and all of the company's executives envisioned the company over the next 10 to 15 years and realized that sustainability (even though they didn't use this term) was intertwined with the lives of its shareholders and other stakeholders and the company's impact on them. In 1998, Natura helped to found and joined Ethos Institute, a Brazilian organization focused on corporate social responsibility (CSR), and learned of the GRI Guidelines. In its 2000 annual report, the company began using the guidelines, making it the first Latin American company to do so. At that time, Natura was a privately held company and thus not obligated to do any external reporting at all (Natura went public in 2004).

The company considered producing an integrated report in 2000 and the idea was discussed by the board. However, it was challenged by the finance function, which argued that, given the state of the company's financial control systems at the time, simply issuing an annual report with high quality financial information was a significant challenge. Interpreting the GRI Guidelines for a CSR report presented an added complexity. The Guidelines were used both to determine content in terms of materiality, inclusion of stakeholders, sustainability context, and scope, and to ensure quality in terms of balance, comparability, accuracy, frequency, clarity, and reliability. Separate reports were issued in 2000 and 2001. Two years later, the company's board decided that it was time to issue one integrated report.

Since its initial public offering (IPO), Natura has worked hard to improve its reporting processes. The company's commitment to continuous improvement, shown in Exhibit 1.3, illustrates the cycle for accomplishing this goal. The cycle begins with sustainable management, which is tied to the company's business strategy. This leads to indicators comprising both GRI indicators and internal indicators determined by management, that are of interest to stakeholders. Indicators form the basis of the communication plan, a multichannel effort that is focused on explaining the strategy and reporting, on a continuous basis, both positive and negative achievements. The

(*continued*)

(*Continued*)

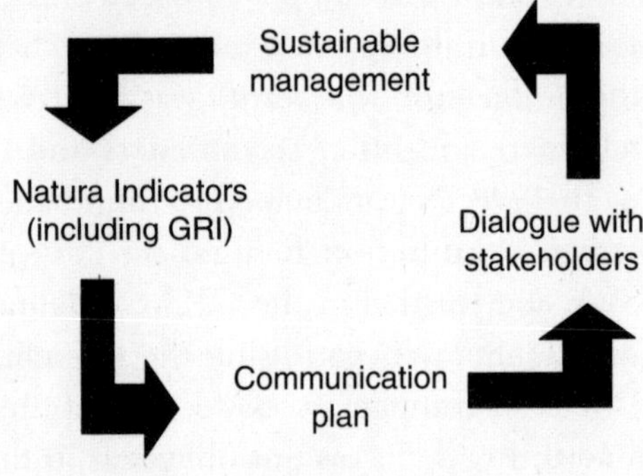

Exhibit 1.3 Natura's Reporting Process

SOURCE: Rodolfo Guttilla, *Natura's Annual Report*, presentation received September 2, 2009.

communication plan then becomes the basis for a multichannel dialogue with the complete range of stakeholders. Natura incorporates all feedback, ideas, and concerns into its sustainable management, thus beginning the cycle again.

With its concerted efforts to communicate with various groups, Natura understood that its reports were not just for an external audience but were important internally as well. "The practice of reporting is necessary, but it is not enough. It's just the beginning of an educational process. Reports will not be effective if they are not seen as a tool that promotes reflection and change in corporate culture," explained Filipe Moura, Government Affairs and Communication of the Board manager.[18]

Despite the prominent role sustainability indicators played in the annual reports, the company got few questions from the financial community about its performance here. "On conference calls with financial analysts, it's unusual to be asked about social indicators or environmental impact. It is not a key issue for them, but they believe that Natura is well managed," said Rodolfo Guttilla, Corporate Affairs Vice President.[19] Echoed Moura, "They look at the short-term perspective, but they know this is our focus. In a 30-minute meeting, it's hard to get to [the sustainability] information. However, we do believe that the price of our shares has something to do with the way we present and deal with our social and environmental performance." Natura was unflustered by the market's lack of attention to its focus on sustainability. Instead, "whenever we go to meetings with shareholders or the media or some other group, there is still sustainability. We believe in it, so we talk about it; it's symbolic of who we are, and it's in our core values," explained Moura.

From its work with Ethos, Natura understood the importance of engaging with stakeholders, and its methods have improved over the years. "All of our stakeholders have different perspectives, so we went to them and said, 'Here are our indicators, what are we missing?' That way, we could understand what they are looking for," explained Guttilla. To reach the company's 6,000 employees, as well as its 850,000 consultants, Natura began producing an abbreviated annual report, a different version for each audience; both groups were quite positive about this move.

The company was also aware of the shifting patterns of communication tools and the importance of the Internet. "We cannot do anything privately or without being noticed by the millions of Web surfers all over the world. In light of this scenario, there is no other path to follow than being completely transparent," observed Moura. One example of transparency was that in its 2006, 2007, and 2008 reports, Natura listed its commitments to each stakeholder group and whether targets had been achieved, partially achieved, or not achieved. Natura was also actively using Web 2.0 tools and technologies to improve transparency. It had recently initiated an effort using social networking technology to improve its degree of dialogue and engagement with its stakeholders on a continuous basis by setting up "wikishops" through the use of an easy-to-deploy open online social media platform, Natura Conecta. Users were able to quickly join, contribute, collaborate, and engage in dialogue with the company in a variety of ways; the Natura Conecta integration provided a nearly comprehensive internal and external social network that was accessible to all Natura stakeholders. "This (2008) is the first year of the Natura Conecta, and we are still testing the

(continued)

(*Continued*)

platform," commented Moura. "As a result, users still have to be approved by the Ombudsman, which serves as the moderator. Even so, we already have more than 4,000 people participating."

The company believed that an ongoing dialogue, rather than an end-of-year conversation when the report was published, would better address all of the issues raised in the annual report. Moura saw this as just a first step toward "the day when society will speak for companies" and that "everybody, writing with us, all together" would produce "a chapter in our report—or maybe the whole report." When this day came, Natura's annual report would become "a kind of 'wikireport'" which would be "a clear and democratic report that can be prepared online with the participation of everybody, everyday, anytime."[20]

Despite all of its efforts to be as transparent and integrated as possible in its corporate reporting, the company was aware that its report still did not show everything that readers wanted, and it looked for ways to reduce this information gap. A table on the Natura product label, for example, displayed information on natural ingredients and the refills a customer could get. "This is the best example of how we tell consumers our commitment. When they buy the product, they can see our improvement, but we're also thinking about how we can make the table better," said Guttilla. For stakeholders with particular interests, the company issued report brochures on specialized topics like carbon and shared them with the media.

The Urgent Need for One Report

We have established the essence of One Report as integrated reporting of financial and nonfinancial information. In some cases, particularly with regard to environmental performance, this information addresses externalities that the company's operations are placing on society. Carbon emissions, water pollution, and ecosystem degradation are very prominent concerns today that are a high priority for many industries. There are various mechanisms for controlling the production of these externalities, such as regulations limiting their release, taxes that seek to internalize their cost, and subsidies that promote alternative technologies. Standards for measurement are essential, and enforcement mechanisms must exist. One of the reasons for the urgent need for One Report is that it will make more apparent, to both the company and its many stakeholders, the relationship between financial and nonfinancial performance and the extent to which financial performance for shareholders imposes externalities on other stakeholders. The result is greater transparency about the company's performance and how it is being achieved—including its social costs and benefits. This function of reporting will change behavior; it is as important as providing information on achieved performance in financial, environmental, social, and governance terms.

We will discuss in Chapter 4 the lack of well-accepted standards, enforced by regulation, as one of the great challenges in reporting on nonfinancial performance. For example, when there is a way of pricing carbon, such as through taxes or a cap-and-trade system, it will be possible for a company to clearly articulate the financial costs of its emissions and the financial benefits from lowering them, taking into account the investments necessary to do so. Harvard University Professor James Engell noted, "Powerfully carried out since the Industrial Revolution and magnified exponentially by population increase, human economic domination of Earth's ecosystems cries out for strict accounting standards to avoid heavier liabilities."[21] A professor of English and comparative literature, Engell is likely not talking about accounting standards per se, but about the general need for better measurement and accountability. Starting with carbon as an example, Ernst Ligteringen, Chief Executive of the GRI, makes the link between financial and nonfinancial accounting even more explicit: "Yesterday's externalities are tomorrow's assets and liabilities. It is obvious that carbon accounting is just the beginning of more fundamental change in what is material to a company's accounts."[22]

Like others, Engell draws a parallel to the financial crisis of late 2008:

> Fueled by good intentions and entrepreneurship, but also by greed and self-interest wrongly understood, the recent financial meltdown took a decade to develop. Fueled by the same human qualities, the environmental meltdown has taken two centuries

> to heat up. It's insidious, pervasive, and fiendishly difficult to calculate, its reversal inestimably harder to achieve. The environmental meltdown is far more dangerous.[23]

Echoing this is the position of The Cambridge Trust for New Thinking in Economics, a British research institute. It calls for two social problems to be solved:

> The first is the obvious degradation of the planet and its atmosphere by over-consumption and over-production through the exploration of resources in pursuit of monetary gain. The second problem is the toxic pollution of the global money supply, also obvious, caused by financial practices over the past twenty years, led by the investment banks of Wall Street and the City of London.

The Cambridge Trust sees both problems as having a common cause, "the pursuit of self-interest," and the solution lies in recognizing "that nearly all economic activity is social in nature, not individual; that human beings are social animals; and that successful economies are based on trust and integrity."[24]

Reducing the probability and effects of financial crises and dealing with the climate crisis require taking a multistakeholder view, and all stakeholders must take a longer-term perspective while retaining a sense of short-term urgency. Greater transparency and the accountability that comes with it are also necessary. In discussing his proposed overhaul of the U.S. financial system, President Barack Obama emphasized that "these reforms are rooted in a simple principle: we ought to set clear rules of the road that promote transparency and accountability."[25] Similarly, Danish Prime Minister Lars Løkke Rasmussen identified transparency as a key element in addressing the challenge of climate change: "Efforts and measures have to be transparent and clear. It is the basis for setting a price on carbon."[26]

The canvas on which Engell and The Cambridge Trust paint is vast compared to the rather narrow focus of One Report; thus we should be modest about what it can do. One Report is not a solution to the climate crisis or the broader environmental crisis; it will not, by itself, reduce social inequality or ensure that all stakeholders' interests are heard; it cannot guarantee proper corporate governance or completely eliminate excessive risk-taking where executives and bankers get the upside and shareholders and taxpayers get the downside; and alone it certainly cannot reduce the risk and magnitude of financial crises caused by systemic risk. But One Report *can* make a contribution in all of these areas. The contribution can be significant if supported by the appropriate economic, environmental, and social policies.

Reporting matters. Reporting communicates to the world the company's performance, both good and bad, and its view of itself. It creates commitments to improve in the future, both through specific targets that are set and from the feedback the company gets from all of its stakeholders based on the information it is making available to them. In addition to reporting, the company should also be listening. Through this process, it will learn and improve.

Like Novozymes, Novo Nordisk, and Natura, a few other innovative companies are already producing One Report and beginning to realize the benefits in doing so. One of them, Van Gansewinkel Group, is a private company and thus not obligated to even report its financial information. However, the company knows that a potential future IPO "will place further demands on the transparency and accountability of our operational management." Therefore, it is "anticipating and acting on those requirements now."[27] Frank Janssen, Vice President of Corporate Communications, further explained the reasons for One Report:

> Our business is turning garbage and waste into energy and useful products. Thus our very business is about sustainability, and so it only makes sense to report in an integrated way. We have also found that the transparency this provides helps us get and keep customers, many of whom are government entities who do waste collection themselves. Through integrated reporting they are able to see that we can create value for both society and our company at the same time.[28]

Of the companies we have been able to identify that are doing One Report, most have been doing this for only a year or two. It is unlikely they know about each other, given the range of industries and countries they are in. This mirrors new scientific discoveries, as explained by Martin Goldstein and Inge F. Goldstein, in which

> . . . there are times when in a particular field there will be a sense of discovery in the air, a shared feeling about the best way to solve some important problem, and many individuals will be working simultaneously in the same direction. The result is that very often a major breakthrough will be made simultaneously or almost simultaneously by several different people, although each may come to it by slightly different paths.[29]

These breakthroughs happen because "their time has come." This is the case for One Report, and none too soon in our view.

Notes

1. The following organizations had representatives at the meeting: ACCA, AccountAbility, APG All Pensions Group, European Laboratory on Valuing Non-Financial Performance, Global Reporting Initiative, Grant Thornton, Harvard University, KPMG, PricewaterhouseCoopers, Railpen, SustainAbility, The Prince's Accounting for Sustainability Forum, UN Environment Programme Finance Initiative, UN Global Compact, and UN Green Economy Initiative.
2. There are many definitions of corporate citizenship, but they all essentially are about a corporation's responsibilities, sometimes defined in ethical and moral terms, that go beyond producing a short-term return for shareholders and take into account social and environmental issues that often have more long-term consequences. Andriof and McIntosh state that "[Corporate citizenship] is becoming closely associated with the idea of 'sustainability.' It is also synonymous with the concept of 'corporate social responsibility.'" Andriof, Jorg and McIntosh, Malcolm, ed. *Perspectives on Corporate Citizenship*. Sheffield, U.K.: Greenleaf Publishing, 2001, pp. 14–15.
3. Novozymes. "The Novozymes Report 2008," www.report2008.novozymes.com, accessed September 2009.
4. Novo Nordisk. *Annual Report 2008: Financial, social and environmental performance,* p. 93.
5. Novo Nordisk. "Materiality," http://annualreport2008.novonordisk.com/how-we-are-accountable/materiality.asp, accessed September 2009.

6. Novo Nordisk describes its Triple Bottom Line approach as one "which ensures that decision-making balances financial growth with corporate responsibility, short-term gains with long-term profitability and shareholder return with other stakeholder interests." "The Novo Nordisk Way of Management," http://annualreport2008.novonordisk.com/who-we-are/nn-way-of-management.asp, accessed September 2009.
7. Novo Nordisk. *Annual Report*, pp. 114–115.
8. Novo Nordisk. "Materiality," accessed September 2009.
9. Novo Nordisk. "Reporting Strategy," http://annualreport2008.novonordisk.com/how-we-are-accountable/reporting-strategy.asp, accessed September 2009.
10. Susanne Stormer, e-mail correspondence with Michael Krzus, September 25, 2009.
11. Natura. *Annual Report 2008*, p. 1.
12. Corbett, Edward P. J. and Connors, Robert J. *Classical Rhetoric for the Modern Student*. New York: Oxford University Press, 1999, p. 1. For a discussion of the role of rhetoric in management, see Eccles, Robert G. and Nohria, Nitin. *Beyond the Hype: Rediscovering the Essence of Management*. Boston: Harvard Business School Press, 1992, p. 10.
13. Natura, p. 5.
14. Corbett and Connors, p. 31.
15. Ibid., p. 15.
16. Ibid., p. 1.
17. The authors would like to thank Philippa Gibson Eccles for her design analysis of Natura's 2008 annual report.
18. Filipe Moura, phone interview with Robert Eccles, Michael Krzus, and Susan Thyne, September 8, 2009.
19. Rodolfo Guttilla, phone interview with Robert Eccles, Michael Krzus, and Susan Thyne, September 8, 2009.
20. Filipe Moura, e-mail correspondence with Robert Eccles, September 2, 2009.
21. Engell, James. "Plant Beach Grass: Managing the House to Sustain It," Phi Beta Kappa Literary Exercises, Harvard University, June 2, 2009. http://harvardmagazine.com/sites/default/files/2009-pbk-oration_1.pdf, accessed July 2009.
22. Ernst Ligteringen, e-mail correspondence with Robert Eccles, September 14, 2009.
23. Engell, 2009.

24. The Cambridge Trust for New Thinking in Economics. www.neweconomicthinking.org/index.htm, accessed September 2009.

25. "Text of Obama's Speech on Financial Reform," *New York Times Online*, September 14, 2009. www.nytimes.com/2009/09/15/business/15obamatext.html, accessed September 2009.

26. Ministry of Foreign Affairs of Denmark, "Address by Danish Prime Minister Lars Løkke Rasmussen at World Business Summit on Climate Change in Copenhagen on Tuesday 26 May 2009," www.ambbeirut.um.dk/en/menu/AboutUs/News/AddressByDanishPrimeMinisterLarsLoekkeRasmussenAtWorldBusinessSummitOnClimateChangeInCopenhagenOnTue.htm, accessed September 2009.

27. Van Gansewinkel Group. "Intro," www.vangansewinkel.eu/en/company/CG-Intro.aspx, accessed September 2009.

28. Frank Janssen, phone interview with Robert Eccles and Michael Krzus, September 23, 2009.

29. Goldstein, Martin, and Goldstein, Inge F. *How We Know: An Exploration of the Scientific Process*. New York: Plenum Press, 1978, p. 255.

Chapter 2

United Technologies Corporation's First Integrated Report

United Technologies Corporation (UTC) is a diversified company that provides high-technology products and services to the building and aerospace industries. It has more than 220,000 employees and nearly $60 billion in revenues. In 2008, it was ranked number 39 on the *Fortune* 500 list.[1] The company traces its roots to the founding of Pratt & Whitney Aircraft in 1925 and has had a strategy of growing by acquisition since its inception.[2] The company changed its name from United Aircraft & Transport Corporation to United Aircraft Corporation in 1934 and to United Technologies Corporation in 1975.

On February 25, 2009, the company issued a press release announcing that it had "become the first among the 30 members of the Dow Jones Industrial Average to publish a fully integrated annual and corporate responsibility report." In the release, the company expressed both its view that corporate responsibility and profitability were mutually reinforcing and its belief that integrated reporting would become commonplace in the future for those who share this view:

> UTC's 2008 Annual Report reflects the belief that corporate responsibility and profitability go hand in hand," said Andrea Doane, director, corporate citizenship and community investment. "For UTC, the evolution to one report is natural, but we believe firmly in the years to come the practice of just one report will be not only widespread, but expected from those who believe corporate responsibility and profitability are inseparable.[3]

Executives at UTC saw publishing a single report as a natural evolution of the company's corporate reporting practices. "Even before publishing a single report, the company had a tradition of packaging both the corporate social responsibility and financial reports in a single folder, which made it clear we were really thinking in terms of an integrated report," Doane said. "A side-by-side look at the two reports made it possible to easily identify and remove redundancies. UTC is a manufacturing company, which drives a process orientation. The visual overlaps in the two reports were viewed as an opportunity for process improvement." When asked if it had been a difficult decision to move to a single integrated report, Doane replied, "It was a logical next step."[4]

While we cannot provide exhaustive proof of this, we believe UTC is the *only* U.S. company to publish One Report for 2008. Starting in 2004, UTC, like many U.S. companies, had issued separate annual and corporate responsibility reports, although they had been combined in a single binder so that an order for one automatically came with the other.

The basic reason usually cited by companies for a greater focus on corporate social responsibility (CSR) is that the increasing expectations of non-share-owning stakeholders create business risks for a company that does not pay sufficient attention to them. Potential employees will not join the company, or current employees will leave; customers will not buy its products; regulators will not grant the company the necessary approvals to introduce new products and build new plants; and the press will write negative articles that will damage the company's reputation and brand. Attention to CSR is viewed largely in terms of managing the downside, although more recently companies are seeing opportunities from CSR, such as creating "green" products and services for their customers.

UTC's First One Report

The title of UTC's 2008 annual report is *More with Less*. In their Shareowner Letter,[5] Chairman George David and President and CEO Louis Chênevert explained the title choice:

> The binding theme in these business and corporate responsibility results for UTC is doing more with less. It is the core operating commitment and value at this Corporation. Looking back at more than a decade's performance, we affirm that startling gains are possible and, indeed, at rates we would not have thought possible at the outset. It's the reason we should all be confident in a long term and bright future for the world's economies and resource consumption even in times of uncertainty and anxiety generally.[6]

Consistent with the company's commitment to Responsibility (other commitments are Performance, Innovation, Opportunity, and Results), its concept that "Successful businesses improve the human condition," and its view that a sustainable company strategy and a sustainable society go hand-in-hand, David and Chênevert discussed both financial and nonfinancial results in their Shareowner Letter. For the former, they focused on the traditional metrics of revenues (a 7 percent increase from the prior year to $58.7 billion) and earnings (a 15 percent increase from the prior year to $4.90 per share), as well as some metrics of particular importance to UTC, such as accelerating a $3.2 billion share repurchase program, restructuring costs of $357 million, and an increase of $100 million in funding for research and development to $1.8 billion.

Key nonfinancial metrics included those regarding both the company's products (e.g., a new jet engine made by the Pratt & Whitney division that promises 12 percent lower fuel consumption and more than 50 percent reductions in nitrogen oxide and noise emissions) and its own operations (e.g., lower lost workday incidences, and reduced carbon footprint and water consumption). In discussing the company's reductions in carbon emissions and the use of water, David and Chênevert emphasized that "these reductions are absolute and are exceptional on business volumes more than twice those 10 years ago."[7]

Belying one of the main objections to One Report (that the result will be an unwieldy long paper document), UTC's combined annual and corporate responsibility report is less than 100 pages long, implicitly conveying the message that it is practicing its belief of "more with less" even in its external reporting. Recognizing that transparency is about making critical information easily available and not about overwhelming the reader with irrelevant details, the company reported its key financial results in a single "At-a-glance" page of bar and pie charts and provided a single-page "Company Overview" describing the products and results of the company's six major business units: Carrier, Hamilton Sundstrand, Otis, Pratt & Whitney, Sikorsky, and UTC Fire & Security. In another two-page "At-a-glance," the company provided its corporate responsibility results in terms of six categories: governance, the environment, customers and suppliers, products, people, and communities.

In a fuller section on corporate responsibility, the company discussed "Focus Areas," describing the company's approach to each of the six categories, with useful links for further detail when viewing the report online; "Recognition" the company has achieved for its corporate responsibility efforts in the form of awards and third-party validation through various types of focus groups and surveys; "2008 Progress and Challenges," where it candidly reviewed successes and failures in achieving previous objectives; and "2009 Objectives," where it clearly lays out quantitative and qualitative objectives for its next fiscal year.

Finally, and before presenting 54 pages of financial statements, notes, and information on the executive team and the board, the company has one page each on its six major business units (plus one on UTC Power for which it does not break out separate financial results). Each page is made up of two sections: "Operations Review" and "Corporate Responsibility Progress and Challenges." Putting these two sections next to each other on a business unit basis nicely symbolizes the company's commitment to achieving high levels of operations and corporate responsibility results and its belief that they are related to each other.

What is missing on these pages is a more specific argument for exactly *how* operations and sustainability objectives are related to each other, along with metrics providing the evidence that they are. (This is typically the case even among companies practicing One Report, and it represents one of the single greatest challenges to more integrated reporting, as discussed in more detail in Chapter 6). Nor is there any commentary in the 22-page "Management's Discussion and Analysis of Financial Condition and Results of Operations" (MD&A) on how the company's corporate responsibility objectives and accomplishments are contributing to its financial results, which seems like an oversight given that the focus of the MD&A section is the effect of operations on company finances. For UTC, as well as for any other company that moves in the direction of One Report, this is the fundamental problem that needs to be addressed.

Reviewing UTC's report for *Ethical Corporation*, Aleksandra Dobkowski-Joy of Framework:CR, a sustainability consulting firm, also suggested that further integration would be useful:

> UTC should explore ways to incorporate more explicit linkages between financial and corporate responsibility performance metrics. For example, research and development could be broken down between standard investment and funds targeted towards solutions that specifically deliver environmental benefits. Similarly, total revenues could be segmented to indicate revenue directly attributable to products and services chosen by customers because of their corporate responsibility components.[8]

Doane too agreed with UTC's commitment "to focus on better integration of information, since too many elements of corporate responsibility stand alone."[9] Despite these criticisms, Dobkowski-Joy was largely complimentary about UTC's effort, stating, "With its all-in-one approach, UTC reaches out to two audiences (stockholders and corporate responsibility adherents) with a wider range of information than either had previously received. Such multifunctional efficiency is the order of the day. Report narratives abound with descriptions of product and service innovations that claim multiple economic and environmental benefits."[10]

A Brief History of Corporate Reporting at UTC

The dramatic nature of what UTC has done in its first One Report becomes even clearer when put in historical perspective. To do this, we studied a small sample of UTC's annual reports, starting with 1958 and then every decade to the 2008 single integrated report. The company actually published its first annual report in 1929, under the name United Aircraft & Transport Corporation, even though it was not required to do so at the time. Following a complicated series of acquisitions, restructurings, and antitrust suits, the company published its first annual report under the name United Aircraft Corporation in 1934. Despite this period of restructuring, it is interesting to note the degree of stability in the businesses UTC has been in (aircraft, aircraft parts and components, and electrical and mechanical products and systems of various kinds), which suggest that regulatory and social forces have had the greatest impact on the company's external reporting, not changes in its strategy and business model. During this 50-year period, there were dramatic changes in content, including greater detail in both financial and narrative information, and format, such as the transition from paper reports obtained by mail to the creation of company Web sites containing documents, pictures, and videos.[11] Exhibit 2.1 illustrates these changes, while Exhibit 2.2 illustrates the increasing amount of financial information; both sets of trends are discussed in more detail next.

1958

The 1958 report totaled 16 pages with seven sections, but it had no had formal table of contents and contained no pictures. The nine-and-a-half-page stockholder letter from Chairman H. M. Horner and President William P. Gwinn reviewed each of the company's major businesses in terms of products, major customers, and number of employees, but not revenues; discussed research activities but without any cost figures (engineering, development, selling, and administrative expenses are a single line item in the income statement that contains a total of five items under "Costs and Expenses"); provided an overview of sales and operating results; reviewed some key balance sheet items such as working capital, inventories, and fixed assets; and commented briefly on federal

Exhibit 2.1 Selected Characteristics of UTC's Annual Reports

	1958	**1968**	**1978**	**1988**	**1998**	**2008**
Report's addressees	Stockholders	Stockholders	Shareowners	Shareowners	Shareowners	Shareowners
Number of pages	16	25	33	64	70	94
Number of sections in table of contents	*	18	12	14	23**	24
Notes to financial statements	No	No	Yes	Yes	Yes	Yes
Word count of the auditor's opinion	122	125	104	217	188	632
MD&A section present	No	No	Yes	Yes	Yes	Yes
Employees thanked in chairman's letter	No	No	Yes	No	Yes	Yes
CR mentioned in any way	No	No	Yes	No	Yes	Yes
Report available on UTC's Web site	No	No	No	No	Yes	Yes
Report furnished to SEC in XBRL	No	No	No	No	No	Yes

*The 1958 report did not have a table of contents.

**The 1998 report had two tables of contents, with 11 and 12 sections respectively.

Exhibit 2.2 Financial Information Provided by UTC's Annual Reports

	1958	1968	1978	1988	1998	2008
Income statement	X	X	X	X	X	X
Balance sheet	X	X	X	X	X	X
Business segment information			X	X	X	X
Comparative stock data			X	X	X	X
Consolidated data			X	X	X	X
Notes to financial statements			X	X	X	X
Management's responsibility for financial statements				X	X	X

income taxes (two sentences), the incentive compensation plan (two sentences), dividends, and capital stock.

The discussion of the company's products was fairly extensive in terms of features and performance (e.g., the Sikorsky S-56 helicopter set the world record for speed at 162.5 miles an hour in 1956). In a few selected cases for the business units, qualitative comments were made comparing sales in 1958 to sales in 1957 (e.g., shipments for United Aircraft Export Corporation in 1958 "did not match those of 1957, the highest in the subsidiary's history") and regarding expectations for 1959 (again for United Aircraft Export Corporation: "At the end of the year the outlook for 1959 indicated that sales will at least equal those of 1958").[12] The letter declined to make any financial projections for the corporation as a whole: "Operating results for 1959 cannot be reliably estimated at this time. Under the circumstances we believe they will be satisfactory." There were no notes to the three pages of financial statements. No mention is made of employees or anything having to do with CSR. The auditor's opinion by Price Waterhouse & Co. appears on the very last page and is a succinct three sentences long.

1968

At 25 pages, the 1968 report included 18 sections, a table of contents, and a few small pictures, including photographs of the Chairman, William P. Gwinn, and the President, Arthur E. Smith. The 17-page shareholder letter from Gwinn and Smith, addressed "To the Stockholders," was very similar to the one of 1958 but with more detail about the company's businesses and support units. There were no notes to the financial statements. No mention was made of employees or any CSR-type issues.

Again, no business segment financial information was given, with the exception of United Aircraft Export Corporation, which had revenues of $418 million, a 67 percent increase over the previous year. Similarly, no cost figures were given for research expenses and "engineering, development, selling and administrative" remained a single line item on the income statement. The discussion of federal income taxes now required three paragraphs filling nearly a half page, but the incentive compensation plan still only merited two sentences.

The "Opinion of Independent Accountants," Price Waterhouse & Co., had the exact same wording, except for a change in date, as in 1958.

1978

Not only was the 1978 annual report longer than previous reports—it was 33 pages and contained more photographs, this time in color, of management—but there were some dramatic changes compared to the reports of 1958 and 1968, starting with the new MD&A section.[13] However, the seven-page "Report from the Chairman," from Chairman and President Harry J. Gray, provided less narrative information on the company's businesses compared to 1968 and focused largely on sales and major new contracts won. In a shift from previous years, the report, including the MD&A, was much more focused on financial results (including business segment revenues, but not profits) and spending on R&D, which was now a separate line item on the income statement, although there were still only eight items under "Costs and Expenses." Consistent with this, and not appearing in the 1958 and 1968 reports, was a page of "Comparative Stock Data" that showed high and low stock prices (for common and four types of preferred stock) by quarter, as well as dividends, for 1977 and 1978.

The financial statement was five pages, compared to three in 1958 and two in 1968, and assets and liabilities were again split into two pages; two new pages, "Consolidated Statement of Changes in Shareholder's Equity" and "Consolidated Statement of Changes in Financial Position," had been added. Another big change was the nine-page "Notes to

Financial Statements" section, which included seventeen notes, of which the last one on "Replacement Cost Data" was unaudited.

Supporting the segment information provided in the Report from the Chairman and MD&A was "Consolidated Summary of Business Segment Financial Data." This table showed revenues, operating profit, identifiable assets, and capital expenditures for each of the three major business segments, plus Other. It also showed the same information for U.S. and International Operations, in which the latter were further broken down into Europe and Other. This segment information was accompanied by a one-page note of explanations of terms and methodology. The last page of the annual report was a somewhat eccentric "Distribution of the Sales Dollar" pie chart showing eight cost and expense categories.

The "Report of Independent Accountants," Price Waterhouse & Co., was not listed in the table of contents. It was now only two sentences long, with the third sentence from the previous reports being eliminated, but the wording of the remaining sentences was exactly the same except for a change in date.

In striking contrast to the 1958 and 1968 reports was the final subsection in the Report from the Chairman called "Good corporate citizenship is practiced." It begins, "United Technologies has pledged itself to be a good corporate citizen wherever—and whenever—it does business." With this self-imposed obligation, the company committed itself to a set of aspirations regarding its employees, customers, suppliers, and the communities in which it does business:

> Within the Corporation, we ensure equality of opportunity in employment and job advancement. We have carefully designed human resources programs to encourage and motivate our people and employment opportunities are extended to the best-qualified applicants, without discrimination. Our people win promotions on their qualifications and abilities as well as considerations for length of service. Outside the Corporation, we maintain the highest ethical standards in our dealings with customers and suppliers, and respect both the laws and customs of our host nations. We believe good corporate citizenship is a prerequisite of good corporate performance.[14]

At the end of his report, Gray also thanks his employees and shareholders.

There is nothing remarkable in this section compared to letters from the chairman today. What *is* remarkable is the discussion of corporate citizenship compared to its complete absence in the 1958 and 1968 annual reports. And, forecasting the foundation argument for the 2008 integrated report, the sentence "We believe good corporate citizenship is a prerequisite of good corporate performance" is striking indeed. Substitute the word "responsibility" for "citizenship" and the sentence is virtually identical to the comment in the press release for the 2008 annual report "that corporate responsibility and profitability go hand in hand."

1988

The 64-page 1988 annual report almost doubled the length of 1978's report, and in contrast to 1978's seven-page Report from the Chairman, the 1988 version had a brief one-page "Letter to Shareowners" from Chairman and Chief Executive Officer Robert F. Daniell. The focus of the letter was financial results in a year in which there were "substantial reductions in workforce and a rationalization of [Pratt & Whitney's] facilities and processes." Daniell also wrote about the need to improve operations at Carrier, Hamilton Standard, and Norden (which was on the block to be sold). Nothing is said about corporate citizenship in this letter, and the only mention of employees was in the penultimate sentence: "UTC's directors, management team and employees remain committed to building our core businesses for maximum shareowner value."

The reviews of the company's three major business units—aerospace and defense, building systems, and industrial systems—contained a large number of color photographs, many full-page ones, and provided substantial detail on segment revenues and information on the primary customers, products, and services of each business segment.

The five-page MD&A section contained an extensive discussion of the financial results of the three-year period 1986 through 1988. The beginning of the section gave a great deal of prominence to two accounting standards: Financial Accounting Standard No. 14 on business segment reporting and Financial Accounting Standard No. 94,

"Consolidation of All Majority-owned Subsidiaries." Prominence was also given to restructuring costs of $148.8 million in 1988 and $592.6 million in 1986, reflecting a great deal of such activity during this period. The "Results of Continuing Operations" was an analysis of changes from 1986 to 1987 and from 1987 to 1988 for revenues; cost of goods and services sold as a percent of sales; financial revenues and other income, net; research and development expenses increased; selling, service and administrative expenses increased; operating profit from continuing operations (after restructuring charges); interest expense; and income from continuing operations after taxes increased.

The two-page "Financial Position" section analyzed the company's balance sheet, with an emphasis on cash flows (referring to Financial Accounting Standard 95, "Statement of Cash Flows"), purchases of fixed assets and divestitures of business units, and debt and equity positions. This section also discussed the debt to equity ratio, a stock repurchase plan, credit lines, and bond rating. Noting ongoing risks, the MD&A stated that "The Corporation is involved in a number of environmental matters at various sites" and that "The nature of these matters makes it difficult to estimate the timing and amount of future expenditures for remedial measures." Finally, the section noted that "Like many defense contractors, the Corporation continues to be the subject of ongoing criminal investigations in connection with its activities as a government contractor" and discussed the consequences should it be found guilty of any wrongdoing, including being debarred from being a government contractor for a period up to three years.[15]

As in the 1978 report, there was a five-year summary of financial results, a table showing high and low stock prices by quarter and dividends, the usual tables of financial results, notes to the financial statements (16 notes over 11 pages), business segment data (revenues, operating profit, identifiable assets, and capital expenditures by product group and geography), and notes to the business segment information.

New in 1988 compared to 1978 was a four-paragraph statement regarding "Management's Responsibility for Financial Statements," which commented that "The financial statements of United Technologies Corporation and its consolidated subsidiaries, and all other information presented in the Annual Report, are the responsibility of the management of the Corporation." It also stated that "Management is responsible for the integrity and objectivity of the financial statements, including estimates and judgments reflected in them. It fulfills this responsibility primarily by establishing and maintaining accounting systems and practices adequately supported by internal accounting controls."[16]

On the same page was Price Waterhouse's "Report of Independent Accountants" which was now longer and substantially reworded. Reinforcing the statement from management, the auditor's opinion stated that "The financial statements are the responsibility of the Corporation's management; our responsibility is to express an opinion on these financial statements based on our audits."[17]

1998

Covering 23 sections over 70 pages, the 1998 annual report is close in size to 1988's, but one big difference between the two is that the former was essentially two documents. The first part held financial information and the MD&A; the second "Year in Review" part contained the letter to shareowners, an "At a Glance" overview of UTC, discussions of the major business units, and, somewhat oddly, replicated pages on Directors, Leadership, and Shareowner Information. The presentation of financial information (including nine pages of notes) was virtually the same as in 1988, although with a bit less detailed segment data. The 1998 report was also available (and still is today) on the company's Web site, a practice begun with the 1995 report.

The seven-and-a-half-page MD&A, signed by Chairman and Chief Executive Officer George David and Senior Vice President and Chief Financial Officer David J. FitzPatrick, was also quite similar in format and content to 1988, including an analysis of three years' worth of performance and a discussion of possible environmental liabilities. Reflecting the growth of globalization, the section noted that "as part of its globalization strategy, the Corporation has invested in businesses in emerging markets, including the People's Republic of China (PRC), the former Soviet Union and other emerging nations, which carry higher levels of currency, political and economic risks than investments in developed markets."[18]

Also reflecting the changing times, and not included in the 1988 report, there was an extensive subsection within the MD&A on "Derivative and Other Financial Instruments" which concluded that "the potential loss in fair value of the Corporation's market risk sensitive instruments was not material in relation to the Corporation's financial position, results of operations or cash flows."[19] Another new subsection was the now-traditional disclaimer about forward-looking statements as defined by securities laws for statements that are not about historical or present facts. "These forward-looking statements are intended to provide management's current expectations or plans for the future operating and financial performance of the Corporation, based on assumptions currently believed to be valid."[20] This sentence was followed by a list of nine items that qualify as such statements, including anticipated uses of cash, cost reduction efforts, the impact of Year 2000 conversion efforts, and the transition to the use of the euro as a currency. The Year 2000, not surprisingly, merited its own separate discussion. Derivatives, disclaimers regarding forward-looking statements, and the Year 2000 discussion are, like the discussion regarding possible environmental liabilities, about managing risks of various kinds. The 1988 annual report contained relatively little discussion about managing risk.

The statement by management on its responsibility for the financial statements was unchanged from 1988, as was the auditor's opinion by PricewaterhouseCoopers LLP, with the exception of the deletion of 1988's last sentence regarding a change by the company to consolidate its wholly owned finance subsidiaries.

The 37-page "Year in Review" document contained 20 full-page color pictures, including one of Chairman and CEO David. The text was large, double-spaced, and no longer in the two-column format used in the previous four annual reports discussed earlier. Also different from these other reports, environmental issues appeared in the reviews of some of the business units, and the report was printed on environmentally friendly recycled and recyclable paper.[21]

David's shareowner letter, which ended with a thanks to the company's 180,000 employees "for first class work," reviewed the company's financial results, the success of its restructuring and process reengineering efforts (resulting in a 49 percent increase in the company's stock price in 1998), and noted that restructuring was continuing. In contrast to the way many companies account for restructuring charges, David noted that "We make it a practice of taking these charges 'above the line,' meeting our commitments even after including one time and unusual events." Using 1978's term "corporate citizenship," David clearly addressed elements of it in four ways. The first was the company's Employee Scholar Program, extended internationally in 1997, which paid for the college and advanced degree costs of its employees. The second highlighted the reception of "the Department of Labor's prestigious Opportunity 2000 award for advancement of women and minorities in our workforce." The third was Carrier receiving the EPA's Ozone Protection Award for the third time in five years. Finally, he devoted an entire paragraph to the company's commitment to the environment: "Our environmental record is enviable. When reporting is finalized for 1998, we will again have achieved meaningful reductions in the two principal measures tracked by our government. Cumulatively since 1988, our hazardous waste generation is 83% lower and chemical releases to the environment 90% lower. We became a founding member of the Pew Center on Global Climate Change and were recognized by the Clinton Administration for this and for our targeted 25% reductions in energy and water consumption."[22]

More on the 2008 Report

Despite its 94 pages and 28 sections, compared to the 1998 report's layout, the 2008 report is much more accessible; its liberal use of "At-a-glance" sections as well as charts, graphs, and color make it easier to find key pieces of information. The downloadable electronic version also takes advantage of Internet technology by providing embedded links to pages on the company's Web site for more in-depth treatments of certain topics. Anticipating our discussion in Chapter 7 regarding an ongoing dialogue with shareholders and other stakeholders, the report asks the reader for feedback on the company's financial and corporate responsibility reporting, and directs the reader to a survey on its Web site. No such request was made in the 1998 report. Like the 1998 report, environmental consciousness is reflected in the production of the report itself, but the description of the paper's composition is even more elaborate.

Unlike any of the previous five reports, there were five sections arranged thematically: performance,[23] efficiency,[24] integration,[25] customers,[26] and discipline.[27] Each of these sections contained vivid pictures and relatively brief text describing what some of the company's business units were doing to accomplish the given theme. A strong element of corporate responsibility was in each theme.

In contrast to the seven-page 1998 MD&A, which largely reported facts with a bit of comparative financial analysis, the 22-page 2008 MD&A provided much more *explanation* of the reasons for the 2008 results (e.g., the general economic environment, the economic environment in specific industries, the price of oil, and exchange rates), the distinction between organic growth and growth by acquisitions, and more detail on actions taken by management (e.g., workforce reductions and other restructuring actions, focus of R&D expenditures, and cost control initiatives). It also contained more discussion about the corporate strategy and business unit strategies and a detailed discussion of cash flows. In short, it contained some real analysis, as intended by the SEC for this section.

Reflecting the growing complexity of accounting standards, which we discuss in Chapter 3, there were long MD&A subsections on "Critical Accounting Estimates," regarding long-term contract accounting, income taxes, goodwill and intangible assets, product performance, contracting with the U.S. government, employee benefit plans, inventory valuation reserves, and "Off-Balance Sheet Arrangements and Contractual Obligations." Separate subsections also existed on "Market Risk and Risk Management" (e.g., derivative instruments, including swaps, forward contracts and options), "Environmental Matters" (e.g., 579 locations with potential liability for remediating contamination and 107 locations where the company is "a potentially responsible party" under the Superfund Act) and "Government Matters" (e.g., a lawsuit by the Department of Justice "claiming that Pratt & Whitney violated the civil False Claims Act and common law" and a contract claim issued by the Department of Defense against Sikorsky regarding alleged overpayments). Further reflecting the increasing complexity in financial accounting and reporting, a full page and a half was devoted to the subsection "New Accounting Pronouncements," which explained the considerable number of rule changes by the Financial Accounting Standards Board (FASB) and their impact on UTC's reporting.[28]

As in 1998, there was a disclaimer regarding forward-looking statements, now formally titled "Cautionary Note Concerning Factors That May Affect Future Results." New in 2008 was the "Management's Report on Internal Controls over Financial Reporting," a requirement of the Sarbanes-Oxley Act of 2002, which mandated that senior management personally "sign off" on the quality of a company's internal controls for financial reporting, upon pain of personal legal liabilities if these controls are later proven to be inadequate, although there was also a disclaimer that "because of its inherent limitations, internal control over financial reporting may not prevent or detect misstatements."[29] This section was signed by President and CEO Chênevert, Senior Vice President and Chief Financial Officer Gregory J. Hayes, and Vice President, Controller Margaret M. Smyth.

The auditor, still PricewaterhouseCoopers LLP, now had a much longer report that covered an entire page. Also required by Sarbanes-Oxley, it contained an opinion that UTC has "maintained . . . effective internal control over financial reporting" rather than previous opinions that simply confirmed the report's accurate reflection of the company's financial situation. Much of the additional length of the opinion was due to sentences regarding internal controls. The opinion also noted that "We conducted our audits in accordance with the standards of the Public Company Accounting Oversight Board (United States)."[30] The board is a creation of Sarbanes-Oxley and is the regulator of the accounting profession's audits; prior to the formation of the PCAOB, the profession was self-regulated.

As had been present since the 1978 report, there were tables showing high and low stock prices and dividends by quarter, followed by an unaudited "Performance Graph" that showed the cumulative five-year total return of UTC shares compared to the Standard & Poor's (S&P) 500 Index and the Dow Jones Industrials. UTC's performance exceeds both, which are about the same. This graph is the one place where comparative performance data are given with a reference point outside the company itself.

One other point should be made about UTC's 2008 report: It was submitted to the SEC as an Extensible Business Reporting Language (XBRL) document. XBRL is discussed in more detail in Chapter 3; here, we simply note that this format makes it easier for users to access and analyze the information in a company's annual report, due to "electronic tags" placed on the data. As another example of its leadership in external reporting for better transparency, UTC was one of the first companies to participate in the SEC's voluntary XBRL filing program; the company has been submitting a report in this format since 2004.[31] The interactive properties of XBRL allow a reader to see definitions of every item in the income statement and balance sheet by clicking on it, to generate charts and graphs in various forms, and download—with a single click—financial information into a spreadsheet for analysis. With a traditional paper or electronic document, the reader would have to manually enter the numbers into a spreadsheet one at a time, with many opportunities for making mistakes.

UTC's Half Century of Corporate Reporting

When viewed in historical perspective and merely focusing on the annual report (ignoring the vast increase in required regulatory filings, voluntary reports for environment, health, and safety and corporate social responsibility, and quarterly conference calls with analysts and investors), it can be seen that some dramatic changes have happened in both content and format in corporate reporting at UTC, as shown in Exhibit 2.3.

Some of the most important changes are the reporting of business segment information, introduction of the MD&A, vastly increased complexity in accounting standards and reporting requirements, and the use of XBRL. UTC's management team in 1958 would probably have had a difficult time imagining any of these things happening, or even understanding the concept of XBRL since it depends on the existence of the Internet. Although it is yet to be fully realized, the impact of the Internet on corporate reporting will be profound. We will explain this in more detail in Chapter 7, in which we will use the Web, rather than a paper document, as the framing for the discussion.

Change is never easy. Arguments can be (and are) always made about why things are just fine the way they are and about the barriers, risks, and costs of change; we address these arguments in Chapter 6. Yet change happens, sometimes incrementally and sometimes radically, sometimes quickly and sometimes slowly. Change is constantly happening in the still largely separate worlds of financial and nonfinancial reporting. We will

Exhibit 2.3 Trends in UTC's Corporate Reporting

Content	Format
• Increasing complexity in terms of the number of separate sections in the report • Increasing number of tables in the financial statements (e.g., addition of statement of cash flows and statement of changes in shareowners' equity) • Business segment information • Comparative narrative analysis of financial results with prior years' • Five-year summary of financial results • Introduction of MD&A section of increasing length due to explanation, rather than simply reviewing, of results • Introduction of the notes section to the financial statements of increasing length • Increasing complexity in accounting standards • Required assertions by management regarding internal controls • Longer but still highly qualified audit opinions • Explicit attention to corporate citizenship issues, broadly defined, in shareowner letter and descriptions of products and businesses • Much more discussion about risk • Introduction of a corporate responsibility (CR) report	• Increasing number of pages • Increasing use of pictures • More elaborate graphics and use of color • Posting of the report, and related information, on the company's Web site • Use of XBRL in furnishing the report • Consolidation of the CR report into the annual report

review each in the next two chapters, respectively, and then make the argument for a much bigger, nonincremental shift to integrated reporting.

Notes

1. *Fortune.* "Fortune 500," http://money.cnn.com/magazines/fortune/fortune500/2008/full_list/, accessed August 2009.
2. "Upon the reorganization of United Aircraft & Transport Corporation in August 1934, United Aircraft Corporation acquired, among other assets, all

the outstanding stocks of Chance Vought Aircraft Corporation, Hamilton Standard Propeller Company, The Pratt & Whitney Aircraft Company, United Aircraft Exports, Inc. and the United Airports of Connecticut, Incorporated and approximately 99.6 percent of the outstanding stock of Sikorsky Aviation Corporation." United Aircraft Corporation, *First Annual Report to Stockholders*, 1934, p. 3.

3. United Technologies Corporation, "United Technologies publishes combined Annual and Corporate Responsibility Report—determined to do 'more with less,'" press release, February 25, 2009, www.utc.com/utc/News/News_Details/2009/2009-02-25.html, accessed August 2009.
4. Andrea Doane, phone interview with Robert Eccles and Michael Krzus, September 17, 2009.
5. It is interesting to note that even in this integrated report, the letter is still addressed to the "shareowner" and not to "stakeholders." This suggests that UTC sees the former as the primary audience of the report and that it does not perceive their interests as being in conflict with other stakeholders.
6. United Technologies Corporation, *2008 Annual Report*, p. 3.
7. Ibid., pp. 2–3.
8. Dobkowski-Joy, Aleksandra. "Joined-up reporting," *Ethical Corporation*, May 2009, p. 41. www.frameworkcr.com/wp-content/uploads/2009/07/UTC.pdf, accessed September 2009.
9. Doane, September 17, 2009.
10. Dobkowski-Joy, p. 41.
11. Because we looked at only six reports over a 50-year period, we cannot document trends per se. Nor do we know what year certain changes appeared and, when they did, whether they remained intact each year after. We know that in some cases this is not true. For example, although the 1978 Chairman's letter discussed "corporate citizenship," in 1988 it did not. However, this simple review vividly illustrates how much things have changed and points to further changes in the future, hard though some of them may be to imagine today.
12. United Aircraft Corporation. *Twenty-fifth Annual Report to Stockholders*, December 31, 1958, p. 9.
13. The SEC introduced MD&A-related reporting requirements in 1968, initially only in the form of a summary and an analysis of earnings and their components. The present and more comprehensively structured MD&A disclosure requirements were adopted in 1980.
14. United Technologies Corporation. *Fulfilling the Promise of Technology: Annual Report 1978*, p. 8.

15. Ibid., p. 38.
16. Ibid., p. 42.
17. Ibid.
18. United Technologies Corporation. *Annual Report*, 1998, p. 3.
19. Ibid., p. 8.
20. Ibid., p. 9.
21. For example, "Carrier emphasizes energy efficiency, quiet operation and environmental stewardship in its new residential and commercial products." (p. 13); "The new WeatherMaker® residential air conditioner using Puron®, a non-ozone-depleting refrigerant, provides the US market with low operating costs and sound levels about the same as a refrigerator's." (p. 16); and "In 1998, a [United Technologies Automotive] plant in Berne, Indiana, earned the Indiana Governor's Award for Pollution Prevention by developing a process that reduces hazardous air pollutants by 80 tons per year. The process also reduces paint use by 80% and clear coat use by 40%." (p. 25). United Technologies Corporation. *Year in Review*, 1998.
22. United Technologies Corporation. *Year in Review*, 1998, p. 3.
23. "Customers have a choice and how we perform determines this. Our products are everywhere and our equipment long lived, so we set goals to exceed industry performance. Whether reducing jet engine noise or generating electricity geothermally, UTC's products bring energy efficiency and conservation to the building systems and aerospace industries. We know everything we do today can be done better tomorrow, resulting in greater value for customers and shareowners." United Technologies Corporation. *More with Less: Annual Report: 2008 Financial and Corporate Responsibility Performance*, p. 7.
24. "Our world has limited resources. Materials, time and energy are scarce and increasingly expensive. To streamline processes and improve product efficiency, UTC applies our Achieving Competitive Excellence (ACE) operating system, carried out by each employee, every day. We call it an operating system because it's not a program with a beginning or end, but rather a way of thinking and performing. From design to manufacture to customer support, our processes and products do more with less." Ibid., p. 11.
25. "We grow by engineering new possibilities. At UTC, integration means people, processes and technologies coming together to multiply the effects of innovation. It's taking the thinking of more than 220,000 employees in 4,000 locations around the world and harnessing it to deliver value to customers everywhere. Sometimes we find solutions in unexpected places, such as applying knowledge gained from modeling the surface physics of advanced materials in jet engine components to improve elevator brake system designs." Ibid., p. 15.

26. "Customers around the world rely on UTC's products and services to make cities more efficient, people more secure and travel more comfortable every single day. We deliver quality and reliability, always striving to reach new levels of customer satisfaction and shareholder value. We use customer feedback continually to recalibrate requirements and improve performance." Ibid., p. 19.
27. "Successful businesses improve the human condition. At UTC, profitability and responsibility go hand in hand, and we measure success through financial, operational, ethical, and environment and safety metrics. We believe the profitability and responsibility elements are equally important, and our record sustains this. As a global company we have global impacts, and we want these always to be net positive and increasingly so." Ibid., p. 23.
28. Ibid., pp. 55–60.
29. Ibid., p. 62.
30. Ibid., p. 63.
31. The SEC's Web site on its XBRL initiatives can be found at www.sec.gov/spotlight/xbrl.shtml, and the voluntary XBRL filings, including UTC's, can be found at http://viewerprototype1.com/viewer. Both accessed August 2009.

Chapter 3

The State of Financial Reporting Today

An analysis of the evolution of UTC's annual reports could lead an observer to conclude that there is a clear trend toward increasing the quantity of information, as reflected in the growing number of elements in the financial statements, the addition of notes and new sections, and the increasing number of pages. In reality, the issue is far more nuanced. From the perspective of a user, quantity is not a bad thing if the result is more useful information. The company preparing its financial report, however, might see increased quantity as a burden in terms of the additional systems and human resources required to produce the report. Additionally, there is the eternal tension between how much information companies want to disclose compared to how much information users want.

The real problem with financial reporting today, however, is not quantity. It is complexity. Complexity in financial reporting refers to the "difficulty for investors to understand the economic substance of a transaction or event and the overall financial position and results of operations of a company."[1] Today, an unnecessarily high level of complexity exists in both accounting standards and disclosure requirements. The result is high burdens on the companies, that prepare financial reports that are, ironically, less relevant and useful for analysts and investors. For example, the United Kingdom's Financial Reporting Council (FRC) noted:

> Concerns about the increasing complexity and decreasing relevance of corporate reports have been growing in recent years. Many people point to the increasing length and detail of annual reports—and the regulations that govern them—as evidence that we have a problem. Others are more worried that reports no longer reflect the reality of the underlying businesses, with key messages lost in the clutter of lengthy disclosures and regulatory jargon.[2]

Similarly, the Global Accounting Alliance (GAA), a coalition of professional accounting associations from around the world, recently issued its own report. One of the two key issues it addressed was the increasing detail and complexity of financial statements, noting:

> It is the resulting detail in financial statements which gets in the way of understanding. One interviewee explained it this way: People talk about the number of pages that are given to the financial statements and then the number of pages that are given to explanations and footnotes, and the explanations and footnotes at times exceed the amount of space for the financial statements themselves.[3]

One suggestion made for reducing complexity concerns the nature of the accounting standards themselves: more rules-based standards, typical of the U.S. Generally Accepted Accounting Principles (U.S. GAAP), should be replaced with more principles-based standards, typical of the International Financial Reporting Standards (IFRS). But this presents a false choice: The issue is not simply rules-based versus principles-based standards. Instead, it is all about finding the right balance between broad principles and detailed rules. A *Wall Street Journal* op-ed piece argued:

> Optimally the mix should be based on the regulatory functions to be performed, the subject matter to be regulated and the litigation risks associated with the regulation. General principles

> have distinct advantages. They are flexible enough to accommodate new financial instruments. They allow detailed rules to be avoided on certain issues, which can be addressed by references to general principles. And they act as safety valves, trumping the application of specific rules that together lead to inappropriate results.[4]

One of the objectives of the current "convergence" initiative of the U.S. Financial Accounting Standards Board (FASB) and the International Accounting Standards Board (IASB) is to develop a single global set of accounting standards that will find the right balance between principles and rules. In their 2002 Norwalk Agreement, the FASB and IASB

> . . . each acknowledged their commitment to the development of high-quality, compatible accounting standards that could be used for both domestic and cross-border financial reporting. At that meeting, both the FASB and IASB pledged to use their best efforts to (a) make their existing financial reporting standards fully compatible as soon as is practicable and (b) to coordinate their future work programs to ensure that once achieved, compatibility is maintained.[5]

SEC Chairman Mary Schapiro signaled her support in September 2009 when she remarked, "It would be ideal if we can have a single set of high-quality accounting standards that worked globally. The reason for that is it would allow for comparability for very large companies in particular and give investors the ability to make comparisons around the world."[6]

The GAA's report also raised the central question of "whether a more principles based accounting regime could provide some or all of the solutions to the complexity issue, through a greater focus on the true and fair view/fair presentation and necessary supporting disclosure."[7] Despite the appeal of principles-based standards for reducing complexity, the report cautioned that there were challenges in adopting this approach, since "both culture and mindset must change within the accounting profession and business around the world if the goals of the consensus demonstrated in this report are to be put into place" and regulators "must accept that there will be variations in outcomes as a result of judgment being used."[8] Higher levels of professional judgment will be required by both the company and its auditor. Even if companies are prepared to exercise this higher level of judgment, complexity will creep in, since it will likely require longer notes of explanation regarding the choices they made. Clearly principles-based standards are not a panacea.

Principles-based accounting standards are about the *content* of financial information. Complementing this content solution to financial reporting complexity is an information *format* called Extensible Business Reporting Language (XBRL). Described in more detail later in this chapter, XBRL is a freely available, open standardized format that applies electronic "tags" to a piece of information, making it easy for users to access and analyze. So-called "taxonomies" or "business dictionaries" are created based on an underlying set of standards, such as U.S. GAAP or IFRS, each of which has its own XBRL taxonomy. XBRL makes it much easier for a user to find and immediately reuse the particular piece of information he or she is looking for and even to quickly link to its underlying definition.

Principles-based standards and XBRL have implications for the company's external auditor. Every listed company must have an independent accounting firm audit its annual financial statements and, in some countries, interim statements. These external audits are crucial in creating confidence among users that the reported financial information is accurate. Principles-based standards require a higher level of professional judgment and potentially create more risk for the audit firm. XBRL raises an incremental set of auditing challenges, largely because it transitions company reports from paper-based documents to electronic reports composed of a much more granular level of information, with specific tags for each individual disclosure item. The audit firm will have to verify the accuracy of these individual tags while still giving an opinion that the financial statements are "fairly presented taken as a whole."

Background on Financial Reporting

Financial reporting by listed companies, whether in the form of a stark black-and-white regulatory report or a glossy, image-building annual report, has for decades been viewed as a company's primary communication with investors and financial analysts, and the basis on which the market allocates capital. This view is both too simplistic and too narrow. It is too simplistic in that most analysts and investors get financial information from data vendors. The analysts and investors then supplement that information in various ways with documents supplied by the company, as well as many other sources of information, such as interviews with company executives, studies done by consulting firms, and the use of experts. It is too narrow in that there are other audiences for these reports, especially the annual report, and companies are cognizant of these audiences when putting these reports together. These other audiences include regulators to determine compliance with rules and regulations; standards-setters to evaluate the application of accounting principles; customers and suppliers for information about the financial health of the company and other relevant background; current and potential employees to determine the company's financial health and whether it is a place where they want to work; and nongovernmental organizations (NGOs) to understand a company's position on environmental and social issues.

To be useful for decision making by all these audiences, financial information needs to be relevant, reliable, neutral, understandable, and comparable. The IASB and the FASB, the two most prominent accounting standards-setting organizations, identified and defined, in separate reports, the qualitative characteristics that make accounting information useful.[9] In December 2003, the American Institute of Certified Public Accountants Special Committee on Enhanced Business Reporting (SCEBR) published a discussion paper that attempted to iron out the relatively minor differences between the IASB and FASB statements and suggested definitions for relevance, reliability, neutrality, comparability, and understandability, terms that were defined in either or both of the IASB and FASB reports.[10]

Another important accounting concept, related to relevance, is "materiality." Both are defined in terms of what influences or makes a difference to a decision maker, but the two terms can be distinguished. A decision not to disclose certain information may be made, say, because investors have no need for that kind of information (it is not relevant) or because the amounts involved are too small to make a difference (they are not material). Magnitude by itself, without regard to the nature of the item and the circumstances in which the judgment has to be made, will not generally be a sufficient basis for a materiality judgment.[11]

Each of these terms has clear value to making financial reporting as useful as possible. Taken together, they all contribute to "transparency," which we define as making it as easy as possible for a user to understand a company's past performance and future prospects. Other common explanations of transparency include getting information in a timely way, getting more detailed information (such as at the business segment level), getting better information on risks, eliminating fraud and other reasons for restatements through more stringent audits, and more reporting of key performance indicators. However, these attributes can be in conflict with each other, and achieving optimal levels across all of them at the same time is usually impossible. For example, making sure that information is timely may require some sacrifice of completeness for data still not available on certain transactions. Or comparability across periods may be sacrificed when a new measurement approach is considered to be more reliable, given a change in the company's business model. Exacerbating these conflicts is the extraordinary complexity arising from the nature of business transactions in a global economy.

Complexity

The problem of complexity will not be easily solved. Companies must use increasingly complex accounting standards to produce financial statements that are difficult and expensive to prepare, require extensive auditing procedures, and are difficult for even the most sophisticated users to understand. Users also experience a great deal of useless "boilerplate" and redundant information, overly condensed information of little substance, and information spread over many pages, which makes it hard to understand and use.[12] Clearly this was not the intention of standards-setters and regulators, so how did this come to pass?

One major source of increasing complexity in accounting standards is that economic transactions have become more complex, such as those involving derivatives, hedges, interest rate swaps, securitization, stock options, pensions, and leases. Another source of complexity is the "interpretive guidance"[13] about how to properly book a transaction asked for by companies and their auditors.[14] This complexity interferes with transparency and raises major challenges for companies that are trying to make their disclosures as useful as possible. Some would argue that companies practice "defensive" accounting in fear of being second-guessed by auditors, who in turn fear being second-guessed by regulators. In addition, some older requirements may no longer be useful and may actually obscure the important information a company is disclosing.

Reducing complexity will require actions at both the regulatory and individual company level. The FRC report recommended "an investigation into the way various sources of regulation are contributing to clutter in annual reports" and noted that "preparers should remember that immaterial disclosures undermine the quality of reports and make a concerted effort to cut clutter."[15]

The regulatory level establishes the context in which companies must operate. Regulations have created much of the current complexity, and regulations will have to reduce it. But whatever the level of regulatory complexity, there are a number of things companies can do to make their disclosures as transparent and useful as possible to shareholders and all the other stakeholders who depend upon them. Academic research shows that there are benefits in doing so, both for investors and companies themselves.[16] For examples on how to improve disclosure, we will review recommendations that have been made for each level. We want to emphasize that, implicitly, these recommendations are largely from a paper-based view of the world, and we will point out the limitations of that view in Chapter 7.

The Pozen Committee

A good example of thoughtful recommendations at the regulatory level for dealing with complexity in accounting and financial reporting is the work completed by the Advisory Committee on Improvements to Financial Reporting (CIFR) to the SEC, frequently referred to as the Pozen Committee, so named after Committee Chairman Robert C. Pozen, Chairman of MFS Investment Management.

The Pozen Committee identified a number of significant causes of complexity, shown in Exhibit 3.1. These causes include the complexity of large companies and the business transactions in which they engage; the way in which accounting standards are developed and applied; educational shortcomings by those who prepare, audit, and use financial statements; the difficulty of providing relevant information in "plain English" due to technical, regulatory, and legal risks; redundancies in

Exhibit 3.1 Sources of Complexity in Accounting and Financial Reporting

Causes of Complexity	Definition
Complex activities	The increasingly sophisticated nature of business transactions can be difficult to understand, particularly with respect to the growing scale and scope of companies with operations that cross international boundaries and financial reporting regimes.
Incomparability and inconsistency	Incomparable reporting of activities within and across entities arises because of factors such as the mixed attribute model, bright lines, and exceptions to general principles. Some accounting guidance permits the structuring of transactions in order to achieve particular financial reporting results. Further, to the extent new pronouncements are adopted prospectively, past and present periods of operating results are not comparable. This is compounded by the rapid pace at which new accounting pronouncements are being adopted, which hinders the ability of all constituents to understand and apply new guidance in relatively short time frames.
Nature of financial reporting standards	Standards can be difficult to understand and apply for several reasons, including: • The existence of opposing points of view that were taken into account when developing standards – most importantly, the attempts by public companies to smooth amounts that vary from period to period, versus the requests from those who want such amounts recorded as incurred • The challenge of describing accounting principles in simple terms (i.e., plain English) for highly sophisticated transactions • The presence of detailed guidance for numerous specific fact patterns • The development of standards on the basis of an incomplete and inconsistent conceptual framework.
Volume	The vast number of formal and informal accounting standards, regulations, and interpretations, including redundant requirements, make finding and evaluating the appropriate standards and interpretations challenging for particular fact patterns.

Exhibit 3.1 (*Continued*)

Causes of Complexity	Definition
Audit and regulatory systems that complicate the use of professional judgment	The risk of litigation and the fear of being "second-guessed" result in: (1) a greater demand for detailed rules on how to apply accounting standards to an ever-increasing set of specific situations, (2) unnecessary restatements that are not meaningful to investors, and (3) legalistic disclosures that are difficult to understand.
Educational shortcomings	Undergraduate and graduate education in accounting has traditionally emphasized the mechanics of double-entry bookkeeping, which favors the use of detailed rules rather than the full understanding of relevant principles. The same approach is evident in the certified public accountant (CPA) exam, as well as continuing professional education requirements.
Information delivery	The need for information varies by investor type and is often driven by legal risk, rather than investor needs. In addition, the lack of a holistic approach to disclosures, the amount and timing of information, and the method by which it is transmitted, may result in complex and hard-to-navigate disclosures that cause investors to sort through material that they may not find relevant in order to identify pieces that are. These factors make it difficult to distinguish the sustaining elements of an entity from non-operating or other influences.

SOURCE: *Final Report of the Advisory Committee on Improvements to Financial Reporting to the United States Securities and Exchange Commission*, pp. 19–20.

disclosure requirements; and audit, regulatory, and legal constraints on applying the professional judgment necessary to adopt a principles-based approach to accounting standards.

The committee suggested a number of ways to reduce complexity, with a focus on some very specific recommendations that could be implemented relatively easily. These recommendations were made with two goals in mind: (1) to reduce the complexity of preparing financial statements and notes and (2) to increase the utility and relevance of information provided to investors. The recommendations included the following:[17]

- The SEC should consider asking the FASB to limit the issuance of new accounting standards that expand the use of fair value in areas where it is not already required.
- Bright lines (absolute thresholds that can easily be manipulated to produce a result that does not reflect economic reality) should not exist in accounting standards, and existing bright lines should be eliminated where practicable.
- Redundancies and overlap of regulatory requirements and accounting standards create confusion and waste and therefore should be eliminated.[18]
- Alternative accounting policies that exist in current U.S. GAAP should be eliminated, and future accounting standards should not provide for alternative accounting treatments.
- Remove existing industry-specific guidance, particularly when such guidance conflicts with U.S. GAAP.

The deliberations of the Pozen Committee were conducted primarily from a United States–centric perspective. However, in the report, the committee argued that its recommendations were relevant to the international community, especially in an environment where U.S. GAAP and international accounting standards are converging:

> As it relates to IFRS itself, we point out how some problems in U.S. GAAP might be avoided in IFRS as it matures, whereas we affirm other efforts of the IASB that we believe are headed in the right direction. More broadly, with respect to matters of convergence, we believe the principles underlying our recommendations will benefit financial reporting regardless of the approach ultimately taken in the U.S.[19]

Reflecting on the work of his committee and what he thought the future prospects were for reducing complexity and improving the utility of financial reporting, Pozen commented:

> We have made good progress in three areas. First is the codification of GAAP to focus on authoritative SEC-FASB pronouncements as opposed to all the "quasi-GAAP" that is floating

around. Second is the tiering of information—through the Internet and hyperlinks—in order to meet the different needs of various user groups. A third area is moving to a multi-dimensional approach to reporting earnings per share, with and without fair market values. This would allow executives and investors to distinguish better core cash flows from fluctuating quarterly values.[20]

Fair Value Accounting

The use of fair value accounting has increased steadily over the past decade, primarily because of investor demands for more relevant financial information to assist their decision making. The credit crisis highlighted the challenges companies face when trying to determine the fair values of assets and liabilities in illiquid markets, particularly when trying to value complex financial instruments. It is possible, however, for companies to provide investors and analysts with better information about the assumptions and rationale underlying fair value estimates through richer disclosures in the financial statements and notes.

The trade-off between relevance and reliability in financial information is an ongoing philosophical debate. Fair value accounting proponents argue that financial statements based on historical cost are not the most relevant because they do not provide transparent information about current market values. Fair value detractors argue that the information provided by financial statements using fair value measurements is unreliable because it is based on volatile, subjective pricing assumptions. They contend that if the information is unreliable, it is therefore inappropriate for use in financial decision making. This perceived trade-off is often at the core of many discussions about the usefulness of fair value measurements.

Recent accounting standards have made strides toward improving consistency and comparability in fair value measurements, enhancing transparency for users of financial statements, and mitigating volatility in reported earnings caused by measuring related assets and liabilities differently. This does not mark the end of the fair value debate; for the foreseeable future, global market participants will continue to debate how and in what circumstances accounting standards and disclosure requirements can be improved to provide users of financial statements with the information they need to make informed decisions. A November 2009 *Harvard Business Review* article suggests the right answer is not by making a simple choice between the two:

> To cut through this complex debate and implement these needed reforms, politicians and business executives must recognize that there is no single best way to value the assets of financial institutions. Some assets may be more accurately measured under fair market value accounting, while others may be better measured under the historical cost approach. For the foreseeable future, banks will continue to be subject to a mixed-attribute system, combining both methods. Accordingly, we should develop reporting formats—such as presenting two calculations of EPS—that help clarify the different types of income included in the same financial statement.[21]

Professors Robert Kaplan and Robert Merton of the Harvard Business School and Scott Richard of the Wharton School of Business have taken an even stronger position in favor of a fair value approach to complex securities issued by banks and other financial institutions. While they acknowledge that doing this "is not trivial," they argue that "these days it is possible for a bank's analysts to use recent market transaction prices as reference points and then adjust for the unique characteristics of the assets they hold." They also state that for these fair-value estimates to be credible, "they need to be independently validated by external auditors" who will probably have to hire independent experts, because many auditors "have little training or experience in the models used to calculate fair-value estimates."[22]

Risk, Executive Compensation, and Corporate Governance

Using fair-value estimates for complex securities is one aspect of the more general topic of reporting on risk. "Risk reporting" is a complex topic for which there is no accepted underlying theory or set of standards. In the United States, companies are required to report on "risk factors" in their annual SEC filing, Form 10-K. Risk reporting has a particular meaning in the context of financial institutions where the issue is what disclosures, both public and to regulators, financial institutions should be making to provide investors and regulators with the information they need to better understand the institution's risk profile and overall systemic risk. For example, risk expert Rick Bookstaber has suggested that electronic

> . . . "tags"—bar codes, if you will—be attached to financial products so that regulators know what products are being held by each bank and hedge fund. This step would allow us to understand the potential for crisis events to have systemic consequences and help us anticipate—and hopefully prevent—the course of a systemic shock. It would allow us to identify situations where investors, even though they might be acting prudently on an individual level, are posing systemic risk through their aggregate positions.[23]

The tags to which Bookstaber refers are equivalent to XBRL.

Another controversial disclosure topic concerns executive compensation, an important aspect of corporate governance. In some countries, such as the United Kingdom, this is a required disclosure in the annual report. In others, such as the United States, it is not required to be included in the company's financial report; however, in 2006, the SEC determined that the "Compensation Disclosure and Analysis (CD&A)" must be included in the annual proxy statement. A press release on the ruling quoted Chairman Christopher Cox as stating, "The better information that both shareholders and boards of directors will get as a result of these new rules will help them make better decisions about the appropriate amount to pay the men and women entrusted with running their companies."[24] More recently, the SEC has proposed further changes to compensation disclosure that link executive compensation with risk: "We are proposing to amend our CD&A requirements to broaden their scope to include a new section that will provide information about how the company's overall compensation policies for employees create incentives that can affect the company's risk and management of that risk."[25]

This proposed rule includes other amendments regarding corporate governance, such as director and nominee qualifications and legal proceedings, company leadership structure, and the board's role in the risk management process. The type of disclosure that is most effective for shareholders and other stakeholders to assess a company's corporate governance practices is even less defined than the disclosures for risk and executive compensation. As we discuss in the next chapter, various efforts are being made in the context of frameworks for environmental, social, and governance reporting. However, since a company's executive compensation policies must be signed off by the board, they are quite telling, as explained by Paul Hodgson of the Corporate Library:

> I think of executive compensation as the window into the board's soul. Decisions about compensation are some of the most public statements that the board makes owing to the necessity to disclose so much data and analysis about the process, particularly in the new CD&A. Publicly-disclosed compensation decisions can be used as a proxy to understand the effectiveness of decision-making in other less public areas. A subjugated board enthralled with the CEO will reveal itself in the compensation package it agrees to.[26]

Report Leadership

Changing regulations takes time, but there are actions that companies can take on their own to address the problem of complexity and improve transparency through their own reporting efforts. Although later in this book we will discuss leveraging the Internet and its constituent technologies to achieve these improvements, today the annual report as a paper document remains centrally important. In this domain, the Report Leadership Group, composed of the Chartered Institute of Management Accountants (CIMA), PricewaterhouseCoopers LLC (PwC), and Radley Yeldar, has made some useful suggestions about how companies can simplify and improve their external communications, even in the current environment of regulatory-based complexity. Exhibit 3.2 summarizes the group's recommendations regarding improving the structure, navigation, and messaging of business reports, based on research into the needs of investors.

Report Leadership recommended that nonfinancial information on strategy, the company's value creation activities, the business environment, and key performance indicators be included, a discussion we pick

Exhibit 3.2 What Investors Want

Structure	Navigation	Messaging
1. Some form of narrative sequence with a beginning, a middle, and an end 2. Clear linkage from markets to strategy to key performance indicators to future goals 3. An integrated structure: • Don't mention one thing as being important and then fail to mention it anywhere else in the report • Don't hide important information away at the back of the report • Don't suddenly introduce a new idea and say it's key to the business halfway through the annual report	1. Clarity 2. Messages backed up by evidence 3. Plain speaking 4. Plain English 5. Balanced discussion of performance	1. A good table of contents, or even an index 2. Summaries of the information included in each section or even each page or spread 3. Individual sections clearly delineated 4. Clear linkage between the narrative section of the annual report and the financial statements 5. Good navigational aids on each page/spread

SOURCE: Report Leadership, *Tomorrow's Reporting Today*, November 2006, p. 6, 8, 10.

up in the next chapter. It also recommended including a forward-looking orientation to give the reader management's view of the company's future prospects.

Companies are often reluctant to provide forward-looking information, citing competitive disadvantage or litigation risk. Nevertheless, there are examples of forward-looking statements in corporate reports. The information is frequently quantitative, for example, earnings-per-share guidance, future capital expenditures, targets for reduction of greenhouse gas emissions and water usage, accident prevention goals, or sales growth objectives. Examples of qualitative forward-looking statements can also be found in discussions about opportunities and risks, such as consideration of the economic environment, raw material availability and pricing, exchange rate volatility, political and regulatory risks, and patent expirations.

While the term is not specifically defined in SEC rules and regulations, some guidance exists.[27] Businesses making forward-looking statements usually include a disclaimer that says the statements are only true at the time they were written, and they further claim that they are under no obligation to update those statements if conditions change or if unexpected events occur. Forward-looking information is generally identified by the use of certain words such as *believe*, *expect*, *may*, *will*, *plan*, *strategy*, *prospect*, *foresee*, *estimate*, *project*, *anticipate*, *can*, *intend*, *target*, and other words of similar meaning.

Building on the work of Report Leadership, a report from PricewaterhouseCoopers in Australia proposed that environmental, social, and governance (ESG) information be included in the annual report and that this information include targets, performance against targets, and quantification of the financial impact of the different aspects of ESG performance.[28] Commenting on this report, Nick Ridehalgh, a partner at PricewaterhouseCoopers, stated:

> It is still early days for comprehensive integration of ESG performance into investor and analyst models, with most sticking to historic financial information, and maybe adding a small premium for perceived management quality. However, assessment of ESG data has started with one major externality (pollution) now being quantified and modeled (carbon equivalent units) as a cost to business due to the proposed emissions trading schemes. When effective management and long term development of scarce resources, whether physical like the workforce and consumables or intangibles like brand and IP, [are] integrated into a company's strategy, then targets against them should be set and performance reported in an integrated fashion.[29]

Consistent with the suggestions of Report Leadership, the FRC report, drawing on the U.K. Accounting Standards Board's *Reporting*

Statement: Operating and Financial Review, offered four "principles for effective communication":

> *Focused*: Highlight important messages, transactions and accounting policies and avoid distracting readers with immaterial clutter.
>
> *Open and honest*: Provide a balanced explanation of the results—the good news and the bad.
>
> *Clear and understandable*: Use plain language, only well defined technical terms, consistent terminology and an easy-to-follow structure.
>
> *Interesting and engaging*: Get the point across with a report that holds the reader's attention.[30]

These suggestions appear to be basic and sensible. They are also often not practiced. UTC's 2008 annual report is a good example of following these suggestions in terms of One Report.

Extensible Business Reporting Language (XBRL)

Reducing complexity in accounting standards and reporting standards is about information content. Complementing this is the format in which this information is provided. Today, investors generally get their information in one of three ways. The first is directly from the company, typically from its Web site, where investors can get annual and quarterly financial reports, press releases, presentations to analysts and investors, environmental reports, and social reports. Even though these documents are downloaded in electronic form, they are all essentially paper documents made readily accessible in PDF or HTML format. Users can also get data from Web sites such as Google Finance, MSN Money, and Yahoo! Finance. In both cases, in order to analyze this information, the typical analyst, retail investor, regulator, or NGO has to manually enter the numbers into a spreadsheet containing the appropriate analytical model.

This process is not only prone to error, but is also very time-consuming, thus distracting the user from the critical task of analysis. As a result, many choose a third way, by buying information (via a subscription) from data vendors such as Bloomberg, Capital IQ, FactSet, or Thomson Reuters. These vendors gather financial statements from all listed companies and provide electronic data feeds to their customers in a structured manner with a proprietary standard, using technologies like Extensible Markup Language (XML), which is often referred to as the "language of the Internet," and Web services.[31] Customers can get a company's latest financial information by simply typing in the ticker symbol of the company in the provider's search bar. This information is then electronically transmitted directly into the user's analytical model. The flaw in this process is that approximately one-quarter of company disclosures from the Balance Sheet, Income Statement, and Statement of Cash Flows do not fit into the general data template created by the data vendor and simply disappear from the electronic data feeds. Finally, the timeline for making the data available is measured in hours or days, due to the manual parsing required to extract meaningful information disclosed within company electronic paper-based reports.

Extensible Business Reporting Language (XBRL), referred to by the SEC as "interactive data," is a freely available standard specifically designed to express business information in a standardized electronic format through the use of electronic "tags."[32] Every piece of business information—such as revenues or short-term liabilities, innovation or strategy, tons of carbon emissions or lost time accidents—can have an electronic tag (called *metadata*) that enables access to this information over the Internet.[33] XBRL is a specific application or "dialect" of XML designed to enhance business information processes. John Stantial, Assistant Controller at United Technologies Corporation, described the kind of information a user can access with XBRL: "If, for example, you apply the tag for gross margin to the gross margin line on your income statement, a tool that can read XBRL would tell you the line item is gross margin, how it is defined, what the balance is, what currency it is in, how accurate it is, what period it covers, and for what company."[34]

As with the data vendors, users can download this information directly into their analytical models. However, there are two critical differences. The first is that the information can be obtained in electronic form directly from the source—the company—rather than through an intermediary. In the United States, the SEC has mandated that all companies tag their required filings with XBRL using a phase-in approach, beginning with the approximately 500 largest SEC Registrants.[35] "XBRL is now mandated or used in voluntary filing programs in Australia, Belgium, Canada, China, Denmark, France, Germany, India, Israel, Japan, Korea, Netherlands, Singapore, Spain, Sweden, Thailand, United Kingdom and United States."[36] In addition, Belgium, Denmark, the European Union, Germany, Korea, the Netherlands, New Zealand, South Africa, Spain, the United Kingdom, and the United States all have active XBRL projects.[37]

The second difference is that the data are the "as is" reported financial statement information, instead of the normalized data available from the data vendors. To provide the information in a relatively small set of fields (typically several hundred), data vendors create general categories and fit in information from each company the best they can. In some cases, the match is an exact one. In other cases, several data points reported by a company might be combined into one field, such as combining "revenue from sales" and "revenue from warranties" into a single revenue item. While some level of granularity is lost, for many users this is not that important, given the type of analysis they are doing.[38]

To use XBRL for corporate reporting, it is necessary to develop taxonomies that include the full set of tags for the type of information being provided. An international not-for-profit organization, XBRL International, Inc. (XII), is responsible for the XBRL technical language; however, because it is an open standard, any organization can create XBRL taxonomies. XII provides an acknowledgement process that ensures the taxonomies meet the specific criteria of the XBRL technical language.[39] These taxonomies are based on underlying content standards. For example, XBRL taxonomies have been developed for both U.S. GAAP and IFRS. The U.S. GAAP taxonomy already includes the disclosure elements commonly used within financial statement note disclosures. It has been proposed that the IFRS taxonomy also be extended to cover the Notes to the Financial Statements. Taxonomies, albeit at a higher level, have also been developed for MD&A disclosures.

In the United States, there are some complaints from the corporate community that the SEC requirement for companies to provide their financial statements in XBRL has introduced an additional layer of complexity and cost.[40] This is likely to be a transitional issue. Furthermore, should XBRL become widespread for internal consolidation and reporting purposes, external reporting using this format would become an easy extension. Some companies have found that using XBRL in internal reporting reduces their costs, which could be an incentive for adoption.[41] For example, through the use of XBRL, UTC was able to reduce the time and cost of their corporate reporting processes by 25 percent 2 years after the company implemented its use by reducing the manual-intensive processes required to prepare the external report.[42]

It is important to emphasize that XBRL is simply an information standard, like HTML, for making it easier to collect, report, and reuse information. It is a format standard for making information content easier to access and use. It does *not* make new information available. Transparency is increased in the sense that it is easier to see the complete detail of all the information provided by the company, but it does not increase the level of detail. It also increases transparency in that it makes it much easier to find the information the user is seeking. Thus, while XBRL does not directly reduce complexity per se, it is a very useful tool for helping to manage it, similar in nature to the way HTML makes it easier to manage the complexity of information available over the Internet. Mike Willis, Chairman of XII and a partner at PricewaterhouseCoopers, explained, "Like other Internet standards, XBRL enables the streamlining of business information processes."[43]

Auditing

Every public company is required to have an audit by an audit firm that meets whatever criteria are relevant in the country of the company being audited. As seen in the example of UTC in Chapter 2, the auditor's opinion, written to comply with professional standards,[44] makes it clear that company management is responsible for preparing the financial statements and that the auditor's opinion asserts that they have done so according to accounting standards. In the United States, any auditing firm that audits a public company must be registered with the Public Company Accounting Oversight Board (PCAOB).[45]

The client for the audit is shareholders, both present and future ones; however, the Audit Committee selects the auditor and the company pays for the audit services. Investors want to know that the financial information on which they base decisions is credible and reliable. Through their audits and auditors' reports, independent auditors contribute to enhancing the reliability of financial information by providing assurance on the reliability of the financial statements and notes. High-quality audits are fundamental to the integrity of the capital markets and, as a result, more than $50 billion in audit fees was paid to the six international audit networks in 2007.[46]

Just as there are accounting standards, so are there auditing standards. In the United States, standards for auditing public companies are set by the PCAOB, while the American Institute of Certified Public Accountants (AICPA) Auditing Standards Board establishes standards for auditing privately held companies. Auditing standards specify what is required to do a proper audit, and audit firms develop their own audit methodologies, increasingly based on information technology. The PCAOB is required to conduct annual inspections of U.S. audit firms that have more than 100 SEC Registrants as audit clients and triennial inspections for firms that provide audit reports for fewer public companies. The PCAOB then issues reports about audit quality and makes recommendations for improvement.[47]

The International Standards of Auditing (ISAs) are published by the International Auditing and Assurance Standards Board (IAASB) of the International Federation of Accountants (IFAC). The six international audit networks[48] base their methodologies on the ISAs, with various modifications and additions to comply with national requirements. More than 100 countries have either adopted or based their national auditing standards on ISAs. According to IFAC, "The European Commission is currently considering a process and timetable for endorsement of ISAs."[49]

A July 2009 study, prepared for the European Commission by the Maastricht Accounting, Auditing, and Information Management Research Center, indicates that differences between the international and U.S. auditing standards are fairly negligible and should not present the challenge now facing the convergence of U.S. GAAP with IFRS. "This is an important study, and its independence is a key factor," said the

Association of Chartered Certified Accountants' (ACCA) head of auditing practice in a statement, and continued: "Comparing the U.S. system with that proposed for Europe is a timely exercise that also holds lessons for governments, regulators and investors." The ACCA also noted, "The report confirms that investors are in favor of one set of auditing standards that are followed on a global basis, so it will be interesting to see the reaction to the study in the U.S."[50]

Auditing a large, multinational company involves many people at a significant cost. The four largest global firms (Deloitte, Ernst & Young, KPMG, and PricewaterhouseCoopers) each have more than 100,000 professionals on staff and are made up of networks of local firms. The term *network* generally refers to member firms, each of which is a separate and independent legal entity with no liability for another such entity's acts or omissions. Network members are generally subject to common quality control, risk management, codes of ethics, and professional practice rules.

One of the reasons for the high degree of concentration in the auditing profession—in 2006, in the United States, the largest international auditing firms audited nearly 98 percent of total public company market capitalization[51]—is that the four largest international audit networks are the only ones that have the global depth of resources to audit the many locations of the world's largest multinational companies. Several hundred or more people with many different specialist skills can be involved in a large audit, with a core team of dozens or more people involved on a full-time, dedicated basis, and often physically located at the company's offices. The annual cost of auditing services can easily be in the millions or even tens of millions of dollars. This is a significant amount of money, but a tiny fraction of the shareholder value lost when a business fails or it is revealed that a company's financial results and stock price were misstated.

One of the challenges facing audit firms is that they are a ready target for lawsuits. When a company suffers a sudden and dramatic drop in its stock price, the audit firm almost inevitably gets sued through some kind of shareholder lawsuit. Audit firms can also be sued when a company goes bankrupt, with the allegation that investors were not given adequate warning in the company's financial results. Audit firms often settle these cases out of court, even though the profession's long-held position is that the standard audit is not designed to detect fraud, particularly collusive fraud at the most senior levels of the organization. It is also difficult to untangle a "failed audit" from a "failed business model."

These lawsuits cost the six international audit networks hundreds of millions every year. As a result, the largest firms in the profession have a goal of "liability reform" that will limit the risk and financial exposure they have to shareholder lawsuits. The issue of liability reform, and related issues regarding the auditing profession, is a complex one.[52] It is also an incendiary topic. The U.S. Treasury Department's Advisory Committee on the Auditing Profession tackled a wide array of issues, ranging from the risk of a catastrophic liability award or series of material settlements against a member firm of one of the global audit networks to the view of many that the threat of private litigation ensures accountability and confidence in our financial markets. Ultimately, the Advisory Committee concluded:

> This Committee's charge is primarily to identify matters impacting—positively and negatively—audit quality and the sustainability and competitiveness of the auditing profession. While the Committee's charge does not include venturing into the general area of litigation policy, some Committee members feel that if, and when, such change is considered, it should go forward in a context broader than just consideration of the impact on the auditing firms. Litigation is clearly of significant concern to the auditing firms but is also of concern to investors and other market participants. And, changes in the litigation environment impacting auditors may potentially affect other market participants. The Committee believes it is important that the litigation system be fair and rational in serving the needs of both auditing firms and the public interest. However, as noted above, Committee members could not agree whether or not the existing litigation system satisfies those objectives.[53]

Liability is also an important issue in providing assurance on other types of information reported by companies, including so-called non-financial information on intangible assets, key performance indicators, and metrics regarding environmental, social, and governance topics. To the extent that demand grows for this type of assurance, the large audit firms will have to determine what role they want to play here. In the short term, the lack of standards for this type of information means that assurance on it cannot be as rigorous as for financial information. However, given the growing importance of nonfinancial information, discussed in the next chapter, standards could well emerge and "real" audits could be done on it.

Notes

1. *Final Report of the Advisory Committee on Improvements to Financial Reporting to the United States Securities and Exchange Commission*, August 1, 2008, p. 18.
2. Financial Reporting Council. *Louder than words: Principles and actions for making corporate reports less complex and more relevant*, 2009, p. 2.
3. Global Accounting Alliance. *Getting to the Heart of the Issue: Can Financial Reporting Be Made Simpler and More Useful?* 2009, p. 17. Members of the GAA are American Institute of Certified Public Accountants; Institute of Chartered Accountants in England and Wales; Institute of Chartered Accountants of Scotland; Institute of Chartered Accountants in Ireland; Chartered Accountants of Canada; Hong Kong Institute of Certified Public Accountants; Institute of Chartered Accountants in Australia; New Zealand Institute of Chartered Accountants; and South African Institute of Chartered Accountants.
4. Pozen, Robert C. "Bernanke's False Dichotomy," *The Wall Street Journal*, May 19, 2007, p. A8.
5. Financial Accounting Standards Board and International Accounting Standards Board. *Memorandum of Understanding: "The Norwalk Agreement,"* September 2002. www.fasb.org/cs/ContentServer?c=Document_C&pagename=FASB%2FDocument_C%2FDocumentPage&cid=1218220086560, accessed September 2009. Subsequent progress updates were issued in 2006 and 2008.
6. Lynch, Sarah N. "Schapiro Says SEC Will Discuss Transition to IFRS This Fall," *Dow Jones Newswire*, September 18, 2009. www.nasdaq.com/aspx/stock-market-news-story.aspx?storyid=200909181521dowjonesdjonline000570&title=schapiro-says-sec-will-discuss-transition-to-ifrs-this-fall, accessed September 2009.
7. Global Accounting Alliance, p. 6.
8. Ibid., pp. 4–5.
9. International Accounting Standards Board. *Framework for the Preparation and Presentation of Financial Statements*, 1989; *Financial Accounting Standards Board. Concept Statement No. 2: Qualitative Characteristics of Accounting Information*, 1980.

10. American Institute of Certified Public Accountants Special Committee on Enhanced Business Reporting. *Quality and Transparency in Business Reporting: A call for action in the public interest*, December 2003, p. 13.
11. Financial Accounting Standards Board, pp. 2, 28.
12. CFA Institute. *A Comprehensive Business Reporting Model: Financial Reporting for Investors*, July 2007, p. 40.
13. FASB completed a project to codify all accounting standards issued by a standards setter, including FASB, American Institute of Certified Public Accountants (AICPA), Emerging Issues Task Force (EITF), and related literature into one topically structured body of authoritative guidance. This will be very helpful in reducing the amount of time and effort required to solve an accounting research issue and improving usability of the literature, thereby mitigating the risk of noncompliance with standards.
14. "The difficulty is the old one of starting out with the best intentions of sticking to principles and becoming progressively boxed in as the business and market situation develops. The accounting keeps getting tested, said one interviewee, and it's always tested at the margin, and because it's tested at the margin interpretations are given. This gradually metamorphoses into what are effectively rules. Gradually, there is a cumulative effect. And that is where the impossible complexity comes from. This was, said several interviewees, particularly the case in the U.S. where companies had, in the past, persistently asked for more and more rulings until the whole system started to buckle. As a result, some said, it was much harder to get useful business information from a set of financial statements." Global Accounting Alliance, p. 9.
15. Financial Reporting Council, p. 45.
16. Healy, Paul M. and Palepu, Krishna G. "Information Asymmetry, Corporate Disclosure, and the Capital Markets: A Review of the Empirical Literature," *Journal of Accounting and Economics*, v. 31, is. 1–3, 2001: 405–440; Gelb, David S. and Zarowin, Paul. "Corporate Disclosure Policy and the Informativeness of Stock Prices," *Review of Accounting Studies*, v. 7, is. 1, 2002: 33–52; Lundholm, Russell and Myers, Linda A. "Bringing the Future Forward: The Effect of Disclosure on the Returns-Earnings Relation," *Journal of Accounting Research*, v. 40, is. 3, 2002: 809–839. Despite this research, there are a litany of reasons companies give for not wanting to provide greater transparency and the greater level of accountability that comes along with it. See: Eccles, Robert G., Herz, Robert H., Keegan, E. Mary and Phillips, David M. H. *The ValueReporting Revolution: Moving Beyond the Earnings Game*. New York: John Wiley & Sons, 1999, p. 22, 202–209.
17. *Final Report of the Advisory Committee on Improvements to Financial Reporting to the United States Securities and Exchange Commission*, pp. 7–10.
18. The Pozen Committee was not the first such group to identify redundancies between GAAP and SEC disclosure requirements and recommend ways to

eliminate them. See Financial Accounting Standards Board, Business Reporting Research Project, Steering Committee Reports Series, *GAAP-SEC Disclosure Requirements*, 2001; and Financial Accounting Standards Board, "FASB Initiates 'Disclosure Framework' Project Aimed at More Useful, Organized, and Consistent Disclosures," news release, July 8, 2009, www.fasb.org/cs/ContentServer?c=FASBContent_C&pagename=FASB/FASBContent_C/NewsPage&cid=1176156338441, accessed August 2009.

19. *Final Report of the Advisory Committee on Improvements to Financial Reporting to the United States Securities and Exchange Commission*, p. 26.
20. Robert Pozen, interview with Susan Thyne, September 9, 2009.
21. Pozen, Robert C. "Is It Fair to Blame Fair Value Accounting for the Financial Crisis?" *Harvard Business Review*, v. 87, is. 11, 2009, p. 92.
22. Kaplan, Robert, Merton, Robert, and Richard, Scott. "Disclose the fair value of complex securities," *Financial Times*, August 18, 2009, p. 7.
23. Bookstaber, Richard. "It's the System, Stupid," *Institutional Investor*, v. 34, is. 5, 2009.
24. Securities and Exchange Commission, "SEC Votes to Adopt Changes to Disclosure Requirements Concerning Executive Compensation and Related Matters," press release, July 26, 2006. www.sec.gov/news/press/2006/2006-123.htm, accessed September 2009.
25. Securities and Exchange Commission, "Proxy Disclosure and Solicitation Enhancements," p. 8. www.sec.gov/rules/proposed/2009/33-9052.pdf, accessed September 2009.
26. Paul Hodgson, e-mail correspondence with Robert Eccles, September 9, 2009.
27. Securities Exchange Act of 1934, Section 21E, "Application of Safe Harbor for Forward-Looking Statements."
28. PricewaterhouseCoopers. *Best Practice Environmental Social and Governance (ESG) Reporting*, 2007.
29. Nick Ridehalgh, e-mail correspondence with Robert Eccles, September 29, 2009.
30. Financial Reporting Council, pp. 39–41.
31. Web services refers to an Internet standard for transporting information between disparate proprietary software application. A W3C standard is promulgated at www.w3.org/2002/ws.
32. "XBRL is a language for the electronic communication of business and financial data which . . . provides major benefits in the preparation, analysis and communication of business information. It offers cost savings, greater efficiency and improved accuracy and reliability to all those involved in supplying or using financial data." XBRL, "An Introduction to XBRL," www.xbrl.org/WhatIsXBRL/, accessed August 2009.

33. While our focus on the application of XBRL is largely on external reporting by companies, it can also be used internally, enabling companies to much more easily and cheaply consolidate data across disparate internal systems than using traditional enterprise resource planning systems. As XBRL is adapted for internal use, its application for external reporting will be even easier, because the information will already be in this format. See Willis, Mike, and Sinnett, William M. "XBRL: Not Just for External Reporting," *Financial Executive*, v. 24, is. 4, 2008, pp. 44–47.
34. Stantial, John. "ROI on XBRL," *Journal of Accountancy*, v. 203, is. 6, 2007: 32–35, p. 33.
35. Securities and Exchange Commission, "Interactive Data to Improve Financial Reporting," Release Nos. 33-9002; 34-59324; 39-2461; IC-28609; File No. S7-11-08, 2009. www.sec.gov/rules/final/2009/33-9002.pdf, accessed September 2009. Technically speaking, XBRL documents are not an official "filing" but are "submitted," and for now companies must still furnish an electronic paper document to the SEC.
36. XBRL. "XBRL International Conference Convened to Demonstrate XBRL in Action Today around the World," http://17thconference.xbrl.org/conference-news, accessed September 2009.
37. XBRL. "XBRL Showcase—Project Details by Country," www.xbrl.org/ProjectDetails/, accessed August 2009.
38. "Benefits and Beneficiaries," www.xbrl.org/BenefitsAndUses/, accessed August 2009.
39. "About the Organization," www.xbrl.org/AboutTheOrganisation/, accessed August 2009.
40. Securities and Exchange Commission, section VI in "Interactive Data to Improve Financial Reporting," 17 CFR Parts 229, 230, 232, 239, 240, and 249.
41. Fujitsu's CIO Hanaoka Kazuhiko presented on the benefits of using XBRL for internal reporting purposes at the 18th XBRL Conference in 2008. See: "How XBRL Transformed Fujitsu's IT Platform," http://18thconference.xbrl.org/sites/18thconference.xbrl.org/files/hanaoka.pdf, accessed September 2009.
42. Stantial, pp. 32–35.
43. Mike Willis, e-mail correspondence with Robert Eccles and Michael Krzus, September 7, 2009.
44. In the United States, the Auditors' report wording is defined by the Public Company Accounting Oversight Board's *Reports on Audited Financial Statements*, Interim Auditing Standards, Public Company Accounting Oversight Board, www.pcaobus.org/standards/interim_standards/auditing_standards/index_au.asp?series=500§ion=500, accessed September 2009.
45. As of August 2009, there were 2,114 firms registered with the PCAOB.

46. Advisory Committee on the Auditing Profession, Department of the Treasury. *Final Report*, October 6, 2008, p V:11–13.
47. The PCAOB is a relatively new organization, formed as part of the Sarbanes-Oxley Act of 2002. Prior to that, the accounting professional regulated itself, and auditing standards were set by the AICPA, which charged a license fee to the firms that used these standards for their audits.
48. The firms comprising the six international audit networks are BDO International, Deloitte, Ernst & Young, Grant Thornton International, KPMG International, and PricewaterhouseCoopers International Limited.
49. International Auditing and Assurance Standards Board, International Federation of Accountants. "IAASB Fact Sheet," http://web.ifac.org/download/IAASB_Fact_Sheet.pdf, accessed September 2009.
50. Association of Chartered Certified Accountants. "Independent study highlights closeness of international convergence of auditing standards," press release, August 21, 2009. www.accaglobal.com/allnews/global/2009/NEWSQ3/News/3242780, accessed September 2009.
51. Advisory Committee on the Auditing Profession, p V:5.
52. Global Public Policy Symposium. *Global Capital Markets and the Global Economy: A Vision from the CEOs of the International Audit Networks*, November 2006, pp. 6–7.
53. Advisory Committee on the Auditing Profession, p. VII:32.

Chapter 4

The State of Nonfinancial Reporting Today

At the same time that the *complexity* of financial reporting has increased, the *need* for nonfinancial reporting has increased. While accurate information on a company's financial performance obviously remains extremely important, it is becoming a less and less complete story in a knowledge economy where an increasing percentage of a company's assets are intangible ones that are not shown on the balance sheet. Past financial performance, while never an unambiguous predictor of future financial performance, is becoming even less so. Managers themselves, and those who are interested in a company's future financial performance (such as analysts and investors), are relying more and more on key performance indicators (KPIs) to make projections about future financial performance. One element of nonfinancial information that is becoming increasingly important is that regarding a company's environmental, social, and governance (ESG) or CSR performance.

A number of frameworks have been proposed on how to use nonfinancial information to supplement financial reporting. In 2003, the Institute of Chartered Accountants in England and Wales (ICAEW) published a report summarizing and asking for dialogue on 11 proposed business reporting models dating back more than 10 years. The ICAEW report concluded, "None of these models, whatever their merits, has so far succeeded in commanding general support. At present, they provide a collection of interesting and challenging ideas, many of which seem to have little prospect of widespread implementation."[1] The same could be said today, although progress has been made and some of these ideas are gaining traction and converging. Consider three of the models reviewed in the ICAEW report: the Balanced Scorecard developed by Robert Kaplan and David Norton, the sustainability reporting guidelines developed by the GRI, and the ValueReporting Framework developed by PwC.

The Balanced Scorecard was developed largely for internal management and reporting purposes, although it is relevant for external reporting as well, as discussed further on.[2] The GRI and PwC began their work at about the same time in the late 1990s, and each had a different focus. The goal of the GRI, discussed further on, was to develop a reporting framework for providing stakeholders with relevant information on a company's economic, environmental, and social performance, with a much stronger emphasis on the latter two.[3] In contrast, the PwC ValueReporting Initiative (now called CorporateReporting) was focused on identifying information in which analysts, investors, and chief financial officers were interested for making investment decisions that went beyond the required financial information but with little attention to ESG factors. In addition to the development of a conceptual framework, PwC introduced industry-specific frameworks, KPIs, and associated XBRL taxonomies.[4] These were developed based on global surveys of analysts, investors, and executives in 16 industries; the survey results identified information, reporting, and quality gaps for industry-specific KPIs and intangible assets.[5]

As environmental and social performance metrics have become more important to investors, the GRI has begun to engage with a broader group of investors than the Socially Responsible Investment (SRI) funds, and PwC has developed its thinking about how ESG might, in practice, be embraced in its CorporateReporting Framework. Nonfinancial information adds a further dimension of complexity to external reporting, particularly since ESG and CSR information is typically contained in a separate report, or even two. Unlike financial information based on accounting standards, which ensure at least some degree of comparability across companies and over time, few standards exist for the measurement and reporting of nonfinancial information, making such comparisons difficult. Questions also exist about the reliability of this information. While some companies have independent assurance done on this information, they are not required to do so.

XBRL is as relevant for nonfinancial information as it is for financial information. As with a piece of financial information, each piece of nonfinancial information has a unique electronic tag. A taxonomy for nonfinancial information can be treated as an extension to the one for financial information. For example, a company could use the IFRS XBRL taxonomy for its financial statements and a compatible XBRL taxonomy for the ESG information it is reporting. A further extension could include company-specific metrics that management felt were especially important given its strategy.

A Typology of Nonfinancial Information

While the term *nonfinancial information* is being used with increasing frequency (see Exhibit 4.1), there is no commonly understood or generally accepted definition of this term, and in practice it is used in many different ways. For some, such as the International Corporate Governance Network, "non-financial business reporting is a wide-ranging term which can include both regulated and voluntary disclosure by companies. From a shareowner and investor perspective, it is information, other than financial statements, which is relevant and material to investment decision making."[6] For others, nonfinancial information is synonymous with sustainability or ESG information. The term is also used to refer to narrative contextual information, such as the MD&A required by the SEC, or to information on intangible assets and intellectual capital. Finally, some people equate nonfinancial information with KPIs. KPIs are generally quantitative measures that permit assessment of the quality, sustainability, and variability of a company's cash flows and earnings. Further complicating this terminology, the term *KPI* is also

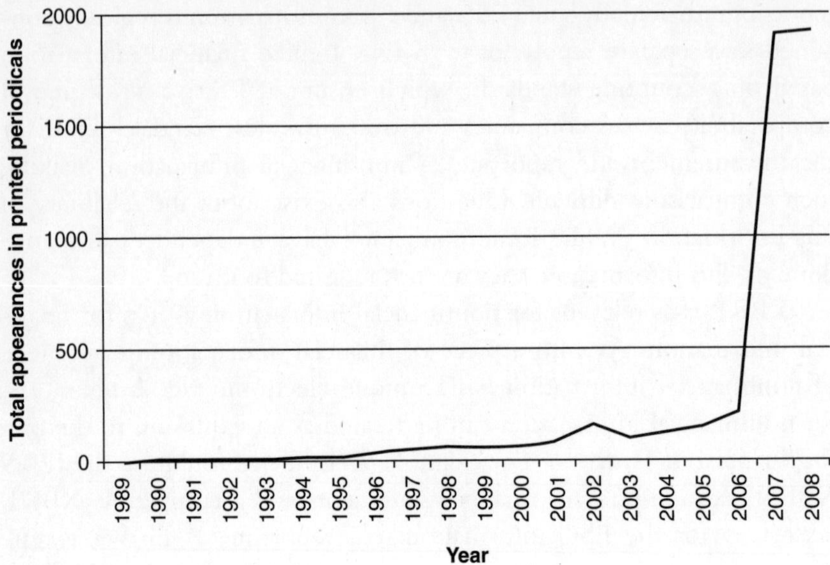

Exhibit 4.1 Increasing Use of the Term *Nonfinancial Information*, 1989–2008*
*For all of our "Increasing Use of the Term . . ." figures, we used the Dow Jones Factiva database to do a yearly word count for the use of the term in all publications included in the database.

often used to refer to financial information that is a leading indicator of other financial information, such as current sales growth as a leading indicator of future profits.

In 2008, AXA Investment Managers and AQ Research conducted a survey of investment professionals to identify the preferred terminology for sustainability information that is integrated with financial information for investment analysis and decisions. The survey asked respondents to rank 16 different terms (see Exhibit 4.2) often used to describe off-balance sheet factors that influence company performance, by inserting each term into the sentence "I now take (. . .) factors into account much more than I used to" and then using a numerical scale to rank each term. By averaging the scores generated by each description, the overall popularity of each was measured.[7]

Given that the focus of the survey was on the term used for sustainability information, it is not surprising to see that "environmental, social, and governance" and "sustainability" were ranked first and second, respectively. But the lack of consensus about terminology in the realm of

Exhibit 4.2 Preferred Terminology for Sustainability Information

Term	Approval Rating
Environmental, social, and governance	3.35
Sustainability	3.23
Responsible investment	3.05
Socially responsible investment	2.83
Social, environmental, and ethical	2.80
Ethical	2.74
Extra-financial	2.73
Enhanced business	2.70
Long horizon investment	2.68
Non-financial	2.47
Value reporting	2.40
Corporate health	2.37
Intangible	2.36
Corporate resilience	2.33
Management commentary	2.24
Non-traditional	2.14
None of these	1.90

nonfinancial information is illustrated by the fact that a number of other terms were ranked fairly highly, and is compounded by the fact that of the more than 350 respondents, 56 percent did not work with "responsible investments." According to Dr. Raj Thamotheram, Director of Responsible Investment at AXA, ". . . having found 16 different phrases to describe the kind of sustainability data that managers say they are now integrating into their mainstream analysis, it's hardly surprising people are confused and that integration is not moving as quickly as it could! If we want mainstreaming to accelerate going forwards, finding one or two consensus terms that embody what integration is about would be a very good move."[8]

Given this wide variation in terminology, it is unlikely that we are going to resolve it in this book. However, for purposes of our own exposition, we want to be clear about the meanings we have for the terms we are using. For us, *nonfinancial information* is a broad term that applies to all information reported to shareholders and other stakeholders that is not defined by an accounting standard or a calculation of a measure based on an accounting standard, such as revenue growth, which we will refer to as "financial information." Thus, nonfinancial can include economic information (e.g., market size in dollars), ratios that use accounting information (e.g., sales per square foot), and accounting-type measures for which no formal standard exists (e.g., core earnings). Nonfinancial reporting is the external reporting of nonfinancial information.

Based on current terminology, the broad category of nonfinancial information can be broken down into three subcategories: (1) intangible assets (including intellectual capital and other intangibles), (2) KPIs, and (3) ESG metrics. The structure of financial accounting with a balance sheet of assets and liabilities, an income statement of revenues and costs, and notes can be used to provide further clarity to the relationships between these three subcategories whose meanings often overlap in practice:

- *Intangible assets* are like assets, in that they are resources used to produce outcomes (stock variables).
- *KPIs* are like revenues in that they are outcomes (flow variables).[9]
- *ESG metrics* can either be an intangible asset or a KPI.

Under these definitions, it can be seen that most discussions of intangible assets and key performance indicators mix up balance sheet and income statement items. Just as financial statements contain notes providing further explanation, nonfinancial measures can have notes of explanation as well. These are especially important due to the lack of universal standards for nonfinancial reporting, although notes rarely appear. For completeness, we will briefly discuss the first two subcategories of nonfinancial information and then focus on the third since it is of central focus for this book.

Intangible Assets

A common motivation of those who study intangible assets is the large gap that exists between a company's market value and its accounting book value. Since 1998, at least five studies have shown that book value is about 25 to 35 percent of a company's market value.[10] The difference is ascribed to intangible assets that, unlike tangible assets, do not appear on the balance sheet.[11]

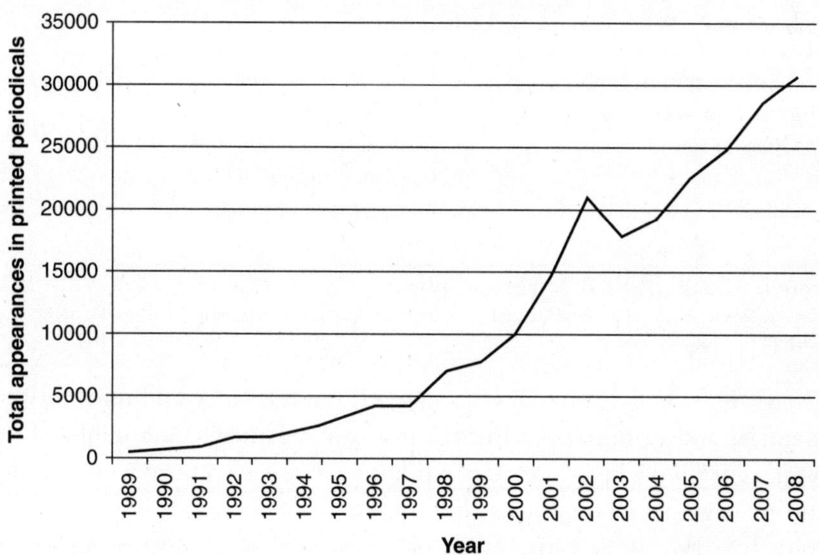

Exhibit 4.3 Increasing Use of the Term *Intangible Assets*, 1989–2008

Like the term *nonfinancial information*, *intangible assets* has no generally accepted meaning and is used interchangeably with the terms *intellectual assets*, *intellectual capital*, and *intangibles*. We will treat them as one, using the term *intangible assets* for the sake of simplicity. As with nonfinancial information, the term is becoming increasingly popular as interest in this topic grows (see Exhibit 4.3).

Intangible assets refer to nonphysical assets with the potential to create value, as opposed to physical or tangible assets, such as inventory, property, plant, and equipment, which are also used to create value. Common examples are human capital (which contributes to quality and thus to price), intellectual capital (which leads to new products), brand (good for market share and profit margins), and customer loyalty (which leads to repeat business and lower sales and marketing costs).[12] There is no universally accepted framework for intangible assets. However, several frameworks or classification schemes have been proposed. A 2006 report by the Organization for Economic Cooperation and Development (OECD) identified five frameworks that had been developed for defining and classifying intellectual assets. Common themes across all frameworks were such things as human capital, relationship capital, and intellectual property.[13]

Exhibit 4.4 Wyatt's Framework for Intangible Assets

Technology resources	1. Research and development and related IP
Human resources	2. Human capital
Production resources	3. Advertising, brands, and related IP
	4. Customer loyalty
	5. Competitive advantage
	6. Goodwill

NOTE: In the above exhibit, *IP* is "intellectual property."
SOURCE: Wyatt, Anne. *What Financial and Non-Financial Information on Intangibles is Value Relevant?* 2008, p. 5.

More recently, Anne Wyatt explored the relevance and reliability of financial and nonfinancial information on measuring intangibles. Her work canvassed a broad range of studies from the accounting, economic, and management literatures. She suggested a framework for intangible assets based on three broad types of "resources" that contains a total of six categories of intangibles, as seen in Exhibit 4.4.

Wyatt noted that these assets are measured by both financial and nonfinancial metrics and by both input metrics (e.g., number of scientists) and output metrics (e.g., number of patents). Illustrating the lack of clarity between *intangible assets* and *KPIs*, what Wyatt would call *output metrics* (e.g., number of patents) are *KPIs* for us. She specifically excluded environmental and social topics, although "arguments can be made that other categories such as environmental and social responsibility are also important."[14]

In terms of external reporting, few companies provide much in the way of information on their intangible assets in any meaningful and rigorous way. They are often referred to in glowing terms in the Chairman's letter or MD&A, such as the claims that the organization has "the best people" and "loyal customers," but rarely are any data given to back up these claims. This is not to say that such statements are irrelevant. They do communicate something about the company's values and focus, and these are important things for shareholders and stakeholders to know, but the information cannot be used in any analytical way.

Some countries are already addressing this issue with various initiatives to improve reporting about intangible assets. The OECD identified several national and regional efforts to encourage reporting of intangible assets as shown in Exhibit 4.5. The study was not intended to be

Exhibit 4.5 Selected Public Sector Initiatives for Reporting on Intangible Assets

Region/ Country	**Scope**	**Application**	**Year**	**Reference**
European Union	All companies	Voluntary	2002	Guidelines for Managing and Reporting on Intangibles, MERITUM Project
European Union	Small and medium-sized enterprises	Voluntary	2006	RICARDIS report, DG Research
Australia	All companies	Voluntary	2002	Australian Guiding Principles on Extended Performance Management, Society for Knowledge Economics
Austria	Public universities	Mandatory	2002	Austrian Universities Act, Federal Ministry of Education, Science and Culture
Denmark	All companies	Voluntary	2003	Intellectual Capital Statements—The new guideline, Ministry of Science, Technology and Innovation
Germany	Small and medium-sized enterprises	Voluntary	2004	Intellectual Capital Statement—Made in Germany, Federal Ministry of Economics and Labour
Japan	All companies	Voluntary	2005	Guidelines for Disclosure of Intellectual Assets Based Management, Ministry of Economy, Trade, and Industry

SOURCE: Organization for Economic Cooperation and Development. *Intellectual Assets and Value Creation: Implications for Corporate Reporting*, December 2006, p. 16.

comprehensive but simply to illustrate that a number of different approaches were being taken. All seven of these initiatives are voluntary, with the exception of Austria, where it is mandatory for all universities.

Intangible Assets at Infosys

Some specific companies are working very hard to provide extensive and rigorous disclosures regarding intangible assets. One example is Infosys Technologies Limited, a multinational information technology company based in Bangalore, India. In its 2008–2009 corporate annual report, Infosys begins the discussion of intangible assets with a brief section titled, "The strength of the invisible," explaining that this disclosure is necessary if it is to lead the debate on what the balance sheet of the future might look like. Management specifically noted that "it is becoming increasingly clear that intangible assets have a significant role in defining the growth of a high-tech company."[15] V. Balakrishnan, the company's Chief Financial Officer, explained, "In knowledge-based companies, the value is derived from the intellectual properties and intangible assets possessed by the company, which do not get reflected in a traditional financial statement. Hence valuing these intangible assets helps investors to understand and appreciate the real intrinsic value of these companies."[16] At the close of its 2009 fiscal year on March 31, the company had a market capitalization of $14.95 billion and assets on the balance sheet of $4.45 billion.[17]

To reduce information asymmetry between Infosys's management and its shareholders, the company made the following additional disclosures relevant to better understanding intangible assets, and specifically stated that "these reports are integral to the Annual Report":[18]

- Brand valuation
- Balance sheet including intangible assets
- Economic Value-Added (EVA) statement
- Intangible asset scorecard
- Risk management report
- Human resource accounting and value-added statement

Commenting on these additional disclosures, the company noted that "we continue to provide additional information even though it is not mandated by law because we believe that it will enable investors to make more informed choices about our performance."[19]

Key Performance Indicators

Key performance indicators (KPIs), another term of increasing use as seen in Exhibit 4.6, are quantitative measures of results, achieved using tangible and intangible assets, which are regarded as leading indicators of financial performance. The basic argument for KPIs is that the income statement is a "rearview mirror," providing information about profitability over a historical period of time. The income statement reflects financial performance based on decisions that have already been made—for example, revenues are a result of successful versus unsuccessful proposals. Thus, a leading indicator for revenues could be percentage of proposals that result in contracts. If the number is going up, assuming the same size of contract and time to deliver it, future revenues will be up as well. By definition, any result is "historical" in that it is a measure of something that has already happened. In that sense, KPIs are also historical, but the difference is that a properly chosen KPI can be a good leading indicator of future financial results, although it may not be a good leading indicator of itself.

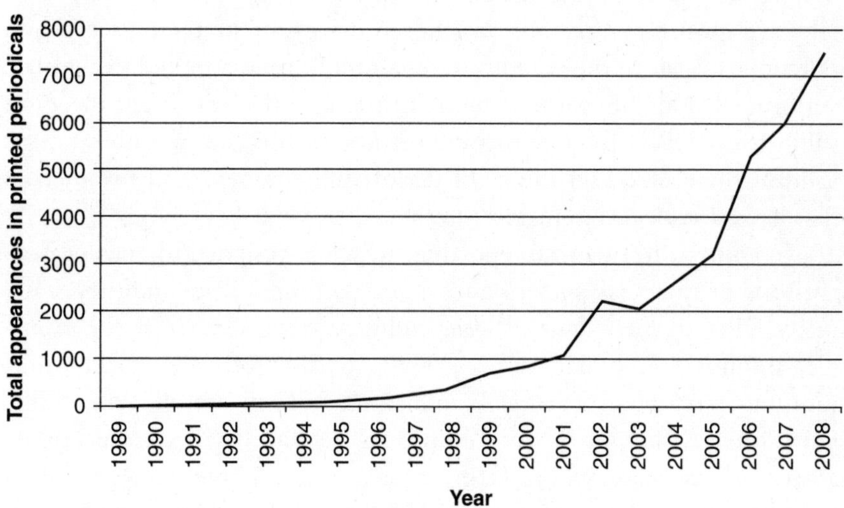

Exhibit 4.6 Increasing Use of the Term *Key Performance Indicators*, 1989–2008

In most uses of the term, KPIs are nonfinancial in that they are not based on accounting conventions. KPIs are metrics regarding things like product quality, employee turnover, new product development success rates, customer retention, and so forth. KPIs, which some also call *operating metrics*, are used by management to implement and monitor the implementation of their strategies.

The relationship between KPIs and financial outcomes can be described in terms of a cause-and-effect model that is essentially the translation of a company's strategy into a set of related metrics. One of the best examples of this is Kaplan and Norton's Balanced Scorecard concept. The Balanced Scorecard views "organizational performance from four perspectives: financial, customer, internal business processes and learning and growth."[20] It emphasizes the need to link these measures to the company's strategy through three principles: (1) cause-and-effect relationships, (2) performance drivers (i.e., leading indicators), and (3) linkage to financials. The next critical step is to view every KPI as an element in an if-then statement that fully describes the strategy of a business unit or an organization.[21]

Determining which KPIs truly are leading indicators of financial results is easier said than done. In a survey of 157 companies, Christopher D. Ittner and David F. Larcker found that only 23 percent "consistently built and verified causal models (diagrams laying out the cause-and-effect relationships between the chosen drivers of strategic success and outcomes)." More often, companies simply "have adopted boilerplate versions of nonfinancial measurement frameworks."[22] To get the most value from KPIs, they advise companies to link metrics to strategy, validate these links, set the right performance targets, and use metrics that have statistical significance.

In contrast to financial reporting, which is designed to enable comparisons of financial performance (e.g., earnings) *across* industry lines, many KPIs are best defined *along* industry lines. Consider, for example, Exhibit 4.7, which displays KPIs for the software, telecommunications, and pharmaceuticals industries.[23] They are all very different. Other KPIs will be very company-specific, based on the unique aspects of its strategy. This logic follows the "Three-Tier Model of Corporate Transparency," suggested by Samuel A. DiPiazza and Robert G. Eccles. Tier One is "Globally Generally Accepted Accounting

Exhibit 4.7 Illustrative KPIs for Three Industries

Software	Telecommunications	Pharmaceuticals
Bugs in products and support	Subscriber mix	R&D pipeline
Customer satisfaction and renewal of maintenance contracts	Churn rate	Market share by therapeutic area
Number and "quality" of users (where quality refers to the likelihood that the name of an existing client will influence the buying decision of prospective customers)	Network operating costs	Revenue from drugs introduced in the previous three years

Principles" (e.g., the convergence of U.S. GAAP and IFRS discussed in the previous chapter), Tier Two is "Industry-Based Standards," and Tier Three is "Company-Specific Information."[24]

Narrative Reporting

Few, if any, companies publish separate Key Performance Indicator reports. However, they are increasingly making this information available on their Web sites, as well as using it in presentations to analysts and investors (which are also often posted on the Web site). Information on KPIs can also be included in the narrative section of the annual report, such as the Management's Discussion and Analysis (MD&A) in the United States or the Operating and Financial Review section (OFR is a "best practice" and not required) for U.K. companies. UTC provides an example of this approach with the KPIs published in its 2008 annual report.

The narrative section is often referred to as providing contextual information to support the financial information presented in the much more structured income statement, balance sheet, and notes. This contextual information—including the company's strategy, plans for implementation, a competitive analysis of the industry, and the general economic environment—helps to explain the financial results and can provide some insight into whether future financial results will be better or worse. While there are guidelines for this narrative information, they are very general and broad. Thus, the content of the narrative section varies tremendously in terms of both quantity and quality. In the best case, it can be as important as the financial information; in the worst case, it can be little more than unsubstantiated claims of goodness and prowess.

The Net Promoter Score at Allianz

A good example of a KPI is the increasingly popular customer loyalty Net Promoter Score (NPS) developed by Frederick F. Reichheld. The concept is based on research that shows a relationship between customer loyalty and profitable growth, since loyal customers promote a company's products and services.[25] The NPS is calculated by subtracting the percentage of customers who are detractors from those who are promoters based on the simple question "How likely is it that you would recommend [Company X] to a friend?" using a 10-point scale.[26]

German insurance and investment company Allianz Group began using the NPS in 2006. Emilio Galli Zugaro, Head of Corporate Communications, explained, "We must understand and meet every customer's expectations in every interaction with the company. If we do this continuously and even exceed them, we build loyalty."[27] Allianz published its overall NPS online, including targets for improvement. The company has a goal of being the customer loyalty leader in its industry, as measured by the NPS.

Allianz's own research confirmed that the NPS was a leading indicator of top-line organic growth. In 2008 alone, Allianz's companies rated better than a peer average and grew top-line revenue by 6.4 percent—an especially good rate for mature markets where growth is usually flat. Allianz Australia Insurance Group Managing Director Terry Towell provided further evidence: "Although we are in the early stages, we're definitely seeing correlations between retention, growth rates, and NPS results in our broker channel. In the past twelve months, we won some significant accounts that would have been beyond our reach previously. We're now much more focused on delivering customer solutions."[28] In 2008, the percentage of Allianz companies with better customer loyalty than the local peer average had tripled to 34 percent since the Customer Focus program was launched in 2006.[29]

Environmental, Social, and Governance Metrics

Environmental, social, and governance (ESG) metrics measure a company's performance in each of these domains. Although commonly lumped together under the theme of sustainability, discussed in more detail in the next chapter, each one of these domains has its own set of forces creating pressures on companies for greater disclosure. Respectively, these are the environmental movement, increasing consciousness about the broader role of business in society, and continuing concerns about lapses in corporate governance. Whether an ESG metric is an intangible asset or a KPI depends on whether it is a resource that produces outcomes, such as goodwill in the community, or an outcome itself, such as lost production time due to accidents. Kaplan and Norton's Balanced Scorecard incorporates the environmental and social components of ESG as regulatory and social processes in the *internal perspective* part of the scorecard, as shown in Exhibit 4.8. These processes contribute to the results in the customer and financial perspectives. Further elaborating on this, Kaplan noted:

> Good ESG performance directly contributes to a company's financial performance. A good ESG reputation helps to attract and retain high-quality employees, thereby making human resource processes more efficient and effective. Reducing environmental incidents and improving employee safety and health improves productivity and lowers operating costs. Finally, companies with outstanding ESG reputations generally enjoy an enhanced image with customers and socially conscious investors. For all these reasons, we strongly encourage companies to include performance objectives for their ESG processes in the process perspective of their strategy maps and scorecards. In that way, ESG performance becomes integrated with all the other components of a company's strategy and used to set priorities for initiatives, guide operational actions, evaluate managers' performance, and stimulate discussion at the leadership team's strategy review meetings.[30]

There are a number of groups actively looking to develop ways of measuring and reporting on ESG, including Asset4, KLD Research and Analytics, and Trucost.[31] Likewise, the Society of Investment

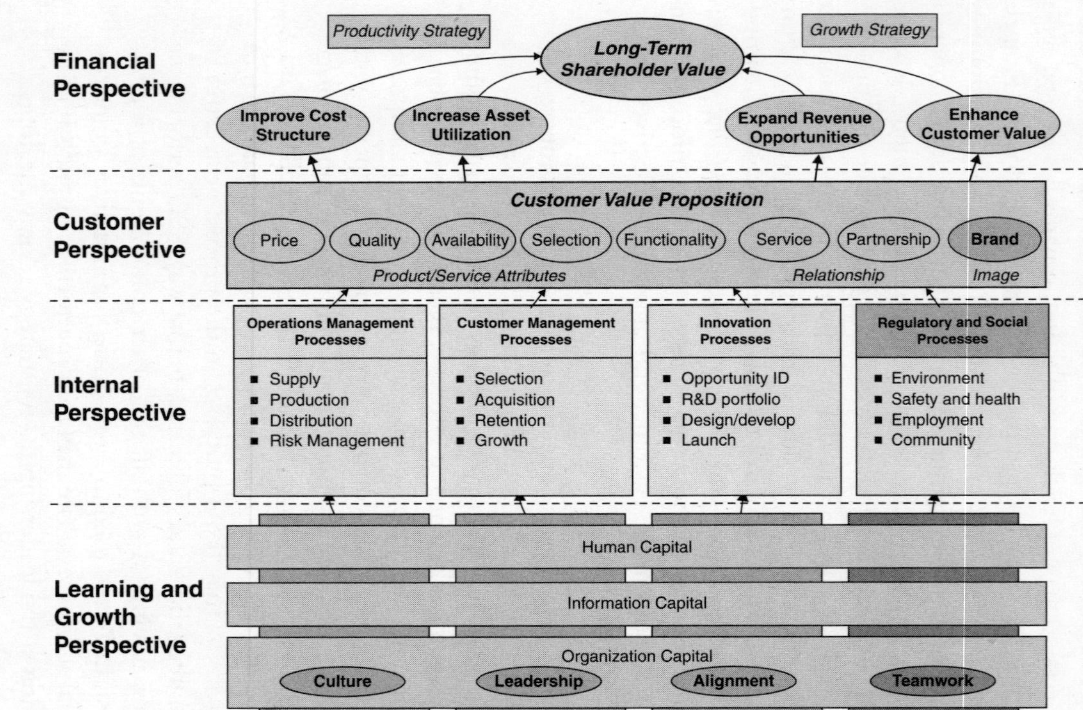

Exhibit 4.8 Environmental and Social Processes in the Balanced Scorecard

SOURCE: Kaplan, Robert S., and Norton, David P. *Strategy Maps*. Boston: Harvard Business School Press, 2004, p. 164.

Professionals in Germany (DVFA) and the European Federation of Financial Analysts Societies established a high-level framework based on the pillars of environmental, social, governance, and long-term viability.[32] The last category clearly indicates their interest in the impact of ESG on long-term corporate performance. Within each pillar are several categories; each category is a "parent" for which there is a "child" relationship with at least one KPI and typically more than one. The DVFA established some generic KPIs considered to be relevant across all industries and also developed industry-specific ESG KPIs for industrial transportation, automobiles, electric utilities, banks, and non-life insurance companies. Exhibit 4.9 shows the "parents" within each pillar, and Exhibit 4.10 shows selected "child" KPIs for the automobile industry. Each KPI is accompanied by a clear definition and methodology for calculation, although in *principles-based* rather than *rules-based* form.[33]

Exhibit 4.9 Overview of Automobile Sector Pillars

E **Environmental**	**S** **Social**	**G** **Governance**	**V** **Long-Term Viability**
ESG 10 Deployment of renewable energy	ESG 19 Investments in accordance with ESG	ESG 24 Contributions to political parties	ESG 25 R&D expenses
ESG 11 NO, SO Emissions	ESG 20 Supplier agreements in accordance with ESG		ESG 26 Patents
ESG 12 Waste	ESG 21 Health & safety of products		ESG 28 Customer retention
ESG 13 Environmental compatibility	ESG 22 Restructuring-related relocation of jobs		ESG 29 Customer satisfaction
ESG 14 End-of-lifecycle impact			

Note: The "parents" are the factors identified as ESG 10 through ESG 29.
Source: European Federation of Financial Analysts Societies. Key Performance Indicators for Environmental, Social, and Governance Issues, p. 29.

Exhibit 4.10 Overview of Selected Automobile Sector Pillar Categories and Related KPIs

Pillar Category ("Parent")	KPI ("Child")
ESG 10 Deployment of renewable energy	ESG 10-1 % of energy in kwh from renewable energy sources as of total energy consumed ESG 10-2 % of energy in kwh from combined heat and power generation as of total energy consumed
ESG 12 Waste	ESG 12-1 Waste by unit produced ESG 12-2 % of waste recycled
ESG 13 Environmental compatibility	ESG 13-1 Average fuel consumption of fleet of sold cars ESG 13-2 Percentage of ISO 14001 certified sites corporates
ESG 21 Health & safety aspects of products	ESG 21-1 Total spending on product safety/revenue ESG 21-2 Percentage of product recalls for safety or health reasons as of total recalls ESG 21-3 Spending on product safety per unit produced
ESG 26 Patents	ESG 26-1 Number of patents registered within last 12 months ESG 26-2 Number of patents registered within last 12 months as percentage of total number of patents ESG 26-3 Number of patents due to expire within next 12 months ESG 26-4 Number of patents due to expire within next 12 months as percentage of total number of patents
ESG 28 Customer retention	ESG 28-1 Percentage of new customers as of total customers ESG 28-2 Average length of time of customer relationship in years ESG 28-3 Share of market by product, product line, segment, region, or total

SOURCE: European Federation of Financial Analysts Societies. *Key Performance Indicators for Environmental, Social and Governance Issues*, p. 29.

Ralf Frank, Managing Director of DVFA, remarked that his organization's approach to defining KPIs for ESG was a necessary step to define clear-cut and measurable indicators that portray the expectations of investment professionals. However, the next goal of DVFA is to encourage corporate executives to give those KPIs a sufficient level of recognition: "We would like KPIs for ESG to become an integral part of the annual general report, ideally within the MD&A, and also see them reported in the risk and opportunity section of analyst presentations."[34] Gunter Verheugen, Vice-President of the European Commission, explained the value of this from an investor's perspective: "There is indeed no other powerful incentive to consider the strategic role of CSR than an investor able to value the role that it plays for the future prosperity and sustainability of a business."[35]

Growth in ESG Reporting

In contrast to intangible assets and KPIs, separate ESG or CSR reports are being issued by an increasing number of companies. Exhibit 4.11 shows the growth in number of CSR reports and Exhibit 4.12 shows the number of reports by country for the period 1992 to 2008. Steve Lydenberg, Chief Investment Officer of Domini Social Investments and

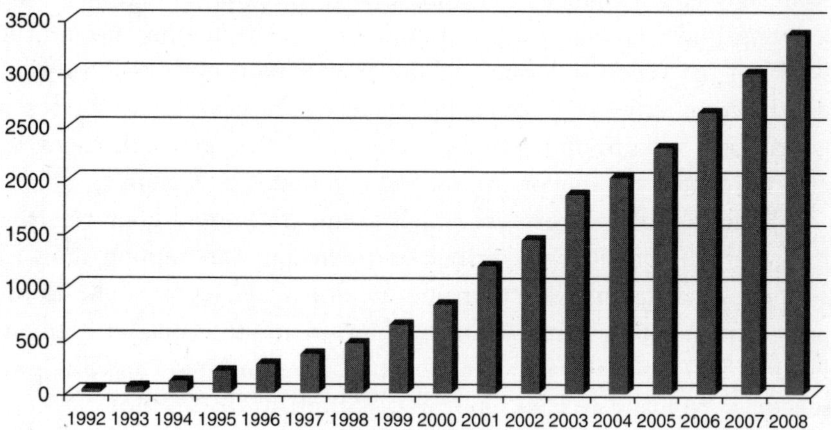

Exhibit 4.11 Growth in Number of Corporate Social Responsibility Reports
NOTE: The authors would like to thank Paul Scott and CorporateRegister.com for access to the underlying data.
SOURCE: CorporateRegister.com.

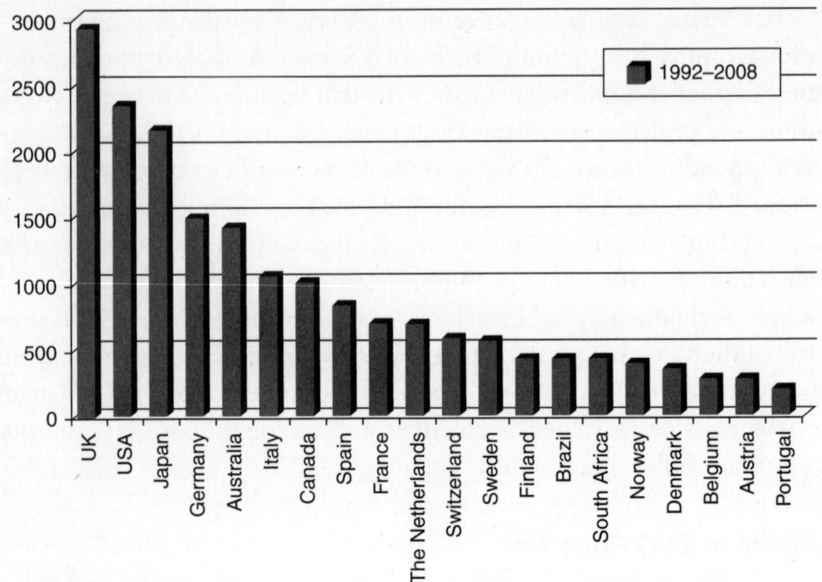

Exhibit 4.12 Corporate Social Responsibility Reports by Country
NOTE: The authors would like to thank Paul Scott and CorporateRegister.com for access to the underlying data.
SOURCE: CorporateRegister.com.

co-author of the forthcoming book *How to Read a Corporate Social Responsibility Report* opined, "This increase in ESG reporting reflects the growing understanding on the part of major corporations around the world of the crucial relevance of this information not only to the financial community as it assesses [its] financial prospects but to society in general as it seeks to understand the impacts of these global firms on the environment, working conditions, and communities in general."[36]

Although these reports are largely voluntary in most countries, this is changing. For example, France and Sweden were among the first countries mandating that companies publish CSR reports. The European Sustainable Investment Forum (Eurosif) and the Social Investment Forum (SIF) have formally called for the European Union and SEC, respectively, to mandate ESG reporting.[37] Similarly, the Investor Network on Climate Risk, representing approximately $1.4 trillion in assets, has asked the SEC to "issue formal guidance on material climate-related risks that companies should disclose and enforce existing disclosure requirements for climate change and other risks."[38]

The usual proliferation of terminology and its attendant confusion and ambiguity exists in this area. Other names for ESG reports are "financial, social and environmental performance" (Novo Nordisk), "environmental health and safety" (Jardine Engineering Corporation), "corporate social responsibility" (Hitachi Group), "corporate sustainability" (UPS), "corporate responsibility" (UTC), "sustainability" (Duke Energy), and "corporate citizenship" (Novartis). Further adding to the confusion, for some companies a "corporate social responsibility" report is largely about its philanthropic activities (The Boeing Company). Finally, ESG is sometimes referred to as "triple bottom line reporting," although their meanings are not exactly the same.[39] Commenting on this terminological variety, Brendan May, Managing Director of Planet 2050, the global CSR and sustainability practice at Weber Shandwick, a United States–based public relations firm, observed, "It is probably too late to do anything about the plethora of terms for a company's broader social obligations. What a company calls it is less important than really doing it. But I'm afraid there's a lot more talk here than real action."[40] Exhibit 4.13 shows the increasing frequency of the phrase "environmental, social, and governance."

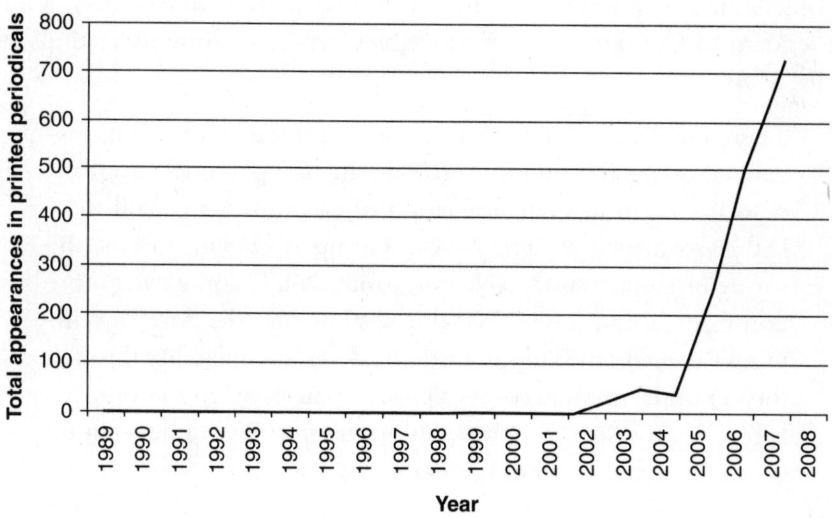

Exhibit 4.13 Increasing Use of the Term *Environmental, Social, and Governance*, 1989–2008

ESG Reporting at BMW Group

In its *Sustainable Value Report 2008*, BMW Group reports a number of what it explicitly refers to as KPIs, which are determined by a "materiality analysis" based on the criteria of "highly relevant for the BMW Group" and "highly relevant for stakeholders." In the "Group-wide environmental protection" section of the report, the company provides information on such KPIs as energy consumed, water consumption, waste for disposal, and volatile organic compounds, all measured per vehicle produced. The company regards these environmental metrics as KPIs because improvements drive overall manufacturing efficiencies that result in lower future production costs. They also contribute to the company's reputation as the world's "greenest" car company: "According to the Dow Jones Sustainability Indexes, the BMW Group is currently the world's most sustainable carmaker. The company has remained the industry leader in these important global corporate sustainability indices for four consecutive years, most recently in 2008. Numerous other ratings and awards also confirm the company's leading role in the field of sustainability."[41]

Studies conducted by the company show that its reputation in this field plays a role in brand awareness and customer satisfaction, thus contributing to revenue growth. According to Bill McAndrews, Vice President of Communications Strategy/Corporate Communications at BMW AG:

> There is a definite trend that key performance indicators of sustainability are becoming more relevant for potential investors, who use them in their evaluation of a company's overall market performance. . . . The BMW Group is convinced that the strong interest in sustainable companies will become even more dominant in the future. For this very reason, the company intends to remain the auto industry leader in sustainability through the continual improvement of processes involved in the vehicle's lifecycle, as well as fully integrating sustainability targets within the entire value chain of the company.[42]

Exhibit 4.14 illustrates how the company has reduced water consumption from 3.03 cubic meters in 2004 to 2.56 cubic meters in 2008.

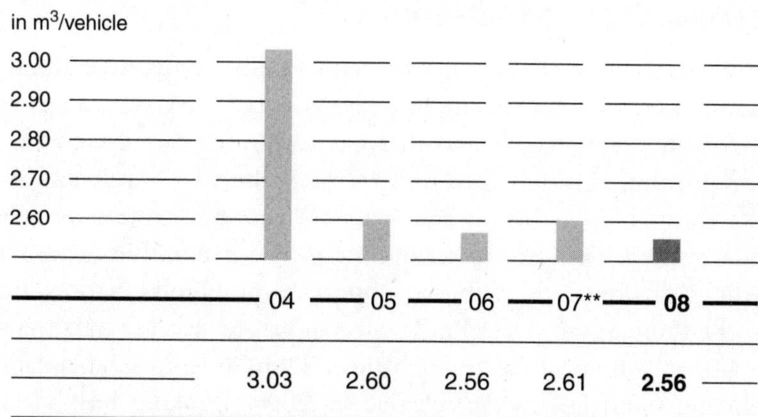

Exhibit 4.14 Water Consumption per Vehicle Produced
NOTE: In 2007, BMW Group expanded data collection from 10 sites to 17.
SOURCE: BMW Group. *Sustainable Value Report 2008*, p. 39.

In addition to reporting on past performance, BMW also sets targets for future performance, in this case a 30 percent reduction from 2006 to 2012, at an average rate of 5 percent per year in its global production network, noting that "This target is subject to changes due to vehicle start of production, end of production or fluctuations in production volumes."[43] In addition, BMW defined water consumption as being both the water used during production and in general use, such as in sanitation facilities; standards in the reporting of water consumption may become of increasing importance as other car manufacturers may measure their consumption differently, making comparison difficult.

Nevertheless, BMW has attempted to make these comparisons since it sees its focus on water consumption as a source of competitive advantage and value creation. Using a methodology developed by Sustainable Value, the company calculated that it had created €3 billion in value based on the difference between its profits of €923 per cubic meter of water consumed and the automobile industry average of €96 per cubic meter.[44] In a study conducted by Sustainable Value of 16 automobile manufacturers, BMW was ranked second, after Toyota, in terms of total sustainable value created.[45] If company size were taken into account, BMW Group would lead in six of the seven years assessed, thus outperforming Toyota.

The Global Reporting Initiative

No discussion about ESG and CSR reporting is complete if it fails to mention the Global Reporting Initiative (GRI). The GRI is a powerful and globally recognized brand that has set the de facto standards for ESG reporting. It was formed in 1997 by Robert K. Massie and Allen White through two Boston-based not-for-profit organizations, Ceres (formerly the Coalition for Environmentally Responsible Economies) and the Tellus Institute, with the support of the United Nations Environment Programme (UNEP). Their goal was to develop a framework for reporting sustainability information. The GRI's first Sustainability Reporting Guidelines were released in 2000. Looking back, Massie reflected:

> The GRI was built on the notion that transparency would allow everyone to see—and thus to accept intellectually and morally—their own responsibility for the choices that we face today and in the future. In this we feel we are beginning to succeed, though much more needs to be done with firms to bring about recognition of the connection between cause and action in the creation of lasting prosperity for all stakeholders.[46]

Today, the GRI is an independent, global organization. It is open to all organizations with an interest in sustainability reporting; these organizations can register to become Organizational Stakeholders with voting rights in the election of Stakeholder Council members. Individuals can register to receive the newsletter, but do not have any voting rights. There are 20,000 Stakeholders from more than 80 countries, representing corporations, governments, NGOs, consultancies, accounting firms, business and trade associations, rating organizations, universities, and research institutes.[47] Remarked White:

> We built GRI in the belief that a globalized world needs a generally-accepted global standard for nonfinancial reporting to achieve the accountability and transparency that all stakeholders need and deserve. A decade after its conception and in the wake of a global economic crisis driven in large measure by a breakdown in accountability and transparency, this core belief has never been more compelling.[48]

The G3 Guidelines (G3), launched in October 2006, are the third generation of the GRI's Sustainability Reporting Guidelines. The G3 consist of broad principles, guidance, and standard disclosure (including performance indicators) that should be included in sustainability reports.[49] The Guidelines include Indicator Protocols (definitions and compilation guidance), Technical Protocols (guidance on issues in reporting), and Sector Supplements (sector-specific Performance Indicators and guidance on how to apply the Guidelines in a specific sector). In broad terms, the G3 Guidelines recommend specific information related to economic, environmental, and social performance. They are structured around a CEO statement; key economic, environmental, and social indicators; a profile of the reporting entity; descriptions of relevant policies and management systems; stakeholder relationships; management performance; operational performance; product performance; and a sustainability overview.

As a sign of its impact, the GRI was aware of 1,002 organizations worldwide that issued sustainability reports based on the GRI G3 Guidelines in 2008. This represented an increase of 46 percent over the 685 organizations that issued reports using the GRI G3 in 2007.[50] The organization has both strong supporters and vocal detractors, reflecting the tensions inherent in a nongovernmental initiative attempting to meet the information needs of a wide range of stakeholders. A critical challenge is whether GRI's well-established Stakeholder community and Framework development processes[51] will permit the level of collaboration with business and mainstream investors necessary for a balanced focus on matters that are material to financial performance, environmental stewardship, and social responsibility. "Comprehensive sustainability reporting enables companies and stakeholders to engage in a constructive discussion about the costs and values associated not only with greenhouse gases, but the wider set of social, economic, and environmental criteria," commented Ernst Ligteringen, Chief Executive of GRI, explaining the draw for businesses and investors to collaborate.[52]

GRI guidelines are created through a multistakeholder process. Its objective is to bring together a wide spectrum of interests—business, civil society, labor, accounting firms, investors, academics, governments, and others—to reach a consensus on the content of the GRI guidelines. Some have expressed the concern that GRI's stakeholder process has become too captive of certain stakeholder groups, which narrowly focus on one issue. For certain NGOs, these can be very narrow indeed, in the belief that performance can be optimized along one dimension without any cost to all the others. Ligteringen countered this concern by noting that "no one group is favored in our multi-stakeholder process" and, further, "companies find value in the broad range of stakeholders included in the GRI's consultative process since just as NGOs can have distorted views about companies, companies can be mistaken in their assessment of different stakeholder perspectives, which some have learned at their peril."[53]

Another concern that has been raised is the lack of involvement from the investment community. Ligteringen countered this view as well when he observed, "In setting the G3 Guidelines, we created a specific investor consultation group comprised of mainstream investors, and their input had a significant impact."[54] At the same time, he acknowledged the difficulty of getting them involved because investors must allocate time and resources to the stakeholder engagement process, and it is not clear that there is an immediate benefit to their asset-owning clients. Sean Gilbert of the GRI also admitted this was a problem, but added, "The FASB and the IASB face a similar challenge in getting investor participation for setting accounting standards."[55]

Another challenge faced by the GRI is ensuring that the financial relevance of the information prepared according to its guidelines is clear. Following extensive consultation with several financial services firms, in a March 2009 report the GRI addressed the critical need for companies to present ESG data in a way that clearly links ESG performance and business strategy. In a press release about the report, Gilbert stated, "As we can see from the number of investors now actively seeking ESG information in order to help them base investment decisions, the dichotomy between sustainability and long-term business value is false,"[56] arguing, as we do in Chapter 5, that the information needs of institutional investors and the broader stakeholder community are converging.

Assurance on Nonfinancial Information

Just as nonfinancial information can be expressed in XBRL similarly to financial information, it can also be subject to various procedures that would result in an expression of *assurance*[57] or *attestation*.[58] These terms may be expressed in either positive assurance (i.e., "in our opinion...") or negative assurance (i.e., "nothing came to our attention..."). We avoid using the word *audit* in this section because in both international and U.S. standards for the auditing profession the term *audit* is only used when applied to historical financial statements and accompanying notes. In most countries today, assurance on nonfinancial information is completely voluntary. However, a 2008 study by KPMG found a clear trend in the number of companies getting an assurance opinion on their CSR report, with more than 50 percent of 2008 reports in France, Italy, Spain, and the United Kingdom having one. The United States had the lowest percentage, at 14 percent, but it was up from 2 percent in 2002; the mean for the Global *Fortune* 250 was 40 percent.[59]

Discussion about providing assurance on nonfinancial information is not new. In 1996, SEC Commissioner Steve Wallman addressed the issue at an AICPA conference:

> We currently provide varying degrees of attestation to information in financial statements, ranging from full audits to reviews of such information. Admittedly, it would be more difficult to attest to much of the information [intellectual and other intangible assets] that might be provided under the proposed model. For example, it may be difficult to arrive at a consensus among auditors regarding whether management's estimates of the value of a brand name are valid. However, although it may be difficult to attest to the value of such assets *per se*, it may be possible for auditors to attest to the procedures used by management to make such valuation estimates. Clearly, this area will need additional thought.[60]

In its 2002 report, *The Future of the Accounting Profession*, The American Assembly argued for new attestation standards. The report stated, "The current standard is appropriate for some, but not all, transactions. Going forward, auditors should be prepared to offer, and investors to accept, more limited attestations when the facts require them."[61]

Assurance on nonfinancial information can be provided by firms that perform financial audits, as well as by other organizations that have the competence and credibility to do so. For example, specialist engineering firms are often called upon to provide assurance on a company's emissions, and boutique consulting firms provide assurance on

CSR reports. Such firms may conduct these engagements using, for example, AccountAbility 1000AS (2008), a freely available international standard that provides the requirements for conducting sustainability assurance.[62] The six international audit networks would seem well-positioned to provide assurance on nonfinancial information, and are already doing so to varying degrees outside the United States, using, for example, International Standard on Assurance Engagement 3000.

One constraint on the auditing profession's ability to provide assurance is the lack of standards for nonfinancial information that would be equivalent to IFRS or U.S. GAAP. Information standards' development is already happening with carbon emissions (see the section titled "The Climate Disclosure Standards Board") and the model being used here could conceivably be extended to other climate-related and environmental metrics, and even more generally. If and when information standards are developed, today's assurance standards may need to be refined or developed anew.

The Climate Disclosure Standards Board

The Climate Disclosure Standards Board (CDSB), a consortium of business and environmental organizations, "was convened at the 2007 Annual Meeting of the World Economic Forum in response to increasing calls for action from corporations and financial markets to address global warming and the associated growth of climate risk information collection and reporting methodologies and initiatives."[63] The purpose of the CDSB is to facilitate the development of a generally accepted international framework for disclosures about climate change-related risks and opportunities, including carbon emissions. It intends this framework, issued as an Exposure Draft in May 2009, to be principles-based, "with the right balance between rules and principles," and to be one that can be integrated "in mainstream financial reports."[64] In our parlance, the framework would include both intangible assets and key performance indicators in the environmental category. Reflecting the growing link between climate issues and financial performance—which will become even stronger with tax or cap-and-trade systems—the CDSB wants to connect "financial and non-financial reporting through a focus on how climate change affects value creation."[65] Appendix II of the Exposure Draft, prepared by PwC, is an illustrative example using the fictional company "Typico plc" to demonstrate how a company might report on its carbon emissions based on the premise that "most companies will include some climate change information in their mainstream financial reports."[66]

The Carbon Disclosure Project (CDP) acts as Secretariat to CDSB and is responsible for advancing the CDSB Framework in association with members of the CDSB Board, Advisory Committee and Technical Working Group.[67] The CDP is a nonprofit organization, sponsored by companies and institutional investors, that conducts an annual survey on behalf of 475 institutional investors of 3,700 companies regarding their climate-related disclosure practices. The CDSB board is composed of CDP, Ceres, The Climate Group, The Climate Registry, the International Emissions Trading Association, the World Economic Forum, and the World Resources Institute. The members of the Technical Working Group include Deloitte, Ernst & Young, KPMG, PricewaterhouseCoopers, the Association of Chartered Certified Accountants, the Canadian Institute of Chartered Accountants, the International Federation of Accountants, the Institute of Chartered Accountants in England and Wales, and the Japanese Institute of Certified Public Accountants.[68]

CDSB's Chairman, Rick Samans of the World Economic Forum, explained, "CDSB is responding to demands for information on how climate change affects business strategies and finances by proposing a single global framework that reflects both the global nature of climate change and the gradual convergence of accounting standards, which form the foundation of financial reporting."[69]

Despite its name and obvious similarity to the FASB or IASB, the CDSB does not intend to be a standards-setting organization in the strictest sense. Instead, it seeks to:

- "Harmonize corporate climate change-related disclosure to form the common approach that is necessary for comparability and

(*continued*)

(*Continued*)

for the implementation of policies under discussion through the UN Framework Convention on Climate Change (UNFCCC) negotiations; and

- Provide conceptual and practical input into deliberations by regulatory agencies contemplating the introduction or development of requirements on corporate climate change-related disclosure."[70]

Through its efforts, the CDSB hopes that standards on carbon and other climate-related disclosures will emerge, providing robust principles for the production of reliable information through voluntary or mandatory channels. Through support from or collaboration with the FASB and IASB, or through other regulatory bodies, the CDSB hopes that the standards will complement the development of an XBRL taxonomy and auditing standards. If and when this happens, this particular type of nonfinancial information will have all of the characteristics of financial information. The membership of the Technical Working Group is a clear signal of the strong analogy the CDSB is drawing between its work and that of its accounting namesakes.

"Global climate risk disclosure standards are important to providing investors information that enables rigorous comparisons between companies," said Mindy S. Lubber, President of Ceres and a founding board member of the CDSB. "If securities regulators implement high quality standards, analysts can incorporate climate risks into financial models, which would be of huge benefit to institutional investors."[71]

Whether and to what extent nonfinancial information should be verified through an assurance process is an important question for shareholders who must pay for it, even though all stakeholders benefit from it. An equity research report by Claudia Kruse and Bramen Singanayagam of JP Morgan Chase & Co. suggested some market interest in audits of nonfinancial information. They argued that incentive schemes should be structured to support a company's strategy and long-term performance and emphasized that the right set of metrics will be industry and company specific. They identified three classes of performance measures: (1) share price–based metrics, for example, Total Shareholder Return, (2) accounting-based metrics, for example, earnings per share, profit, cash flow, or return on capital, and (3) non-accounting metrics, such as customer satisfaction, subscriber additions, and the like. In terms of the third class of performance measures, they noted: "Non-accounting metrics, such as subscriber additions, commonly lack standardized definitions and are generally unaudited. We believe companies should work to develop standard industry definitions to improve comparability and reliability. Where companies use such metrics we would expect them to be assessed by an independent third party."[72]

Whether nonfinancial information should be mandatorily disclosed and assured is an important public policy question that inevitably raises issues about the liabilities to the organizations that provide the assurance. If investors and society determine that ESG results are as important as financial results, they need to decide whether they are willing to pay for assurance that enhances the credibility and quality of this reported information. This will require better standards and, in most cases, improvements to corporate information and control systems. Not surprising, few companies today have internal measurement and control systems for nonfinancial information that are as rigorous and sophisticated as those for financial information. This is something that needs to be addressed. We believe that shareholders and other stakeholders will be increasingly demanding of high-quality nonfinancial information that determines future financial results.

Notes

1. Institute of Chartered Accountants in England and Wales. *Information for Better Markets: New Reporting Models for Business*, November 2003, p. 2.
2. Kaplan, Robert S., and Norton, David P. *The Balanced Scorecard*. Boston: Harvard Business Press, 1996.
3. Global Reporting Initiative. "G3 Guidelines," www.globalreporting.org/ReportingFramework/G3Guidelines, accessed August 2009.
4. PricewaterhouseCoopers, "Corporate reporting framework," www.corporatereporting.com/corporate-reporting-framework.html, accessed August 2009.

5. An *information gap* exists when analysts and investors think a KPI or intangible asset is important but don't feel that they are getting adequate information from companies about it. A *reporting gap* exists when the company sees a KPI or intangible asset as important but admits it is not providing much information on it. A *quality gap* exists when the company regards a KPI or intangible asset as important but doesn't have adequate internal systems for providing reliable data about it. See: Eccles, Robert G., Herz, Robert H., Keegan, E. Mary, and Phillips, David M. H. *The ValueReporting Revolution: Moving Beyond the Earnings Game*. Hoboken, NJ: John Wiley & Sons, 1999.
6. International Corporate Governance Network. *ICGN Statement and Guidance on Non-financial Business Reporting*, 2008, p. 11.
7. AXA Investment Managers and AQ Research, "Investment Professionals vote 'ESG' and 'Sustainability' as top descriptions," news release, July 28, 2008.
8. Ibid.
9. The authors would like to thank Harvard Business School Professor Robert S. Kaplan for the insight on stock and flow variables.
10. See: Eccles, Robert G. "The Performance Measurement Manifesto," *Harvard Business Review*, v. 69, is. 1, 1991, p. 131-137; Lev, Baruch. "Remarks on the Measurement, Valuation, and Reporting of Intangible Assets," *Economic Policy Review*, v. 9, is. 3, 2003, p. 17–22; Ballow, John, Burgman, R., and Molnar, M. J. "Managing for Shareholder Value: Intangibles, Future Value, and Investment Decisions," *Journal of Business Strategy*, v. 25, is. 3, 2004, p. 26–34; Cardoza, Keith, Basara, J., Cooper, L., and Conroy, R. "The Power of Intangible Assets: An Analysis of the S&P 500," *les Nouvelles (Licensing Executives Society)*, v. XLI, is. 1, 2006, p. 3–7; Lasinski, Michael. "Enhanced Business Reporting: Has Its Time Come?" Presentation at the American Accounting Association Annual Meeting 2007, August 17, 2007.
11. Most intangible assets do not appear on the company's balance sheet and, in fact, companies are precluded from doing so, such as research and development. There are a few exceptions, such as goodwill, where an intangible asset appears on company's balance sheet according to a defined accounting standard.
12. Lev, Baruch. "Sharpening the Intangibles Edge," *Harvard Business Review*, v. 82, is. 6, 2004, p. 109–116. "Intangible assets—a skilled workforce, patents and know-how, software, strong customer relationships, brands, unique organizational designs and processes, and the like—generate most of corporate growth and shareholder value. They account for well over half of the market capitalization of public companies. They absorb a trillion dollars of corporate investment funds every year."
13. Organization for Economic Cooperation and Development. *Intellectual Assets and Value Creation: Implications for Corporate Reporting*, December 2006, p. 11.

14. Wyatt, Anne. *What Financial and Non-Financial Information on Intangibles is Value Relevant? A Review of the Evidence*, University of Technology, Sydney, February 2008, p. 6.
15. Infosys Technologies Limited. *Infosys Annual Report 2008–09*, p. 131.
16. V. Balakrishnan, e-mail correspondence with Robert Eccles, September 4, 2009.
17. Worldscope Database, accessed via Thomson ONE Banker, September 9, 2009.
18. Infosys, p. 136.
19. Ibid.
20. Kaplan and Norton, p. 8.
21. Kaplan and Norton provide the following example: "*If* we increase employee training about products, *then* they will become more knowledgeable about the full range of products they can sell; *if* employees are more knowledgeable about products, *then* their sales effectiveness will improve; *if* their sales effectiveness improves, *then* the average margins of the products they sell will increase." Ibid., p. 149.
22. Ittner, Christopher, and Larcker, David. "Coming Up Short on Nonfinancial Performance Measurement," *Harvard Business Review*, v. 81, is. 11, 2003, p. 91, 89.
23. These KPIs are based on discussions the authors have had with experts in each of these industries and are meant as indicative, not definitive.
24. DiPiazza, Samuel, and Eccles, Robert G. *Building Public Trust: The Future of Corporate Reporting.* Hoboken, NJ: John Wiley & Sons, 2002.
25. Reichheld, Frederick F. "The One Number You Need to Grow," *Harvard Business Review*, v. 81, is., 12, 2003: 46–54.
26. Net Promoter. "How to Calculate Your Score," www.netpromoter.com/np/calculate.jsp, accessed September 2009.
27. Emilio Galli Zugaro, interview with Michael Krzus, March 10, 2009.
28. Allianz Australia Insurance Group. "Allianz Australia turning feedback into customer service," https://www.allianz.com/en/press/news/company_news/point_of_view/news_2007-02-13.html, accessed September 2009.
29. Allianz. "Performance Summary," https://www.allianz.com/en/about_allianz/sustainability/performance/performance/page1.html, accessed September 2009.
30. Robert Kaplan, e-mail correspondence with Robert Eccles, September 23, 2009.
31. See: Asset4, www.asset4.com; KLD Research & Analytics, www.kld.com; and Trucost, www.trucost.com; all accessed August 2009.

32. European Federation of Financial Analysts Societies. *Key Performance Indicators for Environmental, Social & Governance Issues: A Guideline for the Integration of ESG into Financial Analysis and Corporate Valuation*, version 1.2, 2009.
33. For example, one of the KPIs under "Environmental compatibility" is "Average fuel consumption of fleet of sold cars," but no specific guidance is given for how to calculate "average fuel consumption" (at what speed?), what is meant by a "fleet," and whether "sold" includes leased cars or not. European Federation of Financial Analysts Societies, p. 29.
34. Ralf Frank, e-mail correspondence with Robert Eccles and Michael Krzus, September 16, 2009.
35. Verheugen, Gunter. "Speech at CSR Alliance event," December 4, 2008. www.csreurope.org/data/files/press/20081204_verheugen_equippedforcsr.pdf, accessed September 2009.
36. Steve Lydenberg, e-mail correspondence with Robert Eccles and Michael Krzus, September 18, 2009.
37. European Social Investment Forum. *Public Policy Position Paper related to Sustainable and Responsible Investment ("SRI")*, April 14, 2009, www.eurosif.org/media/files/eurosif_public_policy_position_paper_2009, accessed August 2009; Social Investment Forum, "Letter to the SEC," July 21, 2009, www.socialinvest.org/documents/ESG_Letter_to_SEC.pdf, accessed August 2009.
38. Investor Network on Climate Risk. "Investors with $1.4 Trillion in Assets Call on the SEC to Improve Disclosure of Climate Change and Other Risks," press release, June 12, 2009. www.incr.com/Page.aspx?pid=1107, accessed September 2009.
39. John Elkington coined the term *triple bottom line* in 1994 to capture the expansion of traditional financial reporting to include environmental and social performance. The concept was later expanded and articulated in his book *Cannibals with Forks: the Triple Bottom Line of 21st Century Business* (Oxford: Capstone Publishing, 1997).
40. Brendan May, e-mail correspondence with Robert Eccles, September 22, 2009.
41. BMW Group. *Sustainable Value Report 2008*, p. 8.
42. Bill McAndrews, e-mail correspondence with Michael Krzus, September 23, 2009.
43. BMW Group, p. 39.
44. BMW Group. *SRI Roadshow Investor Presentation*, November 2008, p. 18. For a detailed description of the concept of sustainable value and how it is calculated, see: Sustainable Value. "Calculating Sustainable Value," www.sustainablevalue.com/theconcept/calculation/howtocalculatesustainablevalue/index.html, accessed September 2009. Value created (or destroyed) is essentially the difference

between the profits generated by a company per amount of resource used compared to an industry benchmark.

45. Sustainable Value, "Sustainable Value," www.sustainablevalue.com/automobile study/sectorresults/sustainablevalue/index.html, accessed September 2009.
46. Robert K. Massie, e-mail correspondence with Michael Krzus, September 28, 2009.
47. Global Reporting Initiative. "About GRI: FAQs," www.globalreporting.org/AboutGRI/FAQs/FAQAboutGRI.htm, accessed August 2009.
48. Allen White, e-mail correspondence with Robert Eccles and Michael Krzus, September 2, 2009.
49. Global Reporting Initiative. *Sustainability Reporting Guidelines*, Version 3.0, 2006.
50. Global Reporting Initiative, "Number of companies worldwide reporting on their sustainability performance reaches record high, yet still a minority," press release, 15 July 2009. www.globalreporting.org/NewsEventsPress/PressResources/PressRelease_14_July_2006_1000GRIReports.htm, accessed August 2009.
51. "All GRI Reporting Framework documents are developed using a process that seeks consensus through dialogue between stakeholders from business, the investor community, labor, civil society, accounting, academia, and others. All Reporting Framework documents are subject to testing and continuous improvement." *Sustainability Reporting Guidelines*, p. 3.
52. Ernst Ligteringen, e-mail correspondence with Robert Eccles and Michael Krzus, September 6, 2009.
53. Ibid.
54. Ibid.
55. Sean Gilbert, e-mail correspondence with Robert Eccles, September 6, 2009.
56. Global Reporting Initiative, "Companies that fail to link their ESG disclosures to corporate strategy fail to connect with investors," press release, March 25, 2009. www.globalreporting.org/NewsEventsPress/PressResources/Pressre lease25March2009.htm, accessed September 2009.
57. International Federation of Accountants. "International Standard on Assurance Engagements (ISAE) 3000: Assurance Engagements Other than Audits or Reviews of Historical Financial Information," *Handbook of International Auditing, Assurance, and Ethics Pronouncements*, 2008 edition, p. 922.
58. American Institute of Certified Public Accountants. "AT Section 101: Attest Engagements," Statements on Standards for Attestation Engagements, p. 2501. Note that these standards, as of April 2003, are now the Public Company Accounting Oversight Board's *Interim Attestation Standards*.

59. KPMG. *International Survey of Corporate Responsibility Reporting 2008*, p. 56–58. www.kpmg.com/Global/IssuesAndInsights/ArticlesAndPublications/Pages/Sustainability-corporate-responsibility-reporting-2008.aspx, accessed September 2009.
60. Wallman, Steven M.H., "The Future of Accounting and Financial Reporting, Part II: The Colorized Approach." Remarks before the American Institute of Certified Public Accountants, Twenty-Third National Conference on Current SEC Developments, 1996. www.sec.gov/news/speech/speecharchive/1996/spch079.txt, accessed August 2009.
61. The American Assembly. *The Future of the Accounting Profession*, 103rd American Assembly, November 2003, p. 13.
62. AccountAbility. "AA1000 Assurance Standard 2008," www.accountability21.net/aa1000as, accessed August 2009.
63. Climate Disclosure Standards Board. "History and Mission," www.cdsb-global.org/history-and-mission/, accessed August 2009.
64. Climate Disclosure Standards Board. *The Climate Disclosure Standards Board (CDSB) Reporting Framework: Exposure Draft*, 2009, p. 2.
65. Ibid.
66. Ibid., Appendix 2, p. 2.
67. "Climate Disclosure Standards Board," www.cdsb-global.org/, accessed August 2009.
68. "Technical Working Group," www.cdsb-global.org/index.php?page=technical-working-group, accessed August 2009.
69. Rick Samans, e-mail correspondence with Robert Eccles and Michael Krzus, September 18, 2009.
70. Climate Disclosure Standards Board, p. 2.
71. Mindy S. Lubber, e-mail correspondence with Robert Eccles and Michael Krzus, September 18, 2009.
72. Kruse, Claudia, and Singanayagam, Bramen. *Management incentives and strategy: Trends, business drivers and metrics across 20 sectors*, Europe Equity Research: J.P. Morgan, April 17, 2006, p. 6.

Chapter 5

Sustainable Strategies for a Sustainable Society

Companies like Natura, Novo Nordisk, and UTC are joined by several others, discussed in subsequent chapters, in producing integrated annual reports for fiscal year 2008. Additionally, all offered supplemental information on their Web sites on financial and nonfinancial metrics and achievements. Although the specific language varied, the core explanation given by each company for why it was practicing integrated reporting was that sustainability or corporate social responsibility was a key aspect of creating value for shareholders. Aracruz, a Brazilian pulp producer, stated in its 2008 annual report:

> Aligning themselves with the new business environment, involving new and influential stakeholders, such as consumers, communities, NGOs, multilateral bodies and universities, is a huge challenge for companies that have perceived that sustainable

> development is the only viable response to guarantee their future. So, like a growing number of companies around the world, we are in the middle of an intensive learning process to adapt ourselves to a new era. Obtaining consistent results on a sustainable basis requires modesty and openness to dialogue, responsibility in the use of natural resources, and profitability. That is the path that Aracruz has been trying to follow.[1]

Publishing financial and nonfinancial information in a single document was one way of strongly signaling this belief, as succinctly expressed in the 2008 annual report of Philips, the Dutch lighting and health-care company: "Now, for the first time, Philips is reporting on its annual financial, social and environmental performance in a single, integrated report. This approach reflects the progress we have made to embed sustainability in our way of doing business."[2]

These explanations of sustainability share the following common elements, although to varying degrees, for each company:

1. *New business model.* Sustainable development for society requires a new business model for companies.
2. *Long-term view.* This model requires a long-term view by the company and, by implication, its shareholders, who are one class of stakeholder.
3. *Multiple stakeholder perspective.* It also requires the recognition of the legitimacy of the interests of other stakeholders, who must also take a long-term view.
4. *Engagement processes.* This new model depends upon processes of engagement for understanding the expectations of all stakeholders.
5. *Value creation for all stakeholders.* This model contributes to value creation for shareholders as well as to meeting the needs of other stakeholders.
6. *Risk of not adopting the new model.* Failure to adopt this new model will put at risk the company's reputation and its ability to create shareholder value and can even imperil its existence.
7. *Benefit of adopting the new model.* Implementing it well can be a real source of competitive advantage.

Sustainability at Ricoh

Ricoh, the Japanese copier manufacturer based in Tokyo and one of the largest firms in its industry, is a sterling example of a company pursuing a sustainable strategy for a sustainable society. It has consciously shaped a business strategy with a very long-term view that incorporates its own obligations to ensure a sustainable society, particularly with respect to the environment. The company recognizes the legitimacy of all stakeholders' interests and works hard to understand them. So far, and to varying degrees, Ricoh seems to be succeeding in terms of the points above on value creation, risk, and benefit, although its continued success remains to be seen over the long term.

Ricoh is also an example of a company facing challenges in getting credit from the market for its efforts, publicized through its external disclosures, raising the question of whether it is doing enough in terms of engagement with this class of stakeholder. However, it *has* gotten recognition from others. In 2009, the company was selected as one of the Global 100 Most Sustainable Corporations for the fifth year in a row.[3] It was also one of the 110 out of 152 surveyed Japanese companies that completed the Carbon Disclosure Project annual survey[4] and was one of the 21 companies to be named to the Carbon Disclosure Leadership Index.[5] One clear benefit the company received for its genuine and recognized commitment to sustainability was that 95 percent of Japanese college graduates who applied for a job there said that this was one of the major reasons in their decision to do so.[6]

Ricoh's commitment to sustainability was embedded in the corporate philosophy of its founder, Kiyoshi Ichimura, who started the company in 1936 as a venture company in a semipublic science research organization called RIKEN.[7] Ichimura was very socially conscious and realized that his inventions would touch the lives of millions of people around the world. He developed a corporate philosophy that reflected this realization, describing this as the "Spirit of Three Loves," meaning to love your neighbor, love your country, and love your work. His explanation of the philosophy, "Everyone starts by loving himself/herself. As time passes, however, this feeling grows and expands to include all people, plants, and animals in the world. This philosophy drives the

Ricoh Group toward better sustainable management,"[8] clearly illustrates Ichimura's commitment to society and the environment.

Over the years, the company's commitment to sustainability, of which the environment was an important element, became more formally embedded in how it was managed as it moved from what it called the Passive Stage (coping with social pressure, starting in 1975) to the Proactive Stage (carrying out its mission as a global citizen, starting in 1990) to the Responsible Stage (simultaneously achieving environmental conservation and profits, starting in 1998). Ricoh's explanation of each stage, displayed in Exhibit 5.1, provides more detail on the company's activities in each step.

In 1976, Ricoh established the Environmental Promotion Section to formulate and implement the company's response to air pollution, which had become a major issue by that time. When global warming and disruption to the ozone layer emerged as important issues in the late 1980s, the company set up six in-house committees, each headed by an executive officer, to deal with different ways in which Ricoh could respond. Following this, an Environmental Administration Office was established in 1990 to promote activities aimed to decrease the environmental impact of the group's manufacturing processes and products. In 1992, after beginning its Proactive Stage, Ricoh introduced its Ricoh General Principles of the Environment, which expressed its commitment to environmental conservation and sustainable management.[9]

That same year, the company decided that all products should be designed and manufactured in such a way that they could be recycled. Tatsuo Tani, Executive Chief Engineer at the time, was put in charge of implementing this policy. In doing so, he ran into a high level of resistance from his fellow engineers due to the amount of effort involved, especially in product design. Searching for a simple way to explain the merits of recycling and how it should best be done, Tani developed the Comet Circle, shown in Exhibit 5.2. The human circulatory system was used as a metaphor, with the arteries representing how resources were taken from the natural environment to make products and the veins representing the collection of end-of-life products whose parts were reused or recycled, with the remaining waste sent to a landfill.

Another major step toward creating a sustainable strategy for a sustainable society was the establishment of the company's "Non Regret

Exhibit 5.1 Ricoh's Three Stages of Sustainability

	Passive Stage	Proactive Stage	Responsible Stage
Purpose	Coping with social pressures ★ Laws and regulations ★ Competitors ★ Customers	Carrying out its mission as a global citizen ★ Self-imposed responsibility ★ Voluntary planning ★ Voluntary activities	Simultaneously achieving environmental conservation and profits
Activities	Passive measures to meet laws and regulations, competing with other companies, and satisfying customer needs	1. High-aiming, aggressive activities to reduce environmental impact ★ Energy conservation ★ Resource conservation and recycling ★ Pollution prevention 2. Improved awareness of all employees	Environmental conservation activities = QCD activities★ Ex.: Reduced number of parts Reduced number of process steps Improved yield and operation rate
Tools		1. ISO 14001 2. LCA 3. Volunteer Leader Development Program	1. Strategic goal management system 2. Environmental accounting 3. Sustainable environmental management information system

★Activities to improve quality, control costs, and manage delivery times

SOURCE: Ricoh, "Sustainable Environmental Management and Corporate Value Enhancement," www.ricoh.com/environment/management/value.html, accessed August 2009.

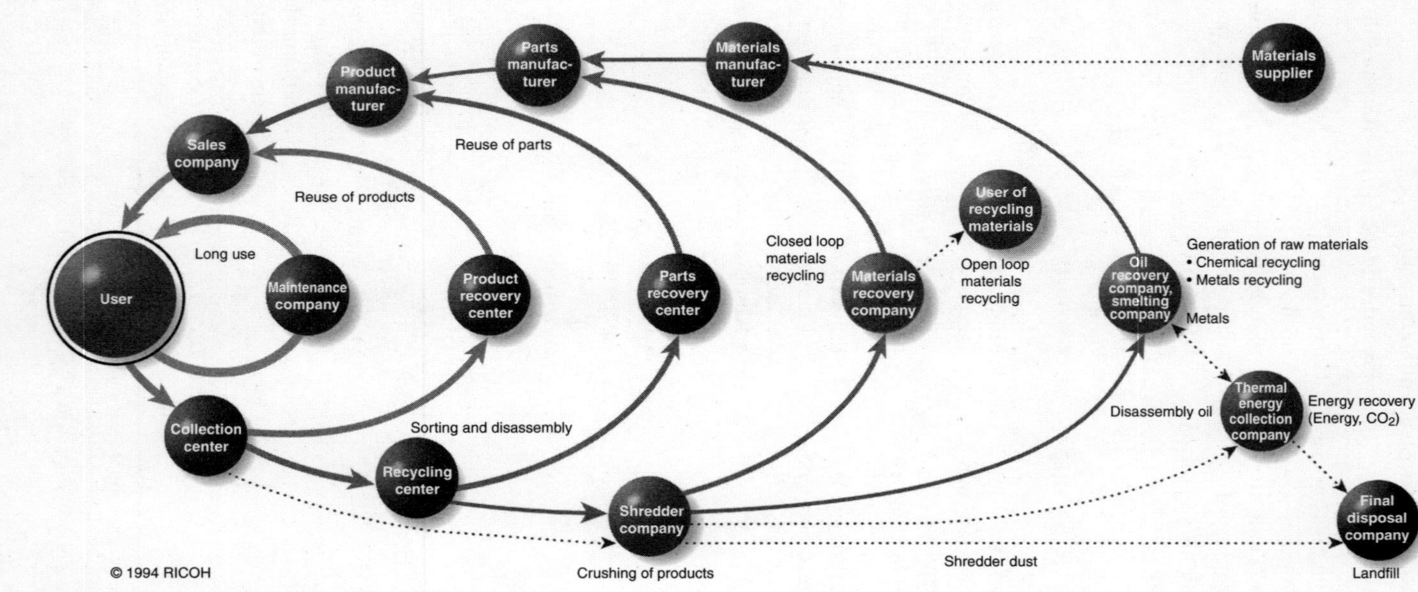

Exhibit 5.2 The Comet Circle Concept

SOURCE: Ricoh, "Concept of Recycling-based Society," www.ricoh.com/environment/management/concept.html, accessed August 2009.

Policy," the stance that even if environmental concerns such as carbon emissions were later proven unfounded and companies were not compelled by either public pressure or public policy to respond to them, Ricoh would not regret these initiatives, as environmental efforts would lead to results such as increase in profits and improvement of company quality. This policy was adopted in 1998, which marked the start of the Responsible Stage. The origin of this policy, that environmental initiatives would lead to cost efficiencies, was the belief of Masamitsu Sakurai, who was appointed CEO in 1996. However, to validate this belief and before publicly committing the company to aggressive environmental targets, he directed Tani to conduct a variety of studies with a small team over one year. Tani, today Director and Division General Manager for the Corporate Environment Division, concluded that "although there were some cases which required more time before we could expect a return from our investment, we felt confident that overall environmental initiatives were economically viable if we worked hard and used ingenuity."[10] Sakurai explained, "When enforcing environmental activities, we should pursue not only environmental conservation but also economic efficiency. In order to continue environmental activity at a high level, environmental activity should not be a mere voluntary activity, but we need to pursue profit generation at the same time."[11]

In 1998, the Corporate Environment Division (CED) was established, and Tani was named its head, reporting directly to Sakurai. The CED worked with all parts of the company to lessen Ricoh's impact on the environment and lower its costs in terms of products, processes, and the company's own facilities.[12] That same year, the company launched an effort to create a recycled copier business based on parts from copiers that were at the end of their life cycle. The business turned profitable in 2006 and represented about 10 percent of copier sales. Ricoh, a leader in the industry in creating this business, expected it to grow to about 20 percent of sales in five years. According to Kiyoshi Sakai, Director and Chief Technology Officer, "Ultimately, we want to build recycling into the business process so that customers would be using recycled machines without thinking about it."[13]

Continuing its trajectory of progressive environmental policies, Ricoh took seriously the phrase "to reduce environmental impact to a level that the Earth's self-recovery capability can deal with and sustain the global environment" from its 2002 Three Ps Balance concept of planet, people, and profit, defining "the kind of society we should aspire to" and its "responsibility as a company to help create such a society."[14] In 2005, the company established its Year 2050 Extra-Long-Term Environmental Vision based on "a perception that advanced nations need to reduce their environmental impact to one-eighth of the fiscal 2000 levels by 2050"[15] and publicly committed itself to achieving these targets even though it was clearly under no legal obligations to do so; there was complete uncertainty about whether other companies would follow its example (few have); and it recognized that its own impact was a miniscule proportion of the global total. Ricoh used the "back-casting method," in which the goal is first set based on how society should be in the future. In April 2009, Ricoh announced its Medium- and Long-Term Targets for Reducing Environmental Impact, in which it set targets to reduce total greenhouse gas emissions throughout the life cycle of its products by 30 percent from fiscal 2000 levels in 2020 (34 percent reduction from 1990) and by 87.5 percent in 2050. The company considered that innovations in production process and product quality as a result of environmental technology development and participation of all employees in *kaizen* (improvement) activities were equally important to achieve the targets.[16]

In addition to these targets for impact reduction, the company also engaged in initiatives to help with "the self-recovery capability of the global environment," including the support of forest ecosystem conservation projects around the world.[17] The company used a "social contribution reserve system" to fund social contribution activities. Ricoh contributed one percent of profits after dividends each year (with a maximum of ¥200 million), an amount approved at the general shareholders meeting in 1998; Ricoh believed that the "unique system responds to shareholders' needs, and carries out the relevant programs."[18]

Thanks to its genuine commitment to environmental sustainability, Ricoh had the strong support of the NGO community focused on environmental issues. Mikako Awano, Head of Corporate Group Fundraising and Marketing at the World Wide Fund for Nature Japan, observed that "Japanese companies are generally hesitant about printing their visions or commitments. In that sense, the fact that Ricoh hammered out the Year 2050 Extra-Long-Term Environmental Vision and reducing environmental impact to one-eighth by 2050 is significant by itself." Reflecting the fact that most NGOs have limited resources, which they direct to companies whose behavior they are going to change, she added, "As Ricoh is already very proactive in environment conservation activities, the company is not one of our main target companies where we are trying to promote environmental activities."[19]

Ricoh's definition of sustainability extended beyond the environment to a broader concept of CSR rooted in Ichimura's "Spirit of Three Loves." The company established a CSR office in 2003 and established the Ricoh Group CSR Charter and Ricoh Group Code of Conduct based on integrity in corporate activities, harmony with the environment, respect for people, and harmony with society. Each of these principles was to be applied to all stakeholders: customers, shareholders, employees, partner companies, and society.[20]

Corporate Social Responsibility

While the appearance of nonfinancial information in the annual reports described above may be new, and although Ricoh first wrote its formal CSR charter in 2004, the concept of CSR, called by many names, is not new. Social responsibility was defined by Howard Bowen (called by Archie Carroll the "Father of Corporate Responsibility")[21] in 1953: "It refers to the obligations of businessmen to pursue those policies, to make those decisions, or to follow those lines of action which are desirable in terms of the objectives and values of our society."[22] In his book, Bowen also cited a 1946 survey by *Fortune* in which 93.5 percent of the respondents agreed that businessmen were responsible for the consequences of their actions beyond their own profit-and-loss statements, but only 29.7 percent said that three-quarters or more of the businessmen they knew had a "social consciousness of this sort."[23]

But Bowen was not entirely a pioneer. Varying discussions on business's responsibility to and role in society had appeared even earlier, including Harvard Business School Dean Wallace B. Donham's *Harvard Business Review* article "The Social Significance of Business," in 1927. Donham claimed that "the development, strengthening, and multiplication of socially minded business men is the central problem of business" and expressed the concern that "unless more of our business leaders learn to exercise their powers and responsibilities with a definitely increased sense of responsibility toward other groups in the community . . . our civilization may well head for one of its periods of decline."[24] Although Donham did not use the term *stakeholder*, which appeared much later, he was clearly referring to them in his reference to "other groups in the community."

In 1975, Robert W. Ackerman of the Harvard Business School used the terms *corporate responsibility* and *corporate social responsibility* in calling for a more effective "corporate response to a dynamic social environment."[25] He regarded this as a managerial, rather than ethical or ideological issue, since social issues (e.g., air and water pollution) were inextricably linked to business operating functions (e.g., manufacturing) and management decision processes (e.g., capital investment allocation).[26] Ackerman was particularly concerned that the growth of the multidivisional form of organization was inhibiting the ability of executives to respond to social pressures and would require innovative management practices. Of particular relevance to this book, he suggested that the common practice of relying only on financial measures of performance would be modified by harder-to-quantify outcomes, such as good employee and customer relations and product and process research, although he addressed this only from an internal measurement and reporting perspective.[27]

By the 1980s, researchers were trying to find a link between CSR and profitability; both Bowen and Ackerman had noted that social responsiveness could be costly, at least in the short term. Joshua D. Margolis, Hillary Anger Elfenbein, and James P. Walsh conducted a meta-analysis of 251 studies presented in 214 manuscripts over the past 35 years examining the relationship between corporate social performance (CSP) and corporate financial performance (CFP) and concluded that "the preponderance of evidence indicates a mildly positive relationship" and that "CSP does not appear to penalize companies financially nor impair their economic functions." They also found that "Doing bad, if discovered, has a more pronounced effect on financial performance than doing good."[28] Their findings are consistent with the view held by many that CSR is more about managing downside risk than it is about dramatically improving performance.

The results of this empirical research are matched by a December 2008 survey by McKinsey, which found that "two-thirds of CFOs and three-quarters of investment professionals agree that environmental, social and governance activities do create value for their shareholders in normal economic times."[29] There was wide variation in the perceptions about how much value was created, ranging from less than 2 percent to more than 11 percent, with some saying these activities reduced value, had no effect, or they didn't know. More respondents saw these activities as creating value over the long term rather than the short term: environmental was 85 percent versus 29 percent, social was 74 percent versus 37 percent, and governance was 84 percent versus 64 percent.[30]

As the literature on CSR grew substantially over the ensuing decades, numerous terms for the same and similar concepts were offered up. Corporate social performance (CSP) became an alternative to CSR and would be joined by *stakeholder theory*, *business ethics*, and *corporate citizenship* in the 1990s as concepts stemming from CSR.[31] Edward Freeman, Jeffrey Harrison, Andres Wicks, Bidhan Parma, and Simone de Colle added the terms *corporate governance*, *corporate accountability*, *sustainability*, *triple bottom line*, and *corporate social entrepreneurship* to this list. To this can be added *corporate philanthropy*, since some companies' CSR reports are simply about this. Not surprisingly, Freeman et al. noted, "After more than half a century of research and debate, there is not a single widely accepted definition of CSR."[32] Yet they also noted that "each of these diverse efforts shares a common aim in the attempt to broaden the obligations of firms to include more than financial considerations"[33] and are broadly in line with Bowen's initial definition. And all are in vivid contrast to Milton Friedman's famous assertion that the only responsibility of a corporation is profits.[34]

Friedman's view is no longer the common one, or at least it is no longer the most commonly espoused one. A 2008 report published by *The Economist* declared that "corporate social responsibility, once a do-gooding sideshow, is now seen as mainstream" even though "nobody much likes the CSR label." The report also noted that "it is often misguided, or worse" and that "too few companies are doing it well." But for those that are, "it is not some separate activity that companies do on the side, a corner of corporate life reserved for virtue: it is just good business."[35] A common phrase used today to express this idea is "doing

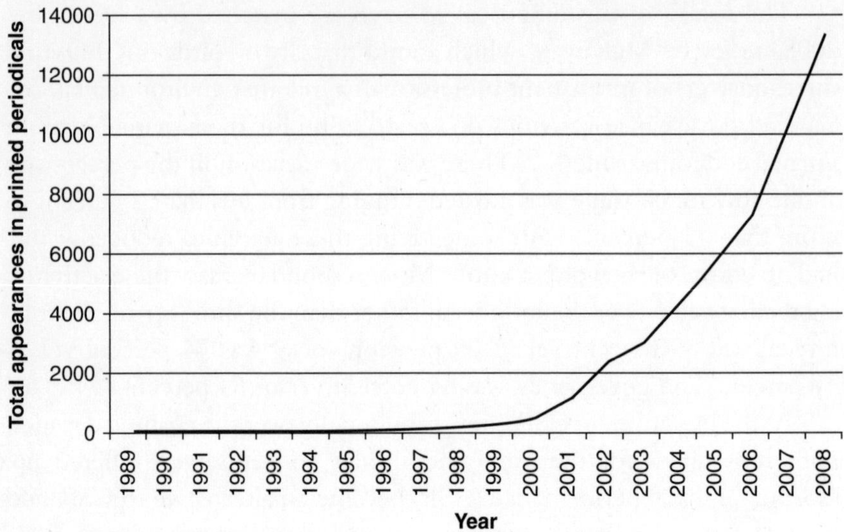

Exhibit 5.3 Increasing Use of the Term *Corporate Social Responsibility*, 1989–2008

well by doing good." As an indication of the growing popularity of CSR, Exhibit 5.3 shows the increased usage of the phrase over the past 20 years.

To varying degrees, those writing about CSR draw a distinction between shareholders and society at large, including its constituent groups like employees and the community, but it was not until Edward Freeman's 1984 book *Strategic Management* that the term *stakeholder* became popular. (Exhibit 5.4 shows the growth in the use of this term.)

Although his book is regarded as the pivotal work in stakeholder theory, Freeman acknowledged that the concept had been developed 20 years earlier.[36] Freeman defined a stakeholder as "any group or individual who can affect or is affected by the achievement of the firm's objectives," and he included "owners" as one type of stakeholder.[37] The basic point of his book, a "deceptively simple" one, was that "organizations must deal actively with their stakeholders."[38] Among other things, and anticipating our discussion about stakeholder engagement in Chapter 7, this involves "'measures of satisfaction' of those groups whose support is necessary for the continued survival of the organization."[39]

Freeman cited the corporate social responsibility literature ("too diverse to catalogue here") as an important source of ideas for the stakeholder concept, since it brought "to the foreground in organizational

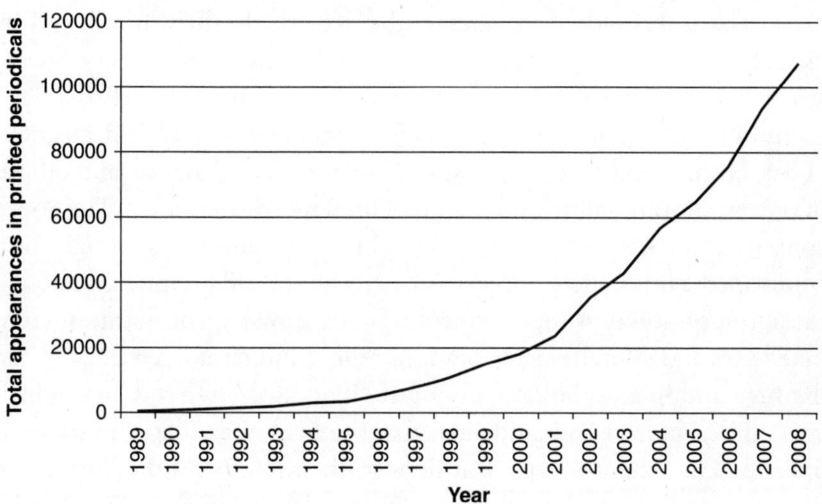

Exhibit 5.4 Increasing Use of the Term *Stakeholders*, 1989–2008

research a concern with social and political issues."[40] However, he also criticized it for failing "to indicate ways of integrating these concerns into the strategic systems of the corporation in a non-ad hoc fashion."[41] Providing some important conceptual foundation for this book, Freeman argued:

> Given the turbulence that business organizations are currently facing and the very nature of the external environment, as consisting of economic and socio-political forces, there is a need for conceptual schemata which analyze these forces in an integrative fashion. We need to understand the complex interconnections between economic and social forces. Isolating "social issues" as separate from the economic impact which they have, and conversely isolating economic issues as if they had no social effect, misses the mark both managerially and intellectually. Actions aimed at one side will not address the concerns of the other. Processes, techniques and theories which do not consider all of these forces will fail to describe and predict the business world as it really is.[42]

Although Freeman did not address the question of external reporting to stakeholders, it is not hard to make the conceptual leap from integrated internal management to integrated external reporting.

Just as stakeholders are affected by a firm, the firm is affected by its stakeholders since its "license to operate" is issued by society. Steven Wartick and Philip Cochran explained the two premises of social responsibility that clarify this connection between society and business: "First, business exists at the pleasure of society; its behavior and methods of operation must fall within the guidelines set by society. . . . This social contract is the vehicle through which business behavior is brought into conformity with society's objectives. . . . The second premise underlying social responsibility is that business acts as a moral agent within society. Like states and churches, corporations reflect and reinforce values."[43] So the firm and its stakeholders are intertwined. Society has values, which are codified in laws and guidelines that the firm must follow in order to operate. The extent to which it does so then reinforces these values to the benefit of society. The firm and society depend upon each other. As Michael E. Porter and Mark R. Kramer put it, "Successful corporations need a healthy society [and] . . . at the same time, a healthy society needs successful companies."[44] A sustainable strategy for a firm requires that it contribute to a sustainable society.

This will require some tough choices, since not all actions that contribute to society will necessarily be to the benefit of shareholders, at least in the short term. Drawing a starker distinction than done by Porter and Kramer in terms of types of CSR, Dean Roger L. Martin of the Rotman School of Management has distinguished between *instrumental* CSR, which explicitly enhances shareholder value, and *intrinsic* CSR, in which "a company's leaders embark on a course of action simply because they think it's the right thing to do, whether or not it serves shareholder interests." He noted that identifying whether a course of action will turn out to benefit "shareholders, society, both or neither" is fairly easy to do in retrospect but often hard to do before a decision is made on which course of action to take.[45] Martin offers a four-quadrant Virtue Matrix to help managers make these decisions. At the *civil foundation* are two quadrants in which actions are largely instrumental in nature. In the *compliance* quadrant, companies do what is required by law or regulation, and in the *choice* quadrant, they voluntarily adhere to norms and customs regarding corporate practice, thereby meeting society's baseline expectations. At the *frontier* are the *strategic* and *structural* quadrants, in which motivations are largely intrinsic in nature. In the *strategic* quadrant are actions that benefit both shareholders and society. The most difficult choices concern the *structural* quadrant, which "houses actions that benefit society but not shareholders, creating a structural barrier to corporate action." Dislodging these barriers can be done through "collective action, either on the part of governments, nongovernmental organizations (NGOs), or corporate leaders themselves."[46]

Sustainability

For many companies today, the terms *corporate social responsibility* and *sustainability* are often used interchangeably. Exhibit 5.5 shows the same curve of increasing popularity of this term as for *CSR*, but in absolute count *sustainability* exceeds *CSR* by a factor of seven.

Unlike CSR, whose origins—as implied in the term itself—are in the business community and those who study it, sustainability's origins are very different. It has roots in the conservationism of the first half of the 20th century, culminating in Rachel Carson's 1962 examination of wildlife destruction and the use of DDT in *Silent Spring*.[47] Her look at

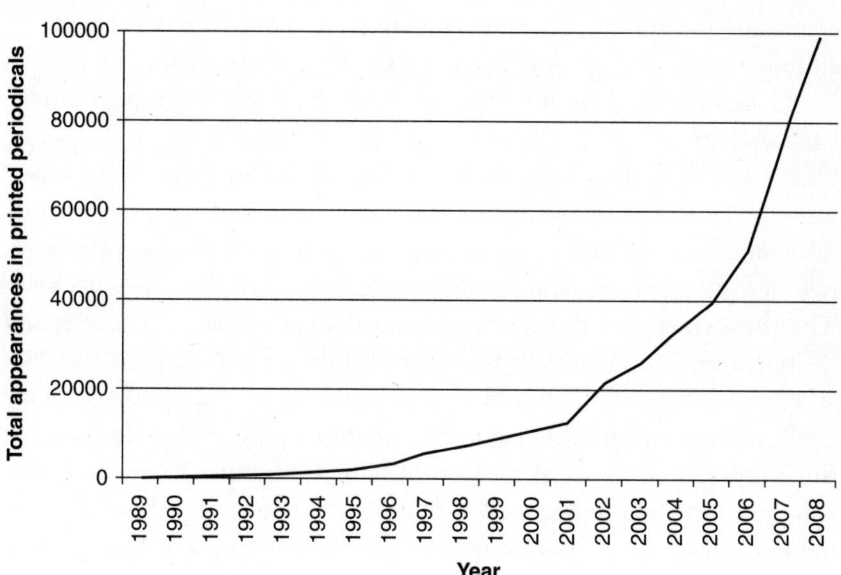

Exhibit 5.5 Increasing Use of the Term *Sustainability*, 1989–2008

DDT as a technology and its effect on nature was eye-opening to the general public. Ten years later, a team of researchers at the Massachusetts Institute of Technology released *Limits to Growth*,[48] their study of computer models used to explore population growth and the demand on resources. They showed that the limits would be reached in the next century.

The 1970s also brought about a shift in focus from the environment to the developing world. Simon Dresner traced the first coining of the term *sustainable society* to the World Council of Churches' 1974 conference on Science and Technology for Human Development. Although the proceedings were not widespread, and the Council rarely gets credit for the definition, it does illustrate the early interest in the concept.[49] Dresner also noted that "The term 'sustainable development' emerged in the World Conservation Strategy of 1980, published by the International Union for Conservation of Nature and Natural Resources."[50] In 1983, the United Nations created the World Commission on the Environment and Development (WCED), led by Norway's Gro Harlem Brundtland; the Commission's publication four years later, *Our Common Future*, became known as simply the Brundtland Report. Its definition of sustainable development is now the most popular and widely used one today: "to ensure that it meets the needs of the present without compromising the ability of future generations to meet their own needs,"[51] although no such consensus exists for the term *sustainability*.

In making the case for sustainable development, the report articulated a clear connection between the environment and the economy: "We have in the past been concerned about the impacts of economic growth upon the environment. We are now forced to concern ourselves with the impacts of ecological stress—degradation of soils, water regimes, atmosphere, and forests—upon our economic prospects."[52] The consequence of this reciprocal dependence between economy and the environment is that there are limits that must be acknowledged, "not absolute limits but limitations imposed by the present state of technology and social organization on environmental resources and by the ability of the biosphere to absorb the effects of human activities." Yet the report was optimistic that limits need not limit economic growth, since "technology and social organization can be both managed and improved to make way for a new era of economic growth."[53]

The concept of sustainable development applies to society as a whole; an important part of society is the world's largest global corporations, which have an enormous impact on society for both good and ill. This means that companies must take limits into account in terms of the vast amounts of resources—natural, financial, and human—they use to create products and services that society needs and wants. What is noticeably absent in discussions about CSR prior to this articulated concern about sustainable development is a concern for limits, particularly with respect to natural resources. There is a concern about the negative impact companies can have on the environment, through waste or pollution, but this is treated as more of an economic or ethical issue, not one that affects the sustainability of society itself. However, now that the concept of limits has become core to the meaning of CSR, it is not surprising that this term and sustainability are used so interchangeably with each other.

Sustainable Competitive Advantage

Before sustainability entered the lexicon of business in the context of CSR, it had a particular and different, but related, meaning in the strategy literature regarding the "sustainable strategy" of a company. Porter's 1985 seminal work established the concept of competitive advantage, stemming from competitive strategy and composed of three generic strategies: cost leadership, differentiation, and focus. Creating and sustaining a competitive advantage requires a long-term focus: "The sustainability of the three generic strategies demands that a firm's competitive advantage resists erosion by competitor behavior or industry evolution;" erosion being a long and slow process.[54]

Pankaj Ghemawat went a step further to identify the three categories into which sustainable advantages fall: "size in the targeted market, superior access to resources or customers, and restrictions on competitors' options" and went on to note that these can and do interact and the more often, the better. Ghemawat's parting advice, "Ultimately, the search for sustainability involves a series of decisions about the degree to which you are willing to commit your business to a particular way of doing things," is about a firm's particular position relative to its competitors.[55]

With Kramer, Porter updated his work to examine the link between competitive advantage and CSR. On the one hand, CSR is a function of risk management. Porter and Kramer referred to this as responsive CSR, a two-part position: "acting as a good corporate citizen, attuned to the evolving social concerns of stakeholders, and mitigating existing or anticipated adverse effects from business activities."[56] In this domain, CSR activities are preventative, such as pollution reduction, and acknowledge areas of the business that may be affected by outside forces, such as energy-use reduction in the face of impending carbon emission caps. Embracing CSR in this manner means that a firm must get it right—missing the mark on basic pollution controls can hurt it financially (in the form of regulatory fines, lawsuits, etc.) and reputationally (in the form of negative media attention and stakeholder activism). This is "managing the downside," which Margolis, Elfenbein, and Walsh found to be particularly important. It is a "necessary but not sufficient" condition for a company to have a sustainable strategy since this requires pursuing the upside as well.

Porter and Kramer see this opportunity in what they call "strategic CSR," which is about creating value: "a small number of initiatives whose social and business benefits are large and distinctive. Strategic CSR involves both inside-out and outside-in dimensions working in tandem. It is here that the opportunities for shared value truly lie."[57] *Inside-out* linkages refer to how "a company impinges upon society through its operations in the normal course of business" and *outside-in* linkages exist because "external social conditions also influence corporations."[58] Here, CSR is closely tied to (and a natural extension of) the firm's activities, creating fertile ground for future products and services or future customers and becoming a key part of how the firm establishes a competitive advantage, thereby contributing to a sustainable strategy in the pursuit of the upside. Doing this requires choices about the company's relationship to society, since strategy "is about choosing a unique position—doing things differently from competitors in a way that lowers costs or better serves a particular set of customer needs."[59] When the right choices are made, strategic CSR "unlocks shared value by investing in social aspects of context that strengthen company competitiveness" and the result is a symbiotic relationship in which "the success of the company and the success of the community become mutually reinforcing."[60] By working in this arena, firms may find an opportunity that puts them in Ghemawat's range of classic sustainable competitive advantage: With success, they may better connect with resources and customers and ultimately restrict competitors' options.

While Porter and Kramer tie CSR into a sustainable strategy based on competitive advantage, Stuart Hart sees a relationship between sustainable development and competitive advantage, because "strategy and competitive advantage in the coming years will be rooted in capabilities that facilitate environmentally sustainable economic activity."[61] Building on another branch of the strategy literature, resource-based theory, Hart calls this a "natural-resource-based view of the firm." It is based on a conceptual framework composed of three interconnected strategic capabilities (pollution prevention, product stewardship, and sustainable development), each of which is associated with a key resource (continuous improvement, stakeholder integration, and shared vision, respectively) and is the basis for competitive advantage (lowering costs, pre-empting competitors, and future positioning, respectively).[62] Just as the concept of sustainable development has come to be a central aspect to the concept of CSR, both are now seen as providing opportunities for establishing competitive advantage. Doing this requires that they be integrated into the firm's strategy and operations and not treated as ancillary philanthropic and public relations activities.

Sustainable Strategies Require Integrated Reporting

The convergence of CSR, sustainable development, and competitive advantage leads to a greater convergence between the interests of all stakeholders, including shareholders. Of course, there will never be complete convergence of interests. Sometimes, innovative solutions can be found that improve the interests of all. At other times, trade-offs will have to be made, and making them will involve difficult choices, since "the dispute among justifiable but competing demands reflects the reality that firms face in society today."[63]

This convergence has implications for a company's external reporting. Putting legal and regulatory requirements and restrictions aside—they are admittedly important, but also can be changed—no good argument can be made for publishing separate financial and nonfinancial (by whatever name) reports. Since a sustainable strategy is about integrating financial and nonfinancial performance, the inevitable consequence of this is that a company should report on how well it is doing this in an integrated way.

Porter and Kramer have a rather jaundiced view of stand-alone CSR reports, claiming that "such publications rarely offer a coherent framework for CSR activities, let alone a strategic one" and instead are based on "aggregate anecdotes about uncoordinated initiatives to demonstrate a company's social sensitivity" that are simply "supporting a new cottage industry of report writers" and the "growth in CSR ratings and rankings."[64] However, these ratings should not be completely dismissed. Aaron K. Chatterji, David L. Levine, and Michael W. Toffel found that environmental ratings not only adequately summarized past performance, but were predictive as well. Specifically, they found that firms that received poor ratings subsequently exhibited worse environmental performance.[65] In another study, Chatterji and Toffel examined firms that were rated for the first time, and found that those that initially received poor ratings "subsequently improved their environmental performance more than other firms, and that this difference was driven by firms in highly regulated industries and for firms with more low-cost opportunities to exploit."[66]

If a company's commitment to CSR and sustainability is a source of competitive advantage, enabling it to have a sustainable strategy for producing current and future financial returns—the claim being made by more and more companies today—then it should report on its financial and nonfinancial performance in a holistic and integrated way. The McKinsey survey cited earlier found that "integrated reports including financial and other data would improve communications" about how CSR activities create shareholder value, and that investment professionals were especially interested in "reports that integrate the financial value of environmental, social, and governance into corporate financial reports." Metrics regarded as most useful in reporting on ESG programs were "those that quantify financial impact, measure business opportunities as well as risks, and are transparent about their methodology."[67] Similarly, companies should report on consciously made trade-off decisions and make clear the resulting financial implications.

Corporate Reporting at Ricoh

Ricoh is a good example of why more integrated reporting is needed. The company clearly has a sincere commitment to CSR and to dramatically reducing its environmental impact, and it believes that these actions will create value for shareholders. This integrated stakeholder view is not reflected in its external reporting. In 2008, Ricoh published an annual report containing typical financial information as well as separate environmental and CSR reports, both of which were called "Sustainability" reports and had some overlap in content, including their respective Web pages. Zenji Miura, Director, Chief Financial Officer and Chief Information Officer, explained that having three separate reports was a conscious decision: "When we first made a decision to produce three separate reports, we thought that it made sense to do so in order to provide full content in all subjects, but perhaps we could rethink this so that more people will have a chance to read about our environmental activities."[68]

Senior executives at the company were concerned that the company had not been getting any real credit from the market for its environmental activities and its stock price lagged that of its major competitor, Canon. Miura elaborated: "Ricoh has always been a good citizen and has acted proactively to conserve the environment. Recently more companies are trying hard to work on environmental activities; however investors are still slow to appreciate such efforts. This is probably due to the difference in time frame [in how] investors look at things. Investors make judgments based on short-term perspectives and do not appreciate Ricoh's strength in the long term. It is also questionable how much our environmental efforts are being appreciated by investors. When I conduct [investor relations] meetings, there are very few questions on environmental issues."[69]

This reaction was despite the fact that Ricoh made a conscious effort to show the economic benefits of its environmental activities. For example, in its environmental sustainability report for 2008, the company provided graphs showing the last five years of performance on Ratio of Eco Profit and Ratio of Eco Effect and accompanying text explained improvement in both areas over the past two fiscal years.[70]

The market remained unconvinced for a variety of reasons. As noted by Miura, time frame was certainly one reason. Whereas the company had medium- and extra-long-term targets for 2020 and 2050, as well as concrete interim targets for 2010 and 2013, sell-side analysts had a time frame of six months or less. For institutional investors, three years was considered a long time, with many operating in one- to two-year time frames and hedge funds in even less.

Lack of data comparability due to the absence of standards was another barrier. Shima Nakao, an equity analyst at AllianceBernstein Japan Ltd., noted, "We do not make investment judgments based on environmental reports, as data provided by companies are not comparable and cannot be converted to financial figures." Putting a pile of environmental sustainability reports from Ricoh and its competitors on the table, she also commented that it was difficult to find what little useful information there was in these many-page reports with lots of prose and few numbers. She suggested that what would be more useful was more basic operating data from Ricoh: "They should also disclose information such as unit shipments of copiers so we can calculate number of machines in the field. Other companies, such as Fuji Film and Konica, disclose this and Canon discloses its anticipated growth rate."[71] Units shipped, a good example of a KPI, was a key line item in analysts' financial models, since it was easy to project sales knowing the ratio of supplies and materials revenues to units.

Hisashi Moriyama, a senior analyst in J.P. Morgan Japan's equity research group who covered the Precision Instruments Sector (of which copiers were a subset), noted the difficulty of using environmental information "because it is very hard to analyze information that cannot be incorporated into our financial models" and added that "companies need to do a better job of explaining the costs and benefits of their environmental activities." He also noted that "we cannot make any investment decision without being able to compare across companies."[72] The lack of standards was a key constraint. A more general issue was the sheer lack of time for doing analysis, given the number of companies he had to follow and the pressures of producing periodic reports on earnings estimates for all of them. Simply put, if the transaction costs of finding and figuring out how to use information were too high, the information did not get used, although Moriyama felt that if a company's profits could be affected by its environmental activities by 5 percent or more, "then we will not be able to ignore the impact in our analysis." Still, he suggested that the main disclosure reason for Ricoh's stock price underperforming that of Canon had nothing to do with its environmental activities but rather its failure to woo foreign investors who could help drive up the company's stock price. He suggested that the company should do road shows in the United States twice a year, as was Canon's practice.

These market analysts acknowledged that eventually environmental performance could contribute to financial performance. Shohei Ura, an equity analyst at Schroder Investment Management (Japan) Ltd., commented, "We analyze companies based on three years' earnings forecasts and qualitative decisions which go beyond three years. One of the important qualitative factors is management quality, which includes environmental, social, and governance issues."[73] Moriyama echoed this, as he also believed that "companies should be given credit for their efforts on environmental issues," although at the present time he felt that "investors tend to consider that environmental efforts do not lead to profits, but are more of a necessary cost to maintaining the company's reputation." He felt this would change in the future, since "Ricoh's environmental efforts should give them a competitive advantage, as investors will no longer be able to ignore the factor as environmental issues become increasingly important."[74]

Despite the lack of market credit for the company's environmental activities, Shiro Kondo, President and Chief Executive Officer, had a rather sanguine view. While he was deeply committed to Ricoh's ambitious and long-term environmental goals, he did not see this as the basis of the company's competitive advantage, which instead he felt was in technology. In fact, he saw the 2050 goal as a good way to foster innovation:

> When the Extra-Long-Term Environmental Vision was being formulated, I was in charge of product development. We held a series of heated arguments with the Corporate Environment Division on the viability of the targets as we did not want to make any irresponsible commitments. However, in the end, we agreed to set goals to reduce our environmental impact to one-eighth by 2050. I thought that setting an ambitious goal would be a good way to induce progress in the level of technology

> development. What we cannot allow to happen is to drop behind in technology development. I think that efforts to conserve the global environment are like the industrial revolution where a drastic change in technology was the key in order to survive. We must compete based on our technology.[75]

Thus, while Ricoh did not see its environmental activities per se as the basis of competitive advantage, such as from a strong demand for "green" copiers, it *did* see competitive advantage coming from the necessary technological innovation to meet the aggressive environmental targets it had set for itself. The company clearly felt its concern for a sustainable society was at the foundation of creating a sustainable strategy for the company itself. But it had yet to convince the market of this, through some combination of insufficiently integrated external reporting and the market's short-term view.

Can One Report guarantee that Ricoh would get more market recognition for what it is doing? There is no way to be sure of this. And in all fairness, the company was already attempting to demonstrate the economic value of its environmental activities and provided a substantial amount of information in its reports and on its Web site. Yet the market was still asking for more persuasive and granular information than the company was providing—even though the company did have that information internally. Buy- and sell-side analysts could also be criticized for not working hard enough to understand the link between environmental and economic performance, using the information that was available. But it is ultimately the company's responsibility to make the case for the financial value of its sustainable strategy and reap the benefits from doing so.

Notes

1. Aracruz, *Annual and Sustainability Report 2008*, p. 14.
2. Philips, *Annual Report 2008: Financial, social and environmental performance*, p. 180.
3. The Global 100 Most Sustainable Corporations in the World are named by Corporate Knights Inc. and Innovest Strategic Value Advisors Inc. and is announced each year in Davos, Switzerland at the World Economic Forum;

the first list was announced in 2005. See www.global100.org for selection methodology.

4. Carbon Disclosure Project. *Carbon Disclosure Project Report Japan 2008*, www.cdproject.net/reports.asp, accessed August 2009. Carbon Disclosure Project (CDP) is a United Kingdom–based organization that collects and distributes information related to carbon emission and how companies are responding to climate change. It has the largest greenhouse emissions data base in the world and provides analysis and information to motivate companies, investors, and governments to take action against climate change (Carbon Disclosure Project. "What We Do," www.cdproject.net/aboutus.asp, accessed May 2009).
5. Ibid. The Carbon Disclosure Leadership Index (CDLI) includes the companies with the highest scores in the two categories of the Global 500 carbon-intensive sectors and the Global 500 non-carbon-intensive sectors, and provides a valuable perspective on the range and quality of responses to CDP's questionnaire ("Carbon Disclosure Leadership Index 2008," www.cdproject.net/carbon-disclosure-leadership-index.asp, accessed August 2009).
6. Tatsuo Tani, interview with Robert Eccles, Masako Egawa, and Akiko Kanno, February 25, 2009.
7. The Japanese word for RIKEN (Rikagaku Kenkyujo) means physical and chemical science institute.
8. Ricoh. *Ricoh Group Annual Report 2008*, p. 66.
9. The Ricoh General Principles on the Environment include a basic policy and an action guideline composed of seven parts: achieve superior targets; develop innovative environmental technologies; encourage all employees to participate in environmental activities; be attentive to product life cycle; improve employees' environmental awareness; contribute to society; optimize communication with stakeholders. *See Ricoh Group Annual Report 2008*, p. 66, for the full text.
10. Tani, February 25, 2009.
11. Ricoh Corporate Environment Division (ed.). *Application of Ricoh's Environment Management*. Tokyo: Niikkageren, 2001.
12. The CED's initiatives included the development of a sustainable environmental management information system that collected data on the environmental impact of operational processes so that better decisions could be made; the implementation of an environmental accounting system to measure the impact of environmental activities on the company's financial performance under guidelines established in 2000 by the Ministry of the Environment (see *Ricoh Group Sustainability Report 2008 (Environment)* for full explanation); and the instigation of mid-term environmental plans that were set every three years and combined environmental management with profit making (the 16th Mid-Term Environmental Action Plan runs from 2008 to 2010).

13. Kiyoshi Sakai, interview with Robert Eccles, Masako Egawa, and Akiko Kanno, February 26, 2009.
14. The Three Ps Balance concept is explained as "the purpose of environmental conservation activities is to reduce environmental impact to a level that the Earth's self-recovery capability can deal with and sustain the global environment. The Ricoh Group, by considering how the relationship among the three Ps (planet, people, and profit) in environmental, social, and economic activities has changed over time, defines the kind of society we should aspire to and carries out its responsibility as a company to help create such a society." (www.ricoh.com/about/csr/env_harmony/index.html, accessed August 4, 2009.)
15. Ricoh, "Extra-Long-Term Environmental Vision," www.ricoh.com/environment/management/vision.html, accessed August 2009. In April 2009, the title was changed to "Long-Term Environmental Vision and Goals."
16. For Ricoh's definition of "integrated environmental impact," see "Evaluation Methods," www.ricoh.com/environment/management/method.html#elu, accessed August 2009.
17. See Ricoh's Forest Ecosystem Conservation Projects Web site for a list of projects and their corresponding non-profit and local community partners (www.ricoh.com/environment/biodiversity/02.html, accessed August 2009).
18. Ricoh. "Social Contribution Reserve System," www.ricoh.com/about/csr_environment/social_contribution_02.html, accessed August 2009.
19. Mikako Awano, interview by Masako Egawa and Akiko Kanno, March 16, 2009.
20. Ricoh, "Message from the President," www.ricoh.com/about/csr/concept/index.html, accessed August 2009; and *Ricoh Group Sustainability Report (Corporate Social Responsibility)*, p. 7.
21. Carroll, Archie B. "Corporate Social Responsibility: Evolution of a Definitional Construct," *Business & Society*, v. 38, is. 3, 1999: 268–295, p. 270.
22. Bowen, Howard. *Social Responsibilities of the Modern Businessman*. New York: Harper, 1953, p. 6.
23. "Fortune Management Poll," *Fortune*, v. 33, March 1946, pp. 197–198.
24. Donham, Wallace B. "The Social Significance of Business," *Harvard Business Review*, v. 5, is. 4, 1927: 406–419, p. 406.
25. Ackerman, Robert W. *The Social Challenge to Business*. Cambridge, MA: Harvard University Press, 1975, p. 1.
26. Ibid., p. 15.
27. Ibid., p. 326.

28. Margolis, Joshua D., Elfenbein, Hillary Anger, and Walsh, James P. "Does It Pay to Be Good . . . And Does It Matter? A Meta-Analysis of the Relationship between Corporate Social and Financial Performance," March 2009, working paper, Harvard Business School.
29. McKinsey & Company. "McKinsey Global Survey Results: Valuing Corporate Social Responsibility," *The McKinsey Quarterly*, 2009, p. 2.
30. Ibid, p. 6.
31. Carroll, p. 268.
32. Freeman, Edward, Harrison, Jeffrey, Wicks, Andrew, Parmar, Bidhan, and de Colle, Simone. *Stakeholder Theory: The State of the Art*. Cambridge: Cambridge University Press, 2010 in press, p. 235.
33. Ibid.
34. Friedman, Milton. "The social responsibility of business is to increase its profits," *New York Times Magazine*, September 13, 1970.
35. Franklin, Daniel. "Just good business: A special report on corporate social responsibility," *The Economist*, January 19, 2008, p. 1.
36. "The actual word 'stakeholder' first appeared in the management literature in an internal memorandum at the Stanford Research Institute (now SRI International, Inc.), in 1963." Freeman, R. Edward. *Strategic Management: A Stakeholder Approach*. Boston: Pitman, 1984, p. 31.
37. Freeman, p. 25.
38. Ibid., p. 246.
39. Ibid., p. 34.
40. Ibid., p. 38, 40. Other relevant literatures he cited are corporate planning, systems theory, and organization theory. See also Carroll, Op. Cit., for a review of the history of the concept and definition of corporate social responsibility.
41. Ibid., p. 40.
42. Ibid., p. 40.
43. Wartick, Steven, and Cochran, Philip. "The Evolution of the Corporate Social Performance Model," *Academy of Management Review*, v. 10, is. 4, 1985: 758–769, p. 759.
44. Porter, Michael E., and Kramer, Mark R. "Strategy and Society," *Harvard Business Review*, v. 84, is. 12, 2006: 78–99, p. 83.
45. Martin, Roger L. "The Virtue Matrix," *Harvard Business Review*, v. 80, is. 3, 2002: 68–75, p. 71.
46. Ibid., p. 74.
47. Carson, Rachel. *Silent Spring*. Boston: Houghton Mifflin, 1962.

48. Meadows, Donella H., Meadows, Dennis L., Randers, Jørgen, and Behrens, William W. III. *The Limits to Growth.* New York: Universe Books, 1972.
49. Much of this section draws on Simon Dresner's analysis of the sustainability's origins in *The Principles of Sustainability* (London: Earthscan, 2008).
50. Ibid., p. 33.
51. World Commission on Environment and Development. *Our Common Future.* Oxford: Oxford University Press, 1987, p. 8.
52. Ibid., p. 5.
53. Ibid., p. 8.
54. Porter, Michael E. *Competitive Advantage: Creating and Sustaining Superior Performance.* New York: Free Press, 1985. pp. xvi; 20.
55. Ghemawat, Pankaj. "Sustainable Advantage," *Harvard Business Review*, v. 64, is. 5, 1986: 53–58, pp. 54, 58.
56. Porter and Kramer, p. 85.
57. Ibid., p. 88.
58. Ibid., p. 84.
59. Ibid., p. 88.
60. Ibid., p. 89.
61. Hart, Stuart. "A Natural-Resource-Based View of the Firm," *Academy of Management Review*, v. 20, is. 4, 1995: 986-104, p. 991.
62. Ibid., p. 992.
63. Margolis, Joshua D., and Walsh, James P. "Misery Loves Companies: Rethinking Social Initiatives by Business," *Administrative Science Quarterly*, v. 48, is. 2, 2003: 268–304, p. 296.
64. Porter and Kramer, p. 81.
65. Chatterji, Aaron K., Levin, David I., and Toffel, Michael W. "How Well Do Social Ratings Actually Measure Corporate Social Responsibility?" *Journal of Economics & Management Strategy*, v. 18, is. 1, 2009, 125–169.
66. Chatterji, Aaron K. and Toffel, Michael W. "How Firms Respond to Being Rated," *Strategic Management Journal*, forthcoming.
67. McKinsey, p. 8.
68. Zenji Miura, interview with Robert Eccles, Masako Egawa, and Akiko Kanno, February 26, 2009.
69. Miura interview, February 26, 2009.
70. Ratio of Eco Profit = total economic benefit/total environmental conservation cost; Ratio of Eco Effect = (total economic benefit + social cost reduction values)/total environmental conservation cost, *Ricoh Group Sustainability*

Report (Environment) 2008, p. 8. *Economic benefit* was defined as benefits obtained by environmental conservation activities that contributed to the profits of Ricoh in some form; *environmental conservation cost* was defined as expenditure on environmental conservation activities that consisted of environmental investments and environmental costs; *social cost reduction values* were defined as financial figures obtained by converting the environmental reduction amount into monetary amount using the Swedish EPS method, *Ricoh Group Sustainability Report (Environment)*, p. 59–60.

71. Shima Nakao, interview by Robert Eccles, Masako Egawa, and Akiko Kanno, February 27, 2009.
72. Hisashi Moriyama, interview by Robert Eccles, Masako Egawa, and Akiko Kanno, February 27, 2009.
73. Shohei Ura, interview by Robert Eccles, Masako Egawa, and Akiko Kanno, February 23, 2009.
74. Moriyama interview, February 27, 2009.
75. Shiro Kondo, interview by Robert Eccles, Masako Egawa, and Akiko Kanno, February 26, 2009.

Chapter 6

It's Time for One Report

The second page of Philips's 276-page *Annual Report 2008: Financial, social and environmental performance* explains why the company decided to combine all of this information into a single report:

> Simplifying our external annual reporting in order to better meet the needs of stakeholders, this year's Annual Report covers both our financial and our social and environmental performance in a single volume. This reflects the fact that sustainability is no mere adjunct to, but rather embedded in the very fabric of our business operations. Our Annual Report 2008 will also be the last to be based on both US GAAP (Generally Accepted Accounting Principles in the United States) and IFRS (International Financial Reporting Standards): as of 2009 we will apply IFRS only.[1]

Due to the recession's impact in 2008, much of President Gerard Kleisterlee's message is focused on financial results, but he does pledge that Philips "will also continue to embed sustainability throughout our operations," indicating that the work in this area is not yet finished and again reinforcing the importance of integrated reporting as a sign of that work. Furthermore, his acknowledgment of the downturned economy's strain on business also expressed the company's commitment to its sustainable strategy: "... these difficult times call at most for a change of tactic, not a change of strategy."[2]

Philips's strategy included a focus on the needs of people: "We want to help people enjoy a better quality of life by focusing on their health and well-being. And this automatically implies helping to build a sustainable society."[3] This focus on health and well-being is supported by the company's product offerings as well as its environmental commitments, and the strategy is evident throughout the report. For example, Philips "has embraced the energy challenge early on, seeing it as a business opportunity that could benefit society at large" by offering energy-efficient lightbulbs and entering a public/private partnership to develop solar-powered lighting for sub-Saharan Africa while at the same time cutting the company's carbon emissions by purchasing renewable-source electricity.[4]

The integrated report also allowed Philips to be explicit about its reporting practices in a single location. Both the U.S. GAAP and IFRS financial statements sections opened with an introduction explaining the Board of Directors' application of the accounting standards, as required by each; so too did the sustainability performance section open with an explanation on reporting. Here, Philips indicated its use of the GRI's G3 Sustainability Reporting Guidelines, including a later table of performance indicators measured.[5] By noting standards and methodology in its One Report, Philips is exemplary in improving transparency for users of the report.

In keeping with its effort to provide information "in a single volume," the company's corresponding annual report Web site is as integrated as the hard copy. This electronic version featured interactive charts and graphs; a one-minute, seven-question survey soliciting reader feedback using both scaled and open response questions ensured complete engagement with users.[6]

The Case for One Report

There are two main reasons why companies should adopt One Report in their external reporting. The first is that it is a key element of taking sustainability seriously, once the company has created a truly sustainable strategy, by responding to the risks and opportunities created by the need to ensure a sustainable society. The second reason is that the simplification from One Report's single message to all stakeholders is a key element of improving corporate disclosure and transparency. Philips cited both of these reasons in its explanation for why it decided to produce a single, integrated report for 2008.

Of course, One Report is not a panacea or silver bullet solution to making sustainability more than a public relations campaign or resolving the complex issues regarding improving corporate disclosure for all stakeholders. Really taking sustainability seriously requires understanding the risks and opportunities created by environmental and social issues and trends and responding to both in a meaningful way. When and where a sincere commitment to sustainability and transparent disclosure exist, an integrated report becomes a cornerstone to improving both, since it provides a point of focus and discipline.

Some simple and pragmatic guidelines can be used to make the company's reporting as useful as possible to all stakeholders. By simplifying the language and avoiding the use of jargon or "legalese," the narratives in One Report are made more accessible to a broad spectrum of readers. Quantitative information in tables that stand out and use of color ensure that the key points of the data are clear and also helpful.[7] Easily navigable corporate Web sites make it easy to find information online, as do internal and external links to related information. By leveraging the spatial qualities of the Internet with drill-down capabilities in which summary data are provided, the company enables the user to get more detailed data one or two levels down. Data presented in an XBRL format make it easy to download and analyze.

It is certainly true that a company can be clearly committed to sustainability without producing One Report. Ricoh, profiled in the previous chapter, is a good example of this. Sustainability is at the core of the company's strategy and how it is managed, yet Ricoh produced three external reports: annual, environmental sustainability, and corporate social responsibility. It is also true that a company can be committed to as earnest disclosure and transparent reporting as possible without being committed to sustainability. In this case, the company would have a classic shareholder-only financial focus and would be striving to do the best job possible in reporting and explaining its financial results.

But *if* a company is truly committed to sustainability (a claim being made by more and more companies) and *if* a company is truly committed to as transparent reporting as possible (another claim being made by more and more companies), *then* the case for One Report is a compelling one. The assertion "What gets measured gets managed" applies here. Just as the Balanced Scorecard provides for better internal management and implementation of strategy by focusing on both financial results and the factors that produce them, One Report adds the discipline that comes from external reporting to the discipline that comes from internal reporting. Reporting on both financial and nonfinancial performance to all stakeholders strengthens management's desire to show good results, particularly if financial and other incentives are tied to these results and commitments are in terms of future goals and targets. This was the case at Natura and UTC; both companies were candid about whether or not past targets had been achieved.

Practicing integrated reporting brings four major benefits to the company. First, it provides greater clarity about relationships and commitments. Second, it leads to better decisions. Third, it deepens engagement with all stakeholders. Fourth, it lowers reputational risk. Taken together, these benefits make the development, implementation, and reporting of a sustainable strategy for a sustainable society mutually reinforcing processes. We discuss each of these benefits in turn next.

Greater Clarity about Relationships and Commitments

It is easy for a company to make the sweeping statement "We believe that sustainability is good for our shareholders" or "By pursuing sound environmental, social, and governance policies we are creating value for our shareholders, all other stakeholders, and society at large." Of course, sustainable strategies are not that easy. Investments to improve energy efficiency and reduce carbon emissions can have a positive return on investment but hurt earnings and cash flow in the short term. Some commitments may actually result in a wealth transfer from shareholders to another stakeholder group, such as paying a "living wage" that is above market labor rates—although this can ultimately benefit shareholders by attracting customers who support this. A sustainable strategy with a multi-stakeholder perspective means that sometimes trade-offs must be made. As Joshua Margolis and James Walsh point out, "Managers face a vexing reality. They must find a way to do their work even as seemingly financial and society demands intensify."[8] Rather than ignoring them or pretending that they do not exist, managers need to directly confront these trade-offs and be clear on the choices they've made and why—recognizing that some stakeholder group will inevitably be disappointed in the decision.

One Report begins with identifying the most important financial and ESG metrics for the company in its given industry and the strategy it is pursuing to achieve its goals. In some cases, revenue growth may be critical; in others, earnings growth is more important. In some cases, reducing carbon emissions may be the most important environmental objective, and in others it may be reducing the amount of water used. Racial and gender diversity can be a priority, but so too is ensuring some minimal amount of training for all employees every year.

The real essence of One Report is in describing what management believes the relationships between these key financial and nonfinancial metrics to be. Most companies have a great deal of work to do in this area. A 2008 KPMG CSR survey found that "Only a minority 16 percent of G250 companies quantified the value of corporate responsibility performance specifically for their analyst and investor stakeholders," an issue that needs to be addressed in order to convince mainstream investors of the company's sustainable strategy.[9] Quantifying the value of CSR starts by answering the following questions: Which ESG topics represent opportunities to improve financial performance, such as through increased revenues for green products or decreased costs through greater energy efficiency? Which ESG topics represent risks and cause spending to protect against the downside in terms of the destruction of shareholder value? Which ESG topics are not risks, but the company is committed to making investments to create value for other stakeholders even if this is at a cost to shareholders? Obviously the dividing lines between these categories of risks, opportunities, and "other commitments" are not well defined. Over a sufficiently long period of time, what looks like an "other commitment" might turn out to be value-enhancing for shareholders, particularly since the state of the world will change in unpredictable ways. One Report gives management the opportunity to clarify the dividing line and explain how other commitments have become value-enhancing activities.

As management develops a better understanding of the relationships between financial and nonfinancial performance through modeling and analysis, improving internal systems and measurement methodologies as necessary, it can re-evaluate what is included in its categories of risks, opportunities, and choices. One Report challenges management to be much more granular about how they are "doing well (for shareholders) by doing good (for stakeholders)." It challenges them to be as explicit as possible in a cause-and-effect sense of how good outcomes on a particular aspect of ESG lead to good outcomes on a particular financial metric. Ideally, the lag times and functionality (e.g., linear, asymptotic, or exponential) will also be specified, although data limitations typically make this very hard to do. Many ESG metrics are still being developed and have not been in place for most companies long enough to explore time-series relationships; we envision that this will change over time. As it does, the capability of companies to develop and implement sustainable strategies for a sustainable society will improve.

Better Decisions

As management attempts to be as explicit as possible about the relationships between financial and nonfinancial outcomes, it inevitably finds that for some, good metrics do not exist, and for others, they are very hard to develop. This can be an excuse for not doing the hard analytical work necessary to specify and validate the relationships that are believed to exist. The better response is to improve poor measurement methodologies and invent new ones for useful metrics that do not yet exist. The result will be better information for better decisions.

In some cases, better information comes from simply combining data that already exist in the firm but are spread across different parts of the company. Some metrics, such as customer satisfaction (like the Net Promoter Score used by Allianz), require going outside the company's boundaries to gather the necessary data. Different measurement methodologies will need to be used, including aggregating data from transactions (e.g., number of calls from whistleblowers), measurement of physical processes (e.g., carbon emissions), and surveys (e.g., of customer and employee satisfaction).

Kaplan and Norton's voluminous body of work on the Balanced Scorecard provides compelling arguments and evidence for how better measurement leads to better management decisions. When information is reported externally, the standards for its reliability are especially high. The higher quality metrics required for external reporting provide higher quality internal information and this results in higher quality decisions. The external transparency of the results of these decisions adds an additional incentive for making them good ones.

Developing greater clarity about the relationships between financial and nonfinancial information, developing the supporting metrics to test and validate these relationships, and then pulling all of this performance information together in One Report requires a high level of internal collaboration across functions and business units. As each unit sees its role in a broader context and begins to better understand the consequences of its decisions on other units, better decisions that craft and reinforce a sustainable strategy will be made for the company as a whole.

Deeper Engagement with All Stakeholders

As companies realize the benefits of better decisions from higher levels of internal collaboration, they will naturally seek to obtain these same benefits from higher levels of external collaboration through stakeholder engagement in order to better understand their expectations, obviously useful for internal decision making. The 2008 KPMG survey found that "understanding key stakeholder expectations" was the most important reason cited for stakeholder engagement by 59 percent of the respondents.[10] External stakeholders can provide useful input to the decision-making process. Initially, collaboration will be between individual internal units and their external counterparts, but eventually this collaboration will become cross-functional and cross-stakeholder in nature.

The implicit theory behind having annual reports that focus on financial performance and separate CSR reports that focus on nonfinancial performance is that these reports are audience-specific and meet each reader's information needs. However, in our world, where companies are facing the demands of many stakeholders, it is essential that *every* stakeholder understands how its interests are related to those of others and to the factors that contribute to the level of performance that is being met. A single-issue focus by a stakeholder is as irresponsible as company's singular focus on short-term profits for shareholders. Just as companies must take a more integrated approach to their external reporting, stakeholders must take a more integrated view about how their interests are related to others' interests.

One Report eliminates the artificial and unhelpful analytical distinction between shareholders and stakeholders. The former are simply one particular type of stakeholder, and all stakeholders have convergent and competing interests to varying degrees. We disagree with the argument that a separate CSR report "empowers" other stakeholders by treating them as a separate and distinct audience deserving of its own report. Instead, it marginalizes them by putting this information in a separate report from the official document that must be audited and filed with the appropriate regulatory agency.

A separate CSR report also marginalizes the importance of nonfinancial information to shareholders. While Socially Responsible Investment (SRI) funds pay some attention to them, primarily for screening rather than resource allocation purposes, most investors find the reports unhelpful because they contain little in the way of information useful for investment decisions. Ricoh, discussed in the previous chapter, is a case in point.

Putting all performance information into One Report in an integrated way challenges all stakeholders to take a more holistic perspective. Shareholders cannot just focus on short-term profits; they need to understand that a company's ability to earn profits over the long term will require investments that come at a short-term cost, or even value transfers that preserve its legitimacy and continued existence in order to earn profits in the future. Conversely, other stakeholders need to understand that companies need to make a profit in order to survive and grow. Failure to do so means that eventually they will not be able to fulfill the needs of other stakeholders or may even fail to survive.

Additionally, One Report ensures that a coherent and consistent message is going out to all stakeholders. It creates the platform for one conversation in which all stakeholders can and must participate. While it is natural for particular stakeholders to want to engage with their corporate counterparts due to a common issue focus—such as environmental groups with environment, health and safety, consumer interest groups with product development and marketing, and community groups with human resources—it runs the risk of creating "splinter groups" or factions along issue lines that make it difficult for the company to communicate and act in a coherent way. The result is often mixed messages to external parties and internal confusion about priorities.

Engagement is not easy. It takes time and effort. It requires listening as well as talking. But it is through engagement that companies remain aware of the interests of their different stakeholders and how these interests are in alignment or conflict with each other. A great deal of engagement is already taking place today in many companies, initiated both by them and by their various stakeholders. Examples include the kind of engagement that comes from active investors—such as on issues of corporate governance, executive compensation, and climate change—and from NGOs—such as on human rights and climate change. Engagement provides the basis for an ongoing dialogue between the company and its stakeholders. The company should also encourage engagement and dialogue among the various stakeholders to help create a single collective conversation rather than many separate and disjointed ones about society's expectations for the company.

Lower Reputational Risk

Not surprisingly, as corporate social responsibility and sustainability have increased in importance, so has managing reputational risk, which is now seen as one of the most important and difficult risks to manage. A survey of senior executives by *The Economist Intelligence Unit* found that, as a priority, reputational risk ranked first and distinctly ahead of regulatory risk and human capital risks, which tied for second. It also found that the key reasons cited for difficulties in managing reputational risk were the lack of established tools and techniques; no identified person with responsibility for the issue; poor coordination between the board, risk management, and corporate communications; and poor communications with external stakeholders.[11] All of these difficulties can be overcome by the process and communication that necessarily go hand-in-hand with CSR reporting. Leslie Gaines-Ross, Chief Reputation Strategist of Weber Shandwick, commented that "In today's multi-stakeholder and multi-channel society, CEOs are increasingly concerned about reputational risk, both for their company and themselves. Now is the time for CEOs to carefully explain their companies to stakeholders, engage in productive two-way conversations, and clearly communicate their contributions to the market and society. If stakeholders are left on their own to unify all the information they need about an enterprise, companies could find themselves vulnerable to misinformation and hearsay and put their reputations at risk."[12]

Robert G. Eccles, Scott C. Newquist, and Roland Schatz cited three major determinants of reputational risk: a reputation/reality gap (the company's external reputation is greater than its ability to consistently meet expectations through actual performance), changing beliefs and expectations (actions considered acceptable become unacceptable as social norms and values change), and weak internal coordination (actions by one group create expectations that another group cannot meet). To manage reputational risk, they cite three corresponding actions[13] and for each of them One Report can play a meaningful role. First, to address the reputation/reality gap, the company needs to objectively assess reputation and reality. An integrated view of the company's financial and nonfinancial performance, provided by One Report, will help identify areas at risk, since it will make clearer the areas where a company's reputation is based on overlapping performance outcomes.

Second is the need to assess and accept the impact of changing beliefs and expectations. These can happen suddenly (such as a major accident that is a catalyst for new safety standards) or emerge more slowly over a long period of time (such as the gradual crescendo of concern about carbon emissions over the past few decades). Through constant monitoring of trends, social attitudes, and the media, the company can improve its awareness of how social norms and values are changing. Through the deeper engagement process, One Report facilitates a dialogue that can identify new themes and concerns across more than one stakeholder group, helping the company become more aware of early-stage changes in expectations that will become more widely held and supported.

Finally, the solution to weak internal coordination is to put a well-defined process in place that includes all of the groups (e.g., investor relations; public relations; corporate communications; marketing;

environment, health, and safety (EH&S); operations; and risk management) whose input is necessary for managing reputational risk. One person needs to be explicitly put in charge of this process to ensure that it works in a collaborative, cross-functional fashion. Similarly, producing One Report requires an integrated process that involves all of these groups and the same degree of collaboration. Given the close relationship between integrated reporting and managing reputational risk, these processes should be coordinated to avoid redundancies and confusion.

One Report for a Sustainable Strategy for a Sustainable Society

There is a natural cycle relating the benefits of One Report to each other, as shown in Exhibit 6.1. In seeking to establish greater clarity

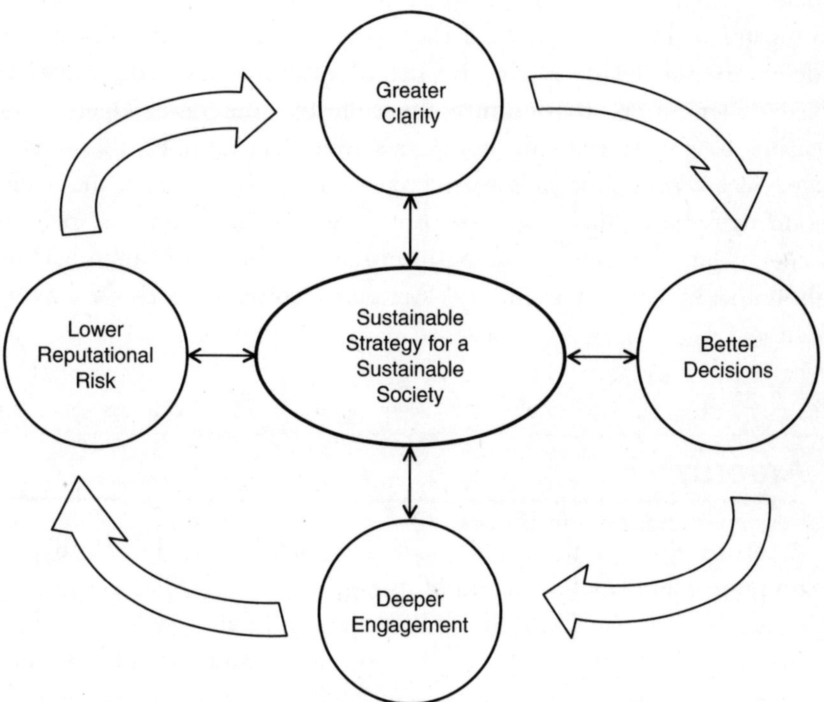

Exhibit 6.1 The Benefits of One Report

about the relationship between financial and nonfinancial outcomes, the company will find it needs better information, which will, in turn, lead to better decisions. Another contributor to better decisions is individual units seeing how their performance affects the performance of others and therefore the company as a whole. The result of this is better internal collaboration. When the company seeks to extend this collaboration externally as another way of obtaining better information, it contributes to the engagement process. Engagement is critical to maintaining a dialogue with stakeholders and critical for tracking changing beliefs and expectations in order to manage reputational risk. Finally, assessing the reputation/reality gap and establishing the required internal coordination for managing reputational risk contributes to greater clarity about the relationship between financial and nonfinancial outcomes.

Similarly, each of these resulting benefits contributes to the development and implementation of a sustainable strategy for a sustainable society. Greater clarity about cause-and-effect relationships enables a company to better understand the impact of its strategic choices on society. Better decisions improve the allocation of resources across all stakeholder groups to optimize the collective outcome. Deeper engagement ensures that the company's strategy is attuned to society's needs as a whole. Finally, lowering reputational risk increases the likelihood that the company is sustainable over the long term as society's values change. Many of the relationships shown in Exhibit 6.1 are illustrated by the experience of Aracruz, described in the following section.

Aracruz

Aracruz Celulose is the world's leading producer of bleached eucalyptus pulp, exporting 98 percent of its output. The Brazilian company is listed on the São Paulo Stock Exchange and the New York Stock Exchange and was named to the Dow Jones Sustainability World Index for the fourth year in a row in 2008–2009. Aracruz's decision to integrate its sustainability and annual reports was "a challenge," according to Carlos Roxo, Director of Sustainability and Corporate Relations. He further elaborated:

> Readers got used to receiving two different reports attached in the same publication: the annual and the sustainability report, which allowed them to find the information related to economic aspects (in the first) and the social and environmental issues (in the latter). Therefore, we didn't know how they would react to the new, single edition format. On the other hand, we thought that there was no other way, since some issues don't fall necessarily into one of the three dimensions (economic, social, environmental), but comprise all the dimensions in a transversal, integrated way (such as governance, risk management, etc.). On top of this, we considered that the medium- and long-term economic results are increasingly dependent on the sustainability performance, and that a non-integrated approach could mislead the readers.[14]

In 2004, the Aracruz board and management decided that rather than approaching singular issues with singular solutions, the company should adopt a comprehensive approach that would encompass a broad range of issues, framed in terms of "sustainability" for both the company and society. In developing a sustainability plan, Aracruz studied the practices of other companies, including its own customers and other major industry players. The company also hired the consulting firm SustainAbility to do a study of their sustainability practices, including interviews with various stakeholder groups. SustainAbility delivered a very frank report to the board that pointed out both strengths and weaknesses.

Based on this work, the board determined that the sustainability plan's first efforts should be to review the company's vision. Roxo explained, "At the time, its vision reflected the prevailing concept that the company's business environment was limited to shareholders, customers, suppliers, employees, and the government, and, similar to the visions of the majority of other companies, was focused on generating benefits for such players." Aracruz's vision now "To offer

(*continued*)

(*Continued*)

products obtained in a sustainable way from planted forests, generating economic, social, and environmental benefits and, in this way, contributing to people's well-being and quality of life" "reflects the interactions with and influence of the traditional players as well as NGOs, consumers, communities, and academia in the current business environment," said Roxo, "and translates the need to generate benefits to society as a whole."

Following that, a commitment was made to a high level of transparency in providing information to all stakeholders based on the principle that any misunderstanding by any stakeholder group was the fault of the company. Finally, stakeholder engagement was seen as absolutely critical. This involved a structured process for surveying the "outside world" to determine what actions and information stakeholders wanted from the company and how to work together with them for mutual benefit. This required a major cultural shift in the company since, as Roxo explained, "the company would have to learn to listen."

Once the sustainability plan was agreed to and its implementation begun, the company then addressed the way it was communicating about it. Since 1997, Aracruz had been publishing a social and environmental report and including it with the annual report in its mailing, but the audiences of each were very different. Luiz Fernando Brandao, Corporate Communications Manager, explained that there was a marked difference between the sustainability and annual reports—the contents of the latter were mostly addressed to business audiences, while the former was read by a much wider audience. In 2006, Brandao voiced the idea of merging the two reports into a single one that would integrate the economic, environmental, and social information that was currently being reported separately. His reasoning was that since sustainability had been integrated into the company's operations, it made sense to have a more integrated approach to reporting. He then had to sell this idea to senior management, and "the crucial moment was helping people understand that one report would give a more integrative view for both the internal and external audiences."[15] Brandao reflected that this was a relatively easy decision inside the company, and although there was some concern about readers' ability to find the information they were looking for in this new format, the first combined report was issued for 2006.

Brandao felt that a single report could be structured under the four perspectives of the company's management system, which followed the Balanced Scorecard methodology—value creation, customer satisfaction, internal processes, and learning and development—that Aracruz had been using since 2002 and that had provided the framework for the company's annual reports ever since. Roxo noted that sustainability was implicit in the Balanced Scorecard approach and was thus a useful framework for putting together a single integrated report.

Deciding on a framework for integrated reporting was easier than pulling together all of the information that needed to be included. Brandao explained that the key to this was a collaborative process that involved "over 30 of my colleagues in different areas like forestry, pulp making, R&D, HR, legal, community relations, marketing, controllership, and investor relations" to provide data. He went on to say that there was a very real benefit to this, since "the way we report helps in our day-to-day management since it makes clearer how different areas need to be aligned with each other." The single report was also causing the company to more rigorously review its processes in the social and environmental areas in the context of their economic consequences. Finally, issuing a single report enabled people in the different parts of the company to have a better understanding of the overall risks to the company created by their activities.

The company was also benefiting from the integrated view the single report gave to external users of the report. Brandao noted that "customers want a sustainable supplier, consumers want sustainable products, employees want a sustainable job, and investors want a sustainable profit." Having a single report provided a clearer vision to all of these groups of the work that Aracruz was doing to meet their expectations.

That said, the company was still wrestling with how to make a single report useful to both investors and other stakeholders, which

(*continued*)

(*Continued*)

remained separate audiences. Feedback from some stakeholders, such as NGOs, had signaled that the report had too much financial information relative to nonfinancial information. At the same time, investors praised the richness of nonfinancial information.

Looking forward, the company had several areas in which it felt it could do a better job with its single report. One of the most challenging was in providing information showing the relationship between financial and nonfinancial outcomes. "This is one of the points we need to take a closer look at," said Brandao. Developing a better understanding of how social and environmental issues affect the business requires better metrics in these domains. It also requires "refining the business case into a sustainability case." Brandao commented, "Consistent metrics are fundamental in making clear to any audience the cause-effect connections between the company's reported objectives and achievements from the triple bottom line perspective. In the same way that investors can easily track a company's financial performance along the years through established, well-accepted indicators, in the new scenario corporate sustainability reporting will increasingly call for the same degree of objectivity in allowing diversified audiences to follow up what is being promised and delivered."

The company was also looking to simplify the report, thereby making it more useful to all users. Their vision was a short and highly integrated report with more detailed information of all types being made available on the company's Web site, including links to relevant sources of information outside the company. The goal, explained Brandao, was to produce a report so that "in 20 minutes of reading the person would have a good sense of the business and its sustainability."

The most immediate challenge was presented by Aracruz's incorporation by Votorantim Celulose e Papel (VCP), which was set to close in August 2009. While Aracruz had developed a smooth process for collecting all of the information necessary to produce its single report, there was some uncertainty about whether the resulting new company would be able to do so for 2009. Historically, Aracruz had started working on its report in September, but in September 2009 they would be at the early stages of a major integration exercise. However, those on the Aracruz side of the incorporation were hopeful that the new board would be supportive of a single report and that for sure, the new company would be producing one by 2010.

The Time Is Now

Both companies and society at large need One Report. Enabling companies to achieve the four benefits discussed earlier, integrated reporting is also an outlet for companies to substantiate the claims they are making about their commitment to sustainability. Pressures from stakeholders will continue to increase, especially around issues regarding limited resources and human rights. Companies will have to keep pace with these rising expectations or risk their reputation, and One Report will help them demonstrate their efforts.

To achieve a truly sustainable society, all stakeholders need a mechanism for engaging in the collective conversation necessary for its creation. One Report's integration of information and clarification on trade-offs will force groups with previously competitive viewpoints to understand that choices have to be made about the most efficient allocation of limited resources—financial, environmental, and social. The sooner a critical mass of companies starts doing this, and the sooner they improve with experience, the faster our progress will be in shaping a sustainable society.

The fact that companies in varying industries all over the world are starting to produce One Report is an early signal of what we believe will be a rapidly adopted new practice in external reporting. Most have been producing integrated reports for only a year or two, although Novozymes has been doing so for seven years and Novo Nordisk for five. It appears that they all came to this idea more or less independently of each other, which suggests a convergence of forces in industries and countries around the world that companies are beginning to respond to in their external reporting practices. Sustainability, and its incorporation into the meaning of corporate social responsibility, is clearly the overarching force here. As companies are learning to adopt sustainable strategies, it is only natural that they begin to adapt their external reporting practices for describing these strategies and their financial and nonfinancial results.

The Prince's Accounting for Sustainability Project

In addition to the efforts of individual companies, groups are being formed to further the practice of integrated reporting in a more systemic way. One such initiative was launched by His Royal Highness the Prince of Wales in 2006. His Accounting for Sustainability Project (A4S) "works with businesses, investors, the public sector, accounting bodies, NGOs and academics to develop practical guidance and tools for embedding sustainability into decision-making and reporting processes." The Prince of Wales established the Project "[t]o help ensure that sustainability—considering what we do not only in terms of ourselves and today, but also of others and tomorrow—is not just talked and worried about, but becomes embedded in organisations' 'DNA'" since the "long term sustainability of many organisations, as well as the societies in which they operate, is threatened by trends such as climate change unless these longer term and broader consequences of actions are sufficiently factored into decisions taken now." A4S sees a better demonstration of the significance of environmental and social factors to a company's financial sustainability within the annual report and accounts as an essential enabler to the increased incorporation of sustainability into investor dialogues and, ultimately, investment decisions. A prerequisite to drive this shift is for business to embed sustainability into strategy and decision making, with external reporting providing an important feedback loop to support this embedding process.[16]

In December 2007, A4S released its Connected Reporting Framework as a "reporting model which presents key sustainability information alongside more conventional financial information to give a more rounded and balanced picture of the organisation's overall performance,"[17] and several U.K. companies are already using the Framework.[18] Although A4S is not calling for One Report per se, the key principles of the Connected Reporting Framework are completely in line with those of One Report and remain core to the further development of the Framework in 2009:

- "Sustainability issues need to be clearly linked to the organisation's overall strategy;
- Sustainability and more conventional financial information should be presented together in a clear and concise manner, so that a more complete and balanced picture of the organisation's performance is given;
- There should be consistency in presentation to aid comparability between years and organizations;
- Reported information should be aligned with that used to manage the business."[19]

A number of accounting bodies from around the world as well as large accounting firms (including Ernst & Young, Grant Thornton, KPMG, and PricewaterhouseCoopers) have provided support to this project. Furthermore, over 150 other public and private sector organizations have provided financial or other support and/or input to the Project's work through the Accounting for Sustainability Forum.[20] Given the platform of A4S's founder, the Project and its Forum have the potential to have a strong influence on a trend for One Report.

King III

South Africa is also moving in the direction of One Report and putting it in the context of corporate governance as an important responsibility of the board of directors. In the third iteration of its corporate reporting rules, the *King Code of Governance for South Africa* (King III) was released in 2009 as well as its accompanying *King Report on Governance for South Africa*; the latter's Principle 1.2 states, "The board should ensure that the company is and is seen to be a responsible corporate citizen." Corollary statements to this principle specify that "The board is not merely responsible for the company's financial bottom line, but rather for the company's performance within the *triple context* in which it operates: economic, social and environmental. It follows that the board should issue an integrated report on its economic, social, and environmental performance."[21]

Chapter 9 of the *King Report* elaborates, in three simple principles, how integrated reporting should be done given companies' dual roles as economic institutions and corporate citizens:

- *Principle 9.1.* The Board should ensure the integrity of the company's integrated report.
- *Principle 9.2.* Sustainability reporting and disclosure should be integrated with the company's financial reporting.
- *Principle 9.3.* Sustainability reporting and disclosure should be independently assured.[22]

King III explicitly recommends integrated sustainability performance and integrated reporting to enable stakeholders to make a more informed assessment of the economic value of a company.[23] Reinforcing our argument about the benefits to companies of issuing One Report, the Code argues that "By issuing integrated reports, a company increases the trust and confidence of its stakeholders and the legitimacy of its operations." Integrated reporting has value inside the company as well: "By issuing an integrated report internally, a company evaluates its ethics, fundamental values, and governance."[24] The *King Report* describes the content and structure of an integrated report, saying that it "should describe how the company has made its money; hence the need to contextualise its financial results by reporting on the positive and negative impact the company's operations had on its stakeholders."[25] In this regard, the report suggests that "Sustainability reporting is becoming increasingly formalised and sophisticated, which is evident in the third generation Global Reporting Initiative (GRI) G3 guidelines" and states that these guidelines provide "excellent guidance."[26] Finally, King III calls for the board to report forward-looking information: "Those who prepare integrated reports should give the readers the forward-looking information they want. Today's stakeholders also want assurance on the quality of this forward looking information."[27] Time will tell, but the King III report could be the impetus for the rapid adoption of One Report in South Africa. Mervyn King believes that will be the case: "The Report will become a listing requirement on the Johannesburg Securities Exchange in June 2010. Several countries now require integrated reporting on a 'report or explain' basis. For example, Denmark has recently amended its financial statements Act requiring a financial and CSR report from its companies on a 'do it or explain why not' basis."[28]

Socially Responsible Investment Groups

In July 2009, two prominent investor groups commented, with some informal coordination between them, on the need for better, integrated sustainability reporting, effectively calling for One Report. In the United States, the 400-member Social Investment Forum (SIF), a membership association for socially and environmentally responsible investment professionals and institutions, submitted a proposal to SEC Chairman Mary L. Schapiro that had two components:

> The first requests that the SEC require issuers to report annually on a comprehensive, uniform set of sustainability indicators comprised of both universally applicable and industry-specific components and suggests that the SEC define this as the highest level of the current version of the Global Reporting Initiative (GRI) reporting guidelines. . . . The second asks that the SEC issue interpretative guidance to clarify that companies are required to disclose short- and long-term sustainability risks in the Management Discussion and Analysis section of the 10-K (MD&A).[29]

Although the proposal does not specifically call for One Report, its recommendation to "provide management's discussion and analysis of how the issuer's ESG performance relates to its overall business strategy and performance" is certainly consistent with it.[30]

The Federation of European Accountants (FEE) and the European Sustainable Investment Forum (Eurosif), SIF's European counterpart, published a joint Call for Action that stated that "the annual report is not the only source of information available to stakeholders: there are press releases, articles and interviews, company websites, road shows etc. However once a year it is helpful to have a calibration and confirmation in the form of sustainability disclosures within the annual report."[31] This "once a year" recommendation followed a Eurosif position paper in which it recommended that "the European Commission adopt three proposals to increase transparency from various segments in the financial chain that would foster a longer-term, more sustainable economy within the EU." In the first proposal, "Transparency from Companies," Eurosif states that "European institutions should mandate disclosure of ESG data by publicly traded, large corporations. Such reporting would be principles-based and use a limited number of standardized Key Performance Indicators (KPIs), some of them being sector-specific." And in the spirit of One Report, "Eurosif recommends that those reporting principles should be integrated into . . . the annual reports."[32]

Bloomberg

In response to increasing investor interest in ESG information and getting it in a way that is integrated with financial information, the Bloomberg Professional® service, a leading source of data, news, and analytics to the financial markets, started providing environmental, social, and corporate governance data in July 2009.[33] Bloomberg's move to include this information as part of its service could be viewed as a signal that financial and nonfinancial information, linked One Report-style, is the future of corporate reporting.

Bloomberg Professional® integrates ESG information with financial statements, valuations, and ratio analyses used to evaluate equity investments. Bloomberg provides data on more than 100 KPIs for a global set of 3,500 public companies. It also provides company risk data, sustainability news, research, indices, funds, energy and emissions markets data, legal and regulatory factors, as well as robust screening, scoring, and other portfolio optimization tools. The user has access to the latest ESG information (both quantitative data and policies) provided by companies in whatever reports (e.g., annual, CSR, sustainability, EH&S, etc.) it is contained in or in reports provided by others, with links to the underlying source of the information so that the user can get any explanations provided by the company or other data source of how the metric was calculated and any narrative explanation that accompanies it.

The integrative nature of the offering is reflected in other ways, including:

- Templates for comparing peer companies in terms of market value and financial ratios and a variety of ESG metrics such as emissions, diversity policies, and governance metrics
- Similar templates for risk analysis
- Comparing buy/sell recommendations and consensus earnings estimates with ESG metrics

- Screening tools that combine financial and ESG data
- Scoring tools for ranking securities based on various weightings of financial and nonfinancial data.[34]

Explaining Bloomberg's decision regarding its ESG offering, Curtis Ravenel, Bloomberg's Global Head of Sustainability Initiatives, said:

> Based on a number of studies, we believe that ESG data will be considered fundamental data in three to five years. Mainstream investors will require the ability to integrate ESG data into their traditional investment analysis process. Having a robust ESG product on Bloomberg not only increases its value for existing users but also opens opportunities for us to become a leader in this field.[35]

That Bloomberg sees a business opportunity in providing integrated information suggests that companies would be well served to provide it in an integrated fashion themselves to make sure that they are presenting their view and not simply letting the market develop its own. Gary Turkel, Bloomberg Equities Product Manager, acknowledged the merits of "companies providing information in a more integrated way" but that "investors will want to evaluate the relationship between ESG and financial performance themselves and then integrate all these data into their investment process."[36]

A Broad Stakeholder View

The growth in sustainability reporting raises the question of whether those who advocate and support this activity would, like investors, want to see this information integrated with financial information or whether they would prefer to see separate CSR reports. An argument can certainly be made that they would prefer to get the information of interest to them in a separate report, untainted by the complicated financial reporting described in Chapter 3, but a 2007/2008 survey by KPMG and SustainAbility of 2,279 businesspeople, NGO members, labor leaders, investors, consultants, academics, and others provides conclusive evidence that broad public opinion across all stakeholders strongly supports the idea of One Report: 70 percent of respondents agreed with the statement "Future sustainability reporting should be integrated with the annual report." Civil society (i.e., NGOs and labor leaders) had the highest agreement rate at 80 percent in favor of integrated reporting. Further evidence of the perceived value that would come from One Report is that more than 70 percent of respondents agreed that "Future sustainability reporting should include more information about the economic impact" and more than 80 percent felt that "Future sustainability reporting should give more information about the processes around sustainability management." In contrast, less than half thought that "Future sustainability reporting should move toward stakeholder reporting" and less than 20 percent felt that "Future sustainability reporting should move towards issue reporting."[37]

Based on the survey results, KPMG and SustainAbility suggested a "2020 Vision" for sustainability reporting, shown in Exhibit 6.2. In addition to calling for the end of separate sustainability reports, as this

Exhibit 6.2 Sustainability Reporting in the "2020 Vision"

The end of sustainability reports	Fully integrated in annual reports and other corporate communications
Seamless accessibility	Information embedded in a variety of hard copy, PDF, and web-based communications
Stakeholders' roles integrated	Reporting developed based on continuous stakeholder dialogue linked to the business agenda, and fully reflected in reporting
Translation into business	Sustainability elements are translated into business targets, linked to company strategy
Sustainability and innovation	Discussion in the report of how process and product innovation has been incorporated to take account of sustainability needs
The business case is established	Clarity of approach to sustainability issues has obviated the need to demonstrate the value of sustainability to the business
More and more active readers	The number of users of sustainability reports has increased to a majority of all relevant readers, as does their use of reports for decision making
Trust and reliability	Globally accepted standards and stronger, relevant assurance activities build comparability and trust in reporting

SOURCE: KPMG and SustainAbility, *Count Me In: The Readers' Take on Sustainability Reporting*, p. 39.

information will be fully integrated into annual reports and other corporate communications, the vision points out the importance of linking sustainability to financial outcomes, the integration of all stakeholders' interests, ongoing dialogue with stakeholders, leveraging technology and using multiple formats for providing information, the role of product and process innovation in building sustainable strategies for a sustainable society, and globally accepted standards on which assurance can be given.[38]

Further support from stakeholders for One Report is evident in a subsequent SustainAbility presentation by Research and Advocacy Manager Katie Fry Hester. Based on interviews at a number of prominent organizations, including companies, NGOs, financial institutions, sustainability consulting firms, and universities, Hester predicted that:

- Sustainability reporting will be *integrated* into mainstream communications channels, an implicit attribute of products, branding, contracts, etc.
- Stand-alone, explicit reporting will either *disappear or dramatically shrink in size*, focusing on the intersection of business strategy and material issues.
- Comprehensive tracking of multiple sustainability indicators will evolve into an *internal management system*, not a report.
- *Emerging markets* reporters have the opportunity to leapfrog to positions of leadership.[39]

Hester also conducted a workshop with participants from 31 well-known European and American companies regarding the "Reporting Job Description for 2011." Based on this workshop, she elaborated on the aforementioned predictions. First, the integrated annual report will be supplemented by tailored reporting for specific audiences (e.g., NGOs, employees, and customers), consistent with our view that One Report does not preclude more detailed and tailored communications. Second, information will be available on a real-time basis in multiple formats. Third, the person responsible for sustainability reporting will (1) report directly into the C-Suite, (2) coordinate much more extensively with other functions and business units, (3) communicate directly with the financial community, and (4) have much more technology support.[40]

The degree to which companies will achieve the benefits we claim from practicing integrated reporting depends upon how receptive the capital markets and society as a whole are to the idea. The support given to Accounting for Sustainability, the recommendations of King III, the letters written by SIF and Eurosif, Bloomberg's new ESG offering, and the interest of civil society in integrated reporting identified in the survey conducted by KPMG and SustainAbility suggest that these benefits will be high. One Report is an idea whose time has come.

Objections to One Report

Despite the evidence provided in this chapter supporting the idea of One Report, there are arguments that can be made against it. Because One Report is a new idea and only a handful of companies are implementing it, there is little in the public domain in the way of analysis of this practice or criticism of the concept; virtually no academic literature exists on this topic. Based on conversations we have had while doing the research for this book, we expect that this will change—especially within academic circles. The objections can be organized into three arguments: (1) the market's efficiency means there is no reason for companies to change their reporting practices (capital market perspective); (2) if there was a clear benefit, companies would already be doing it since they are optimally managed (company perspective); and (3) doing so will actually hurt the development of a sustainable society (stakeholder perspective).

Each of these arguments is based on deeply held theories and beliefs, not easily rebutted by facts, and so we have no illusions that our counterarguments will be persuasive. We should also acknowledge that our own perspective is based on three deeply held beliefs about which we want to be explicit. The first is that markets are not completely efficient, and opportunities always exist to improve capital allocation through better information. The second is that management practices can always be improved through innovation, which inevitably involves risks and costs—especially to first movers—but they can achieve some long-lasting benefits as well. Third, shareholders' and other stakeholders' interests are neither completely congruent nor completely at odds with each other and all stakeholders have an obligation to take a broad view as the context of their own particular interest.

The Markets Are Efficient

The first objection to One Report is not about the relevance of integrating financial and nonfinancial information. Rather, the point is that to the extent nonfinancial information is value-relevant, the market is already taking this into account, and it is reflected in the company's stock price. Thus, there is no reason for companies to "package up" this information in a single report. Furthermore, if in fact the nonfinancial information is not relevant, why put it in the annual report or 10-K?

There is some merit to this argument. Goldman Sachs has created a large proprietary database of financial and nonfinancial data that it uses in its analyses as part of its GS SUSTAIN initiative (see the section titled "GS SUSTAIN"). This effort dates back to 2003 and allows the company to account for global trends in ESG in firms' management and strategies. Earlier, we noted that Bloomberg is now providing ESG data via its Bloomberg terminal. Individuals can also access this information directly on companies' Web sites or through many organizations that consolidate and provide such information for a fee or even for free. The information is out there, the argument goes, and the users can integrate it themselves or pay someone else to do it. In efficient markets, investors will use information if it is valuable to them.

GS SUSTAIN

Evidence of the strong connection between sustainable company strategies and concern for a sustainable society is the GS SUSTAIN initiative, launched by the large global bank Goldman Sachs Group, Inc. The origins of this initiative go back to 2003, when Goldman Sachs joined a group of investors forming the Asset Management Working Group (AMWG) of the United Nations Environment Program Finance Initiative (UNEP-FI) "to identify environmental and social issues likely to be material for company competitiveness in the global energy industry, and to the extent possible, quantify their potential impact on stock prices." Goldman Sachs then developed its

(*continued*)

(*Continued*)

own proprietary ESG framework "for helping to identify sustainable advantage" through a "quantifiable and objective picture of performance." It includes data on corporate governance; social issues with respect to leadership, employees, and wider stakeholders; and environmental management. The firm incorporates the 10 principles of the UN Global Compact "to the extent possible in every sector" and believes that "leadership on these issues is crucial" to successful long-term financial performance.[41]

Goldman Sachs integrated ESG into its fundamental sector and company analyses because there are a number of strong global trends that are making effective management of ESG issues essential for establishing strategies that create a long-term sustainable advantage. Goldman Sachs believes these key trends to be:

- Changing GDP
- Population is growing and aging
- Urbanization rates are increasing globally
- Resource constraints and environmental impacts are imposing challenges
- The millennial generation creates a different workplace
- Consumers changing in the old world; new consumers in a new world
- Interconnectivity increases communication of the flow of news and ideas
- NGOs continue to focus on companies
- Shareholders are becoming more active
- UN Global Compact provides a mechanism for engagement with stakeholders
- Industry structures are changing rapidly and this change will accelerate in the future[42]

Integration of financial and nonfinancial information is at the foundation of Goldman Sachs's approach since the firm notes that it has "found no correlation across sectors or within sectors between any of our ESG metrics and share price performance."[43] It is only when superior management with respect to environmental, social, and corporate governance translates to sustained industry positioning and return on capital that it contributes to sustainable long-term returns. Thus, Goldman Sachs is looking to identify companies that demonstrate sustainable and sustained competitive advantage by leading its peers across all indicators of corporate performance: management quality, industry positioning, and return on capital.[44] Goldman Sachs takes the view that ESG performance "is a good overall proxy for the management quality of companies relative to their peers" and thus provides insights into which ones have the "ability to succeed on a sustainable basis."[45]

Goldman Sachs has assembled a proprietary structured database that incorporates financial and nonfinancial data gathered from a wide variety of sources, including companies themselves. Based on the models it has built using these data, the firm identified its "GS SUSTAIN Focus List" of more than 80 global companies across mature and emerging industries. In the two years since its launch in June 2007, the Focus List outperformed the MSCI World index by 18 percent.

Commenting on Goldman Sachs's future plans for integrating ESG across its Global Investment Research division, Marc Fox, Vice President of GS SUSTAIN Research, noted, "GS SUSTAIN research identifies the implications to investors of the key structural trends facing the global economy, environment, societies, and industries. The GS SUSTAIN framework applies objective measures to identify companies well-placed to sustain competitive advantage and superior returns on capital over the long term (three to five years) as they evolve in response to a rapidly changing, globalizing world."[46]

We are hardly going to take on the eternal and complex debate with its extensive literature about whether the markets are efficient. Instead, we simply note that substantial research dollars are spent on both the sell and buy sides under the presumption that the market is *not* efficient and that through gathering information and doing analysis it is possible to identify stocks that are under- or overpriced. This then raises the issue of how these resources are best expended. Anything the company can do to reduce the transaction costs of getting information means that more resources can be spent on analyzing it. The fact that most mainstream investors spend little, if any, time looking at sustainability reports[47] means that either they find the cost in time not worth getting it or that the information is not worth using. By integrating nonfinancial information with financial information in One Report, management reduces search costs. It also can also help make the case for the relationship between financial and nonfinancial results. Of course, users will still want to do their own analyses, but seeing management's analysis is a useful starting point.

Companies Are Already Optimally Managed

We turn to the objection that if there were a benefit to companies in doing One Report, this would be common practice already.[48] Just as the first objection, based on efficient market theory, assumes completely rational decisions without resource constraints at the market level (a rather large assumption after the latest financial crisis), this second objection assumes the same for management. Without reviewing the extensive literature on how managers make decisions, we simply note the obvious fact that managers are not omniscient and the quality of their decisions varies according to many factors. More important, we note that management practices are always changing as the state of the world changes and innovations in management practice develop. These innovations typically start in a few companies and then become widespread, sometimes for real benefits and sometimes as management fads. To say that companies would have already adopted a practice if it made sense to do so is to take the untenable position that at any given point in time companies are as well-managed as they could be. If this were the case, change would never happen—and yet it always does.

Of course, change involves risks and costs, particularly for the innovators. In the case of One Report, the risk we hear most often is that both shareholders and stakeholders will either be overwhelmed with information they do not want in a comprehensive One Report or will not get the information they do want in a briefer One Report. It is easy to set this objection aside, since nothing about One Report precludes providing more detailed financial and nonfinancial information, and technologies like XBRL can be used to make it easy to find the information of interest.

Cost concerns come in two ways, the first trivial and the second more substantive. The first is that long paper documents are expensive to prepare and print. This is a specious argument for three reasons. First, One Report doesn't have to be long; UTC's is fewer than 100 pages. Second, printing separate reports is also expensive. Third, to the extent allowed by regulation, documents can be posted on the company's Web site, where any printing costs are shifted to users. More important, as explained in the next chapter, One Report is about much more than a single paper document.

The more substantive cost concern involves the coordination costs from having many different functions working together to produce a consistent message in One Report. Substantial coordination costs are inevitable if a company is going to truly embed sustainability into its strategy and operations, but the benefits of doing so, described earlier, are enormous. If anything, most companies have too little interfunctional coordination, not too much—at the risk of their reputation and performance in general.

First movers certainly face advantages and disadvantages with risks and costs, some fleeting and some longer-lasting. Which dominates depends on the particulars of the situation and how well the innovation is managed. Innovations spread through both mimicry and their demonstrated benefits learned about in such ways as publications, consulting firms, and executive education programs.

One Report Hinders the Development of a Sustainable Society

The third objection is that integrated reporting reinforces companies acting only for "instrumental" or "utilitarian" reasons and not for the common good *in and of itself*. This argument assumes that shareholder and other stakeholder interests are mostly *not* aligned, and that overall social welfare will be increased only if value is transferred from shareholders to other stakeholders. In this case, if companies only pursue sustainable strategies that create value for shareholders, there is a risk that One Report will make it easier for companies to see that some of their sustainability decisions are actually value-destroying for shareholders and, as a result, will reduce their commitment to these activities. We have argued that when shareholders' and other stakeholders' interests are in conflict, at least in the short term, management needs to make some difficult choices. In the end, these choices are based on values, but these decisions also need to be informed by the better analysis that comes from integrated reporting.

Another, and somewhat more cynical, argument for why One Report will inhibit the adoption of sustainable strategies for a sustainable society is based on the view that companies are transferring wealth from shareholders to other stakeholders, but that the cost of this transfer is small. As long as other stakeholders can be kept at bay with a CSR report that reveals little about the true costs involved, there is a risk in moving to One Report. Creating an integrated report would make it easier for other stakeholders to see these investments in sustainability in the context of the company's other investments, which will lead to more pressure on management to be more responsive to other stakeholders. This, in turn, will lead to more value destruction for shareholders, and managing the competing claims of shareholders and other stakeholders will simply become more difficult. This, of course, assumes that these stakeholders are easily fooled and "bought off," which seems unlikely in light of the growing size and sophistication of the NGO community.

The Bottom Line

Markets are not completely efficient, better management practices are always being invented as the world changes, and tough choices are informed, not avoided, by better information and analysis. Integrated reporting is a better management practice that will increase market efficiency and improve resource allocation across all stakeholders in order to create a sustainable society. The case for One Report is clear and compelling.

Notes

1. Philips, *Annual Report 2008*, p. 2.
2. Ibid., p. 12.
3. Ibid., p. 9.

4. Ibid., pp. 27–28, 184.
5. Ibid., p. 180, 190.
6. Philips, "Annual Report 2008," www.annualreport2008.philips.com, accessed August 2009.
7. For more on the visual representation of data and information, see: Tufte, Edward R. *The Visual Display of Quantitative Information*. Cheshire, CT: Graphics Press, 1983; *Envisioning Information*. Cheshire, CT: Graphics Press, 1990; *Visual Explanations: Images and Quantities, Evidence and Narrative*. Cheshire, CT: Graphics Press, 1997; and *Beautiful Evidence*. Cheshire, CT: Graphics Press, 2006.
8. Margolis, Joshua D. and Walsh, James P. "Misery Loves Companies: Rethinking Social Initiatives by Business," *Administrative Science Quarterly*, v. 48, is. 2, 2003: 268–305, p. 296.
9. KPMG. *International Survey of Corporate Responsibility Reporting 2008*, p. 31.
10. Ibid., p. 31.
11. The Economist Intelligence Unit. *Reputation: Risk of Risks*, white paper, December 2005, p. 5, 22.
12. Leslie Gaines-Ross, e-mail correspondence with Robert Eccles, September 22, 2009.
13. Eccles, Robert G., Newquist, Scott C., and Schatz, Roland. "Reputation and Its Risks." *Harvard Business Review*, v. 85, is. 2, 2007, pp. 104–114.
14. Carlos Roxo, phone interview with Robert Eccles, Michael Krzus, and Susan Thyne, August 7, 2009.
15. Luiz Fernando Brandao, phone interview with Robert Eccles, Michael Krzus, and Susan Thyne, August 7, 2009.
16. Accounting for Sustainability. "Project Aims and Mission Statement," www.accountingforsustainability.org/aboutus/, accessed August 2009.
17. Accounting for Sustainability. "What is the Connected Reporting Framework?" www.accountingforsustainability.org/output/Page159.asp, accessed August 2009.
18. BT and Aviva issue separate CSR reports, but these do contain some financial information, and the companies' Connected Reporting Framework is placed in the Annual Report and Accounts page on their Web sites. Accounting for Sustainability, "The CRF – Examples from Published Reports," www.accountingforsustainability.org/output/page97.asp, accessed August 2009.
19. Accounting for Sustainability, "What Is the Connected Reporting Framework?"
20. Accounting for Sustainability, "Forum Members," www.accountingforsustainability.org/forum/, accessed August 2009.

21. Institute of Directors in Southern Africa. *King Report on Governance for South Africa 2009*. September 2009, p. 22.
22. Ibid., pp. 108–110.
23. Institute of Directors in Southern Africa. *King Code of Governance for South Africa 2009*. p. 12.
24. Ibid.
25. *King Report on Governance for South Africa 2009,* p. 109.
26. Ibid., p. 109–110.
27. *King Code on Governance for South Africa 2009*, p. 13.
28. Mervyn King, e-mail correspondence with Robert Eccles, September 27, 2009.
29. Social Investment Forum, letter to Mary L. Schapiro, July 21, 2009, p. 2. www.socialinvest.org/documents/ESG_Letter_to_SEC.pdf, accessed August 2009.
30. Social Investment Forum, "Proposal," p. 3.
31. Federation of European Accountants and Eurosif, "Call for Action: Sustainability Disclosures in Financial Information Can Be Improved," July 2009, p. 2. www.ibr-ire.be/fra/download.aspx?type=1&id=4074&file=3505, accessed August 2009.
32. Eurosif, "Public Policy Position Paper related to Sustainable and Responsible Investment ("SRI")," April 14, 2009, po. 1–2. www.eurosif.org/content/download/1361/7711/version/1/file/Eurosif+Public+Policy+Position+PPape+2009.pdf, accessed July 2009.
33. Clients pay a monthly subscription for access to more than 27,000 functions and unlimited data. ESG data is included in the core product and integrated into the Financial Analysis function for equity traders and portfolio managers.
34. "Environmental, Social & Governance," Bloomberg Coverage, August 29, 2009, Version 1.00.
35. Curtis Ravenel, e-mail correspondence with Robert Eccles, September 25, 2009.
36. Gary Turkel, e-mail correspondence with Robert Eccles, September 25, 2009.
37. KPMG and SustainAbility conducted the survey for the Global Reporting Initiative. SustainAbility is a strategic business consultancy and independent research center. "Count me in: The readers' take on sustainability reporting," www.globalreporting.org/NR/rdonlyres/3F57ACC8-60D0-48F0-AF28-527F85A2A4B4/0/CountMeIn.pdf, accessed August 2009. All data in this paragraph are from the detailed responses to survey question 15 regarding statements about the future of sustainability reporting.

38. The report notes that readers want assurance on both the company's report (around 50 percent) and even more so on the organization's sustainability performance (around 65 percent). See graph showing response to question 14, "Is it important that some form of assurance is given?" www.globalreporting.org/CurrentPriorities/GlobalReadersSurvey/Q14.htm, accessed August 2009.
39. Fry Hester, Katie. "Beyond the Sustainability Report—Communicating Accountability." *Sustainable Brands International*, December 10, 2008, p. 9. www.sustainability.com/downloads_public/insight_general/Communicating Accountability_KatieFryHester_10Dec2009.pdf, accessed August 2009.
40. Ibid., pp. 16–21.
41. Goldman Sachs Group, Inc. "Introducing GS SUSTAIN," June 22, 2007, p. 5.
42. Ibid., p. 12.
43. Ibid., p. 5.
44. Ibid., p. 7.
45. Ibid., p. 5.
46. Marc Fox, interview with Robert Eccles, July 6, 2009.
47. Fry Hester, p. 15.
48. If markets are efficient, then a company's stock is properly priced, and there is no reason for management to do anything else beyond what they are required to do by regulation.

Chapter 7

The Internet and Integrated Reporting

Consider this possible vignette. 朱丽 (Zhu Li) is head of Corporate Communications for Shanghai-based 彩裳 (Cai Shang, or Colorful Clothing Company). Cai Shang (CS) is a large public company, listed in Shanghai and cross-listed on the New York Stock Exchange with a market cap of RMB25 billion (around $3 billion). This women's apparel company has its own labels and does contract manufacturing for a variety of low- and medium-end U.S., European, and Japanese apparel companies, as well as private department store labels. Zhu Li, 43 years old, is a married mother of an 8-year-old girl; her husband, 赵峰 (Zhao Feng), works for a major Chinese bank. Zhu (Zhu is her last name; Chinese convention is to list the given name second) owns stock in Cai Shang. She is also collaborating with local government agencies and international NGOs regarding child labor issues.

Prior to leaving the office today, Zhu received notification from CS's legal department that the large contract they have been negotiating with a French fashion company was approved and signed. It is a substantial contract, worth RMB20 million per year over the next five years. Since it is the first contract CS has received from a prestigious fashion house, it has the potential to create opportunities with other such high-end brands down the road. As a Chinese citizen, Zhu takes great pride in this contract, because it is yet another example of how the country is now seen as a place where work of the very highest quality is done.

Zhu stays late at the office to put together the media release, since she wants this information in the news cycle and on RSS feeders before the markets open in New York and before they close in Europe. She is able to do this quickly, using the company's document collaboration site to enable all departments to contribute to press releases, which the CEO then signs off on once Zhu considers it finished. On the commute home, Zhu checks stock prices on her cell phone and is pleased to see a noticeable uptick in CS's stock price—investors clearly like the news of the contract. She is happy to see that the French apparel company's stock price is up as well, indicating a win-win for both companies. Nearing home, Zhu accesses prices for CS's competitors and saves the data so she can take another look after dinner.

Later that night, once dinner with her family is finished and her mother-in-law has put her daughter to bed, Zhu pulls out her netbook to check on a number of things. Zhu wants to briefly monitor the dialogue surrounding the media release, which includes statements from the CS and the French company's CEOs that mention the size of the contract in revenues (but provides no estimates of profit margins). Pulling up the stock data she saved earlier, Zhu first does some analysis to make sure the price changes aren't simply due to general market movements in the industry. Comparing the changes to each company's competitors and some industry indexes, she sees that the positive differences are statistically significant. However, using some internally developed analytical rules, she can tell from a three-dimensional visualization of the analysis that the increase in CS's stock price is greater than can be explained by just the additional revenues from the contract. The market clearly believes this contract will lead to more business for the company. Zhu then uses other rules to model the impact of these additional revenues on existing capacity to ensure that the company can do this work in its existing facilities. The capacity appears to be there, but it is tight. Zhu next models employee satisfaction, a key performance indicator that the company publishes by manufacturing site on a monthly basis alongside other metrics, including quality, safety, employee turnover, hours of training, and carbon emissions. Zhu anticipates that this analysis might be useful later in the inevitable dialogue that will emerge in the social media as news of this contract rapidly spreads.

Zhu smiles to herself, knowing that she has successfully managed several potentially negative impacts on the good news for CS through her robust management of the social media and political spheres in which her company operates. Two months ago, she pushed CS's CEO to encourage employees to join an online community where people come together to create collaborative models to help companies achieve their environmental and social goals while pursuing genuinely profitable endeavors. Knowing the French fashion house contract was still being negotiated and that working conditions and human rights were of utmost importance to many of the NGOs monitoring the manufacturing facilities of CS and other companies in the industry, Zhu sends a post to this collaborative user community, saying that because of its rapid growth, CS is increasingly concerned with labor issues, and the company wants to hear the community's thoughts. One user responds with a comment on how Chinese regulations on child labor are increasingly a major topic in recent trade negotiations with other countries. Another replies to that post with a strategy about how to help avoid this potential risk, and several other users work together to develop an analytical model and implementation plan for this strategy. The user community, which includes a number of individual and institutional investors, votes this strategy as the most viable and well-thought-out one of the five that were presented as options for CS to pursue.

Backed by the reaction of the user community, and identifying with their concerns as a mother, Zhu makes a pitch to her executive team to help refocus their organizational practices, cut costs, and move away from potential child labor pitfalls a month before the new deal is announced. Sure enough, a week before CS's new contract is announced, the Chinese government issues tighter regulations on child labor with which all apparel companies in China will need to comply in one year. Instead of scrambling to find a viable solution, Zhu is pleased that she has leveraged the company's stakeholder community, including her own input, to help find a viable and truly sustainable path for her company going forward.

After the executive team endorses her pitch, Zhu writes an entry regarding the company's labor practices for the blog on the company's Web site, which she started with the heads of human resources and manufacturing. She notes that the reaction of the user group and the responsiveness of her executive team helped mitigate the issue in a timely fashion. The blog post is an instant hit! Not only does it spread quickly across various social media networks in which Zhu is a member, it also has an adverse effect on several of CS's competitors that were less proactive in addressing child labor issues. However, even given her large social media campaign, Zhu is still bothered by one foreign blogger, who points out that CS's sales have increased dramatically over the past two years and that it is operating at capacity and questions whether the company will be able to add additional work to its existing sites, all of which are being monitored by several NGOs, including China Labor Watch. The blogger's post on whether the company will resort to "gray outsourcing" (subcontracting work to manufacturing companies in China and other low-labor-cost countries that are not being monitored and audited) comes up in her personalized RSS reader, which monitors news feeds, blogs, and other relevant sources of information.

To ensure that this conversation does not get out of control, Zhu sends a message to her CEO, saying that the company needs to respond to this issue tomorrow. In her message, she includes a link to the analysis she did on capacity availability, but she suggests that the head of manufacturing confirm her data. Realizing any company message will have to respond to concerns outside of China, Zhu also prepares a short video interview of herself in both Chinese and English for CS's YouTube channel for her CEO to review. (Zhu would not have been able to get this job without being fluent in English, and her overseas MBA training certainly helped her here.)

Knowing that her work over the past few weeks has put CS in a strong position to handle public reaction, Zhu scans the headlines in her RSS reader, including one article put out by a prominent Chinese business news organization. The reporter questions whether the contract really exists and wonders whether this press release was simply a ruse to boost CS's stock price due to rumors it was looking to acquire a regional retailer in the United States. Unsure whether she should respond to this claim or not, Zhu uses a free online social networking tool that identifies other journalists who tend to write follow-on stories based on this reporter's work, and writes a script to have her reader follow any stories issued by these reporters in the next 48 hours. Realizing the seriousness of the charge, and anticipating the call she would get tomorrow from the Shanghai Stock Exchange, Zhu forwards this story to her contact there, along with an authenticated signed copy of the contract in a secure document format.

Feeling tired after a long day that is ending on an exciting but somewhat stressful note, Zhu decides that any further work can wait until tomorrow. While some of the company's reporting and engagement practices are standard practice today in most large Chinese companies, she remembers how controversial some of them were the first time they were suggested. The much bigger issue, she realizes, is that without some self-discipline, she could be online all the time, reporting and gathering information, doing and sharing analyses, and engaging with a wide range of stakeholders on topics of mutual interest. Before heading to bed, Zhu shoots a quick e-mail to a United States–based firm associate, informing her of the online blogging for which she is tracking the most relevant portions of the conversation in CS's online repository. She asks her counterpart to update and respond to any relevant commentary overnight, and says they will meet up for a quick Web chat when Zhu awakes. Zhu plugs her cell phone into its charger, checks on her sleeping daughter, and goes to bed.

A Web-Based Perspective on One Report

This story of Zhu Li may strike many readers as incongruent or even irrelevant in a book arguing for One Report. What does a day in the life of a corporate communications professional have to do with producing a document that integrates both financial and nonfinancial information, while also explaining the relationships between different types of performance outcomes? While the answer today is "not much," we believe that will change, and rapidly. When discussing the topic of corporate reporting, it is natural to think in terms of documents. After all, it is documents, nearly all paper-based, that are required by regulators, such as the annual report and 10-K in the United States.

Reporting connotes paper, whether delivered by mail or posted as a PDF on a company's Web site.

While paper documents will not go away any time soon, if ever, more and more people are accessing information online. Even more significantly, they do not want to be simply passive consumers of information supplied or "pushed out" by some person or some organization, but instead expect to become engaged in an ongoing dialogue that involves reacting to the information, supplying their own information, and doing and sharing analyses typical in the context of an online group of ever-evolving and shifting members. Real-life examples can be found for every technology-based scenario in the Zhu Li vignette, albeit admittedly not in a corporate reporting context, which remains largely passive and paper-based.

Corporate passivity needs to change in order for the full promise of One Report to be realized. Integration of different types of performance information and engagement with all stakeholders—both key hallmarks of One Report—are most fully realized in a digital world, including Web 2.0 tools and technologies. When these are used for corporate reporting purposes, there will be a natural shift in "reporting" from an outbound communication only to an ongoing dialogue between a company and its stakeholders. As this dialogue broadens and increases, One Report will shift from being a single document prepared by the company itself, such as UTC's 2008 Annual Report, to a socially constructed online representation of One Report, the direction Natura is already going with its integrated report. Other companies already practicing integrated reporting are also taking steps in this direction, as described in the following sections. There are also companies seeking to improve transparency through these means, even if they are not yet producing One Report, also described later in this chapter.

A Primer on Web 2.0 in the Business World

The Internet—and the subgroup of Web 2.0 sites and services, such as blogs, collective intelligence, mash-ups, podcasts, RSS feeds, social networking, Web services, and wikis—is increasing being used by companies in how they manage their businesses today.[1] A 2009 McKinsey global survey found that 69 percent of respondents reported that "their companies have gained measurable business benefits, including more innovative products and services, more effective marketing, better access to knowledge, lower cost of doing business, and higher revenues."[2] The survey identified the most popular technologies in terms of achieving measurable benefits and areas of greatest benefit according to internal purposes, customer-related purposes, and working with external partners/suppliers. Blogs and video sharing were the top two technologies for all three purposes. Increasing speed of access to knowledge was the top benefit for internal and external partner purposes, while increasing marketing effectiveness was the greatest benefit for customer-related purposes.[3]

An earlier McKinsey study of 50 early adopters identified six critical factors that determined the success of Web 2.0 initiatives:

1. The transformation to a bottom-up culture needs help from the top.
2. The best uses come from users—but they require help to scale.
3. What's in the workflow is what gets used.
4. Appeal to the participants' egos and needs—not just their wallets.
5. The right solution comes from the right participants.
6. Balance the top-down and self-management of risk.[4]

This same study argued that Web 2.0 could have "a more far-reaching organizational impact than technologies adopted in the 1990s—such as enterprise resource planning (ERP), customer relationship management (CRM), and supply chain management." The study also noted that, in contrast to these other technologies, Web 2.0 is not technically complex, is a relatively lightweight overlay to the existing infrastructure, does not necessarily require complex technology integration, and requires a high degree of participation. Web 2.0 technologies "are inherently disruptive" and "are interactive and require users to generate new information and content or to edit the work of other participants."[5] Rather than simply being the recipient or processor of information, in a Web 2.0 world the user is actively involved in the generation of the information itself, both individually and collectively.

Web 2.0 is as much about behavior as it is about technology, as illustrated in Exhibit 7.1. Our vignette on Zhu Li contains examples of each "description" and "category of technology" shown in this table. Broad collaboration was seen in the internally developed analytical rules

Exhibit 7.1 The Behavioral Implications of Web 2.0

Web 2.0 Technologies	Description	Category of Technology
Wikis, commenting, shared workspaces	Facilitates co-creation of content/applications across large, distributed set of participants.	Broad collaboration
Blogs, podcasts, videocasts, peer to peer	Offers individuals a way to communicate/share information with broad set of other individuals.	Broad communication
Prediction markets, information markets, polling	Harnesses the collective power of the community and generates a collectively derived answer.	Collective estimation
Tagging, social bookmarking/ filtering, user tracking, ratings, RSS feeds	Adds additional information to primary content to prioritize information or make it more valuable.	Metadata creation
Social networking, network mapping	Leverages connections between people to offer new applications.	Social graphing

SOURCE: Chui, Miller and Roberts. "Six ways to make Web 2.0 work," *The McKinsey Quarterly*, p. 2.

for analyzing stock price changes and the impact of additional revenues on outcomes like employee satisfaction and quality. Zhu's video in both Chinese and English and the various blogs in which she participates are examples of broad communication. The winning strategy developed for the company's child labor policies illustrates the use of collective estimation. The RSS reader that caught the streaming news story questioning the veracity of the contract is an example of metadata capturing and processing to a user. Finally, social graphing comes into play when Zhu sets up her RSS reader to follow stories by the other journalists.

Web 2.0 and Transparency

Missing from these studies, among others, is any mention at all of the implications of Web 2.0 for corporate reporting purposes. This is not surprising for two reasons. First, this is a rather specialized application, although it does affect a large number of people in different stakeholder groups. However, "successful companies already use Web 2.0 for business applications such as communicating with suppliers," and it is an easy extension to add other stakeholders in the context of communicating the company's results.[6] Second, companies are currently doing very little with Web 2.0 and reporting. Today's standard practice for using the Web for corporate reporting purposes is for companies to make PDF documents, such as their annual and CSR report, available on their Web site, so that the reader can view or print at their discretion. This limited online activity, and interactivity, is hardly what Web 2.0 is about in a corporate reporting context.

The real value of Web 2.0 for corporate reporting is the much higher degree of transparency it makes possible. Don Tapscott and David Ticoll were among the first to recognize this in their bestselling book *The Naked Corporation: How the Age of Transparency Will Revolutionize Business*. The basic thesis of their book was that achieving high levels of performance that are sustainable over the long term will require companies to practice a high level of transparency. They defined transparency as "the *accessibility of information to stakeholders of institutions, regarding matters that affect their interests*." Tapscott and Ticoll cited the success of market economies and globalization; the rise of knowledge work and business webs; the spread of communications technology; demographics and the rise of the Net Generation; and the rising global civil foundation as drivers for transparency and its accompanying requirement of trust. They emphasized that transparency "is far more than the obligation to disclose basic financial information" and that companies should become more transparent for their own self-interest since "armed with new tools to find information about matters that affect their interests, stakeholders now scrutinize the firm as never before, inform others, and organize collective responses." They concluded that companies are "becoming naked" and, in what has become a famous phrase from their book, "If you're going to be naked, you'd better be buff!"[7]

Nakedness comes in degrees. David Wheeler, Barry Colbert, and Edward Freeman developed three value levels of the firm:

- *Level 1.* Avoiding the unacceptable destruction of economic, social and ecological value through a compliance culture that ensures adherence to laws and regulations

- *Level 2.* Value is created through a relationship management culture but trade-offs are made, typically after investors are satisfied, and
- *Level 3.* Maximizing the simultaneous creation of value in economic, social and ecological terms through a "sustainable organization" culture[8]

Tapscott and Ticoll used this framework as the foundation for their three levels of transparency.[9] Although we do not see the distinction between Levels 2 and 3 as being clear-cut, because sometimes trade-offs have to be made (recall our discussion in Chapter 5), we do agree with Tapscott and Ticoll that the current trend toward a broad stakeholder-based perspective is forcing companies to become more transparent. Even though their book was published before the term *Web 2.0* became popular and before some of its technologies had broad adoption or even existed (such as prediction markets and social networking sites), Tapscott and Ticoll recognized the importance of the Internet, since it "raises transparency to a whole new level," not just through the "one-way, centrally (and corporately) controlled, single message" of broadcast media, but also "from Weblogs and e-mail to mobile phones and hand held computers."[10]

For Tapscott and Ticoll, corporate reporting was only one aspect of transparency, albeit an important one, which they saw changing. Thus in one sense their book is on a broader topic than this one. At the same time, when the concept of One Report is extended beyond the idea of a single paper document to an idea about Web-based communication and engagement, it becomes a corporate-reporting-based way of achieving much of what Tapscott and Ticoll called for. A Web 2.0-based concept of One Report recognizes that information flows must go both ways and that a collective conversation about the company is going on whether the company likes it or not. Employees and former employees blog about their work experience; suppliers and customers Twitter about companies' business practices and ethics; engineering studies of products are neatly sorted by a search engine; and RSS feeds send corporate updates to the marketplace itself. One Report is a way for the company to become part of the conversation being held about it by presenting an integrated report in a way that facilitates dialogue and engagement.

The Essential Elements of Web-Based Integrated Reporting

The essence of One Report is the integrated presentation of financial and nonfinancial information and the relationships between different types of performance outcomes. There are severe limitations to this presentation when it is only done in a paper document in which one page follows the next; this presentation even raises the question of how one can specify whether a company is practicing One Report, since integrated reporting is a matter of degree, not simply the existence of a single paper document.

When the Web is used to provide information, much higher degrees of integration are made feasible. Not being limited to the linear nature of the paper format, the company can provide many different presentations regarding financial and nonfinancial outcomes and the relationships between them at various levels of detail through the drill-down capabilities the Web provides. A single integrated report can provide greater detail of particular interest to various stakeholders, and the Internet makes it possible to provide users with tools that enable them to analyze the company's data themselves.

Finally, the Internet and its associated Web 2.0 tools and technologies also make it possible to shift from a one-way information push to a mutual conversation and ongoing dialogue between a company and all of its stakeholders, thereby adding much greater dimension to the idea of One Report. This higher degree of integration and interaction is made possible by an online presence that is user-friendly, engaging, collaborative, and secure. Doing this well typically involves Web sites beyond that of the company, since much of the collective conversation is taking place throughout a plethora of other channels on the Internet such as social media sites, blogs, and news sites.

User-Friendly

User-friendly Web sites are designed in a way that minimizes the user's effort to find relevant company information while at the same time delivering the information in a format that is more elaborate than a static Web site or a PDF document. Such user-friendly sites are simple and easy to navigate, and they typically include a detailed site map or intuitive menu structure. They have an overall insightful design and an interface that is appealing to a wide variety of audiences. Ideally, they also easily display in multiple language character sets and are accessible to people with disabilities; they also include links to other pages that contain more in-depth information on a given issue and can provide a description of what each page offers.

Additionally, a corporate Web site that is user-friendly offers tools that enable the user to control the range and level of data or information visible to them. A further step is making it easy for the user to decide exactly what information he or she wants—even putting it into a customized document. For example, the Philips Web site allows users to save and download the chapters and sections of the annual report that they want as a PDF, thus personalizing their information search.[11] Financial statements are available in either IFRS or U.S. GAAP, and can be downloaded as either a PDF or into an Excel spreadsheet. Once downloaded, these customized reports and data sets can be used and analyzed completely externally from the Web site.

The United Kingdom–based global bank HSBC, a participant in Accounting for Sustainability's Connected Reporting Framework Project, is another example of a company with a user-friendly site. The company is deeply committed to sustainability and has this embedded in its operations. "Sustainability" is one of nine main tabs on the company's home page, and the "Our Approach" section there clearly articulates that the bank has a multi-stakeholder view regarding its role in society, recognizes the existence of limits, articulates its long-term view, and realizes the importance of climate change as an issue for society. The bank voluntarily subscribes to the Equator Principles, which "set the standard for socially and environmentally responsible project finance and form a core part of our environmental and social risk management approach."[12] Explained Francis Sullivan, HSBC's Deputy Head of Group Corporate Sustainability, "As a global bank, managing risk—whether economic, social or environmental—is integral to the way we operate our business. We have the systems, people and policies in place to make sure this happens throughout our operations."[13]

The Sustainability page is easy to navigate with prominent links to important publications like its *Sustainability Report 2008* and the *Climate*

Confidence Report 2008. It contains links to relevant external Web sites (including the UN Universal Declaration of Human Rights, UNEP Finance Initiative, UN Global Compact, Global Business Coalition on HIV/AIDS, Global Sullivan Principles, OECD Guidelines for Multinational Enterprises and the Equator Principles), prominently displays key data, makes effective use of pictures, provides a page of interesting case studies regarding the bank's activities around the world, and is frequently updated. Rachael Morgan, Head of Communications and Reporting in Group Corporate Sustainability, reflected on the site's effectiveness: "Our Group company Web site provides one important way that we can communicate with our stakeholders around the world on our approach to sustainability. It allows us to share our strategy, to give examples of 'sustainability in practice,' and to report on the progress we are making."[14]

Engaging

Engaging Web sites let the user complete his or her own analysis of the information provided on the site, sometimes integrating it with other data as well, using analytical tools provided by the company or through other commercially available tools or widgets embedded on the site. In this setting, users can generate their own content and often manipulate that content within the Web site itself. Typical user-generated content today, although still relatively uncommon, is analysis of information presented by the company using tools that the company makes available. A higher level of sophistication is reached when the user can upload their own data to the company's Web site to be analyzed with company-provided data.

Two varying examples of engaging design of corporate reporting Web sites are found at Microsoft and SAP. Microsoft relies on increasingly normal modularized features—manipulation of stock and investment data—but takes them to the next level using a graphically appealing and easy-to-use platform. Exhibiting its SilverLight technology,[15] Microsoft enables users to drill down into its own stock graphs, segmented by business unit, sector, and other various organizational structures, and export all of the data into Excel format for further manipulation and analysis.

SAP's "SAP 2008 Sustainability Report" Web site bridges the gap between Microsoft and the need for more robust data analysis. On the SAP Sustainability Collaboration Forum page, the user is invited to "Join the Carbon Conversation" by registering for free to exchange views with others about SAP's sustainability objectives, actions, and performance.[16] In this workspace, SAP openly advertises full (not just segmented) Excel files to download and perform full data analysis and manipulation; the Web site also offers a robust platform that allows readers to self-explore and analyze SAP's sustainability performance via interactive charts and graphs. While the reports and graphs are not totally without constraints, in functionality they are far beyond the capabilities of most corporate Web sites today. SAP labels the various slices of interactive reporting on its Web site as "dashboards" and leverages SAP BusinessObjects technology to deliver them. SAP additionally creates an enriching user experience by supplementing these dashboards with clear performance icons and targeted write-ups focused on the specific reporting area, providing insight into SAP's point-of-view and initiatives for improving performance. This level of interactive presentation is truly One Report in nature and is an excellent model for helping users access and analyze information in a unified digital space. Scott Bolick, SAP's Vice President of Sustainability, reflected on the company's sites:

> Providing an online, interactive 2008 Sustainability Report created ongoing and consistent traffic from new and returning visitors. We have already seen a fivefold increase in visitors versus our static 2007 Sustainability Report which we believe is primarily due to the richer user experience provided by our online analytical dashboards. The benefit to us is clear—greater breadth and depth of relationship with our stakeholders. We therefore see a trend toward leveraging Web 2.0 tools and technologies even more to provide informative, interactive and collaborative reporting.[17]

Collaborative

A company's collaborative online presence can be established when the company provides its own tools, a platform from another Web site, or has a "location" on an independent Web site that allow users to exchange and share information with each other. Collaboration is achieved through discussion forums, blogs, podcasts, and other similar Web 2.0 tools and technologies that take stakeholder participation to another level by facilitating and encouraging user-generated content. Users can thus freely make comments, give suggestions, and pass judgments on the company's performance.

An even more sophisticated form of collaboration takes place on social media platforms, where stakeholders can engage in a direct dialogue with staff and representatives on a real-time basis. This contributes to a bidirectional information flow that not only enhances the company's transparency and accountability but also provides it with the most up-to-date information about the preferences and aspirations of its stakeholders. Although this form of dialogue can be quite challenging from a company's perspective, when taken promptly into consideration, this information can be a driver for business improvement and innovation. In other words, the company collaborates with its stakeholders to achieve mutually beneficial outcomes. The section on Timberland, which follows, is a leading example of collaboration using Web 2.0 tools and technologies. The company's Web site is also one that is user-friendly and engaging.

Another interesting example of using social networking Web sites for interacting with a wider and larger part of the stakeholder community is Marks and Spencer's (M&S) presence on Facebook. The British retailer leverages the public's wisdom by encouraging stakeholders to "become a Fan of" the company. Mike Barry, Head of Sustainable Business, explained why M&S turned to Facebook: "The key to becoming a sustainable business and a sustainable society is to create a tribe—the 60 million members of British society are potential members of a tribe that needs help in understanding how to be sustainable."[18] As of September 2009, more than 34,000 Facebook users had become Fans of M&S, whose Fan page contains the usual Wall postings, discussions, news, events, and photos sections. Some of the discussion topics are directly customer-oriented, such as "What NEW product would you like M&S to do?" and "If you don't, tell us why you don't shop at marksandspencer.com?" Other topics were targeted toward a broader range of stakeholders and solicited opinion on topics such as the environment, the company's sustainability plan, and changes M&S could make, all of which invite a direct dialogue with company representatives. When asked how this conversation will evolve, Barry said, "Someday, sites like Facebook will expand beyond dialogue with customers; M&S will engage in a conversation with a very wide range of external stakeholders, including competitors, in order to create the wide range of partnerships that will be needed to build a sustainable retail sector."

Although Marks and Spencer did not go so far as to use its Fan page to make decisions, other companies have done so. The low-cost retailer Target ran a Facebook campaign with the primary goal of expanding its presence in the social media space. To accomplish this goal, Target allowed its user community to vote and decide what charity organization Target would strategically align itself with from a variety of choices. Target gave away three million dollars a week for several weeks in amounts corresponding to each charity's percentage of the overall vote. Target successfully built online brand presence and gained notable increases in market exposure, given the large number of users that became Fans of the company on Facebook. It is not hard to imagine how a company can use a similar approach to determine what information its stakeholder community wants to use and in what form.

Marks and Spencer, Target, and Timberland are all examples of what Tapscott and Anthony Williams in their book *Wikinomics* call *mass collaboration* or *wikinomics* (they use these terms interchangeably), both "a new way for people to socialize, entertain, and transact in self-organizing communities of their choosing." For them, wikinomics "is based on four powerful new ideas: openness, peering, sharing, and acting globally," which "are replacing some of the old tenets of business."[19] As with *The Naked Corporation*, this book covers a much broader landscape than corporate reporting. But corporate reporting is an important part of what companies do, and this process will be subject to the same forces of wikinomics as the rest of the enterprise. Rather than trying to control the message in a paper document and carefully scripted quarterly calls, integrated reporting companies should open themselves up to the power of the Internet and Web 2.0 tools and technologies and reap the benefits in doing so.

Timberland

Headquartered in Stratham, New Hampshire, The Timberland Company makes and sells outdoor clothing and footwear. The close link between the company's products and the environment led to the awareness that protecting the environment was vital for Timberland's business success and should become intrinsic to the way the company operates; its commitment to sustainability and corporate social responsibility can be traced back to 1992. At that time, under the guidance of Chief Operating Officer Jeffrey Swartz, Timberland joined Business for Social Responsibility, teaming up with other businesses to initiate social change. Around the same time, the Path of Service Program was launched, and employees were offered 16 hours of paid leave to perform service in their communities every year. To reflect its understanding that "how we make our product is as important as what we make," in 1993 Timberland signed a set of environmental guidelines from the Coalition for Environmental Responsible Economies (Ceres).[20]

Timberland issued its first Corporate Social Responsibility Report in 2000 and six years later supplemented it with a Facility Report that included baseline performance information for the Recreational Footwear Company factory in the areas of global human rights, environmental stewardship, and community involvement. Owned and managed by Timberland, the factory is located in Santiago, Dominican Republic.[21]

As part of Timberland's continuous efforts toward improved CSR, in 2008 the Corporate Social Responsibility team developed a CSR Strategy that set long-term goals for the company. "A main driver for our decision to launch the new strategy," CSR and Sustainability Reporting Manager at Timberland Beth Holzman explained, "is our belief that transparency and accountability are key to the company's success and that as a business we can have a positive impact on the world."[22] The Strategy is based on four pillars—energy, products, workplace, and service—and the goals associated with each pillar are, respectively, to reduce carbon emissions; design sustainable

(*continued*)

(*Continued*)

products at a lower costs with less harm to the environment; promote fair, safe, and nondiscriminatory workplaces; and, finally, to serve the community through engaging the employees in volunteer activities.

The CSR Strategy was accompanied by changes in Timberland's CSR reporting, including the move to publish a complete CSR report every other year, summarizing the company's work in sustainability for the previous 24 months. Additionally, Timberland would report CSR key performance indicators on a quarterly basis. "While we do not issue an integrated financial and sustainability report, we want to make sure that we issue our CSR reports in the way we issue our financial report," said Holzman. Among the indicators are data on energy, products, workplace, and service. These reporting changes are used to achieve an enhanced level of disclosure and a higher level of engagement with the stakeholder community. They are aided by other tools, such as the Nutrition Label, seen in Exhibit 7.2, and the Green Index, both created with substantial feedback from the public, which give consumers clear, easy-to-understand, product-specific information about the impact of their footwear choices on the environment, including climate impact, chemicals used, and resource consumption.[23]

Another important aspect of Timberland's CSR reporting is the use of Web 2.0 tools and technologies. The company uses a social media platform where stakeholders and interested parties can engage in a direct dialogue with Timberland staff. Timberland's platform includes company podcasts and videos, quarterly reports, its Earthkeeper blog, news and events announcements. Using the power of social networking, this platform gives stakeholders the opportunity to discuss the company's CSR performance through a focused discussion around the four pillars. Stakeholders use the opportunity for direct dialogue to comment on a recent initiative, propose a certain strategy, applaud efforts in a given area, or ask very specific questions. In a discussion from May 2009, for instance, a Vietnamese representative of a global environmental organization was able to acquire information that would allow her to collaborate with Timberland to promote CSR in Vietnam. (See Exhibit 7.3 for the complete

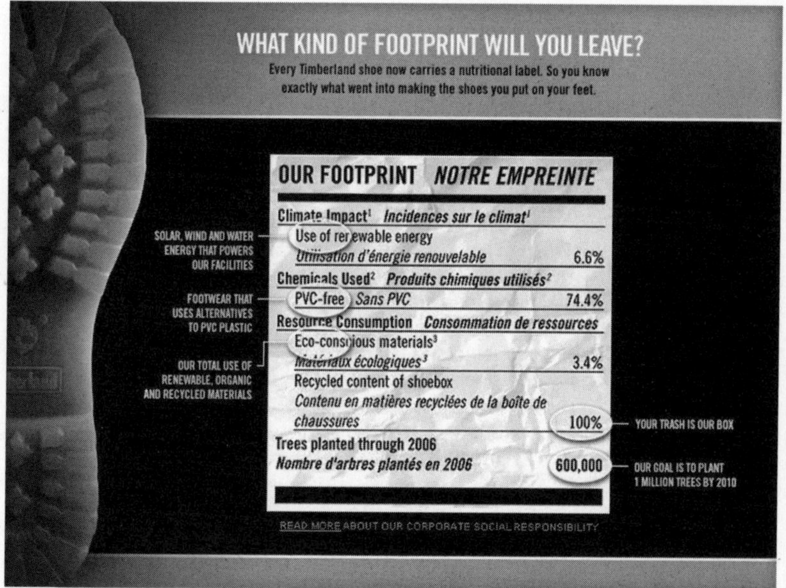

Exhibit 7.2 Nutrition Label
SOURCE: Timberland, "Nutrition Label," www.timberland.com/shop/ad4.jsp, accessed September 2009.

dialogue.) Although Timberland is eager for users to post comments more frequently, Holzman sees the social platform as rapidly gaining in importance. She noted, "My biggest dream and also my biggest nightmare would be that I would come in one day and have no capacity to do my strategy management job because I will have so many comments to respond to online."

Timberland's use of Justmeans, a social media portal for companies to help manage their sustainability initiatives, represents one of the company's many efforts to engage in conversation with its diverse stakeholders and respond to their different needs. "We want to create a two-way dialogue and to scale and broaden the diversity of stakeholders we interact with," notes Holzman. Although she agrees that the flow of information from stakeholders to the company can be quite difficult, she finds it instrumental for the company's progress. "Transparency and accountability are core to our mission to equip ourselves and others to make their difference in the world. That is

(*continued*)

(Continued)

Timberland | Posted: 27 May 2009

Hello Fabrice. Yes, we have several sourcing partners in Vietnam and we do have a Code of Conduct Specialist based in Ho Chi Min City who works with our suppliers to both assess factories in that region and also work with management to improve the lives of workers and their surrounding communities. We would indeed be interested in exploring possible opportunities to further promote CSR in Vietnam. Please send me an email at csrinfo@timberland.com to discuss specifics and local contacts. Also, we aim to use this online platform as a way to engage many types of stakeholders to learn from each others' CSR efforts; for this reason, would you be willing to post a follow-up comment with more about your organization and the opportunities you're looking to explore (or have successfully engaged) with international buyers to promote CSR in Vietnam?

Posted By: Colleen Von Haden

Fabrice Hanse | Posted: 26 May 2009

Hello, being based in Vietnam and working for an international organization to promote CSR among businesses operating in Vietnam, I am trying to get in touch with a Timberland representative in the country/region as I know you are sourcing a lot from here. I would like to start a dialogue and maybe use Timberland as a national case study to foster a local dialogue on international buyer/local suppliers' respective responsibility and opportunities to promote CSR in Vietnam. This is related to the Global Compact local network and we also work in partnership with the government. Could you help me identify a relevant person? Thank you very much.

Exhibit 7.3 Stakeholder Dialogue on Justmeans
SOURCE: Justmeans, "Timberland," www.justmeans.com/viewcompanyprofile?id=122&sublinkid=0&page=2#, accessed September 2009.

why we appreciate feedback both from partners and from critics because we see this as the only way to evolve and innovate."

To ensure the quality and timeliness of its interaction with stakeholders, Timberland employs a variety of engagement approaches. These approaches, detailed in Exhibit 7.4, vary from quarterly shareholder calls along with the quarterly CSR reports to partnerships with different NGOs and community organizations to open discussions and meetings with the public. "As our relationship deepens with these individuals and organizations, the understanding of our impact on the world increases," summarized Holzman.

Exhibit 7.4 Type of Engagement by Stakeholder Group

Stakeholder Group	Engagement
Employees	The Global Employee Survey Civic engagement: Path of Service program and Service Sabbatical Integrity Line (a 24-hour confidential hotline)
Customers	Surveys and focus groups Nutritional label and Green Index Civic engagement: Serv-a-palooza, Earth Day
Communities	Civic engagement: Earth Day, Serv-a-palooza Employee membership on nonprofit boards Corporate investment
Shareholders	Annual and quarterly reports Annual shareholder meetings Quarterly analyst calls, conferences, and regular meetings
Suppliers	Factory assessments and capacity building Human rights initiatives Annual supplier summit
Non-governmental organizations	Direct collaboration or joint programs on CSR objectives Annual planning and review Focused feedback on CSR activities Meetings and conferences
Media	Press releases Meetings and briefings
Government entities	Engagement on regulatory issues Adherence to laws where we operate
Business colleagues	Industry alliances and associations CSR ventures (consumer and community) Conferences and trainings

Source: Timberland, "Stakeholder Engagement," www.timberland.com/corp/index.jsp?page=csr_transparency_stakeholders, accessed September 2009.

Secure

As with all other Web applications, a Web-based approach to One Report must deal with security issues. Many of these already exist with today's more limited paper-based reporting format, but the momentum toward new online-enabled formats, like XML-based reporting, typified by XBRL, opens the door to new security-related technical standards that can both mitigate existing issues and provide new solutions for enhanced reporting in the future. In discussing security, we like the motto "No PAIN, no gain" where PAIN is a mnemonic for some of the most important aspects of security: privacy, authorization and authentication, (data) integrity, and non-repudiation.[24]

Privacy, both for individuals and companies, is important even while traditional external reporting by its nature is public. Information that is finding its way to the One Report, such as the financial reporting in advance of public exposure, as well as certain information within the One Report (underlying detail, tax, and other reporting that is compliance-necessitated but not public information) may need to be kept private. In particular, the underlying detail(s) may contain personally identifiable information, such as customer and employee information. To reduce the risk of exposure, standards like XML Encryption[25] can be used so that access to information is limited to those who are authorized to have that access.

Authorization speaks to whether or not the person making a statement is permitted to do so. *Authentication* speaks to the identity of the publisher—it is necessary to know they are who they say they are. For example, when looking at a report, the reader wants to see that the right party made a statement, that no one else changed the statement, and that the statement was signed off on by people with the necessary authorizations. XML Signature can ensure that no one has changed the report—the digital equivalent of a corporate seal.[26]

Data *integrity* is a term used to indicate the information is whole and unaltered. Information can be altered maliciously, by an attacker, or accidentally, through communication and human errors. XML Signature cannot stop data from being changed, but it can immediately provide an indication that information that fell under the signature has been changed.

Once something has been published, *non-repudiation* is a concept indicating that the publisher cannot deny or refute that they published the document or that the document is valid. This is important, as events subsequent to the publication of the document may alter its meaning in a different context. For example, if a company issues a restatement, it should not be able to alter the original Web-based financial statements that contained the error.

One additional concept important to security is time-stamping. Time-stamping securely keeps track of creation and modification times of documents, informing creators and users of the version they are viewing and allowing them to verify the authority and authenticity of the document, even over time.

With tools like XML Signature and Encryption, the concepts of PAIN can be provided at the file or document level. In addition, the XML security standards permit security across and inside documents, permitting the One Report expressed in an XML language like XBRL to selectively unfold to different audiences at different times. This provides enhanced control and security features to both companies, who want to ensure they are the stewards of their content, and to end users, who want to ensure that the content they are receiving from the company is genuine and unaltered by some third-party.

Web 3.0 and Integrated Reporting

Just as Web 2.0 is a paradigm shift away from paper documents, Web 3.0 promises an even bigger advance because of its focus on integrating data from many diverse sources. During the late 1990s and early 2000s, there was much debate about what exactly the future of the Internet would be. This debate culminated largely under the banner of Web 2.0, epitomized by its modularization of Web functionality (the ability to take something quickly from one site and integrate it nearly seamlessly into your own site), the rise of user-generated content, and social media sites. Throughout this chapter, we have highlighted the impacts of many of these various Web 2.0 tools and technologies on corporate reporting and engagement and discussed how the convergence of information online and the ability of users to generate, analyze, and disseminate content has the potential to dramatically reshape the corporate reporting landscape.

New Web 3.0 digital technologies, the so-called Semantic Web, will enable both humans and machines to make complex queries across large sets of diverse data on the Web. Instead of someone asking a search engine to do a simple search query, a data browser can learn and understand the context the user is seeking in doing a query. According to Dr. Ivan Herman, Semantic Web Activity Lead for the World Wide Web Consortium,

> With the semantically-enabled web of data one could make a complex query such as "Within walking distance from the conference center and hotel where I am staying in Washington, D.C., show me the art museum with information about the Impressionist painters and recent academic articles about them; three-star restaurants with menus, pricing, phone numbers, and recent reviews from people in my social network; and the park locations and times where I can walk my dog." When public data is exposed using Semantic Web technologies, organizations and individuals will benefit from access to countless databases and content management systems worldwide. This approach maximizes the "network effect of data."[27]

This same capability is relevant to One Report. When browsers, online software suites, and search engines begin to understand and remember contextual information about a user and their requests, the type and amount of data available on the Web will have a direct relation to what is shown to the user. For example, if a user is curious about the trends in IBM's stock price and how they relate to one of the company's sustainability initiatives in Latin America, and this same user always likes viewing the data in downloadable charts and graphs, the new Web 3.0 technologies might look instantly for that type of data from IBM. However, if IBM made the decision to not post that type of data on the Web, and third parties were the only sources of that data, the user might end up getting only the third-party account as viable information. As the user makes more and more queries from a One Report perspective, the Semantic Web and artificial intelligence embedded in the Web will provide users with their own versions of One Report, whether the company is practicing it or not. Sound implausible? Some experts believe that the Web 3.0 scenarios described here are less than five years away. "Semantic Web technologies, such SKOS, RDF, OWL, and SPARQL, that help organize, describe, and query data, are already being deployed commercially," said Herman. "The next levels in the technology stack, such as rules, are just around the corner."[28]

The implication for companies is clear. As Web tools and technologies and user communities and capabilities grow, companies can choose to be in control of their content, data, and information circulating throughout the digital space, or allow third parties to represent their view in the most accessible manner. The latter will happen anyway, but we believe companies should be as proactive as possible in making sure that their own view is part of Web 3.0—and whatever the successive generations are after this. If they do, integrated reporting will enable companies to be the primary stewards of their information and message, while empowering their stakeholders to engage with the company and each other through a user-friendly, engaging, collaborative, and secure online experience.

Notes

1. For a definition of these terms see: McKinsey & Company. "How businesses are using Web 2.0: A McKinsey Global Survey," *The McKinsey Quarterly*, 2007, p. 6.
2. McKinsey & Company. "How companies are benefiting from Web 2.0," *McKinsey Global Survey Results*, 2009, p. 1.
3. Ibid., pp. 3–4.
4. Chui, Michael, Miller, Andy, and Roberts, Roger P. "Six ways to make Web 2.0 work," *The McKinsey Quarterly*, February 2009.
5. Ibid., pp. 1–2.
6. McKinsey & Company. "Building the Web 2.0 Enterprise," *The McKinsey Quarterly*, 2008, p. 10.
7. Tapscott, Don and Ticoll, David. *The Naked Corporation: How the Age of Transparency Will Revolutionize Business*. New York: Free Press, 2003. pp. 22, 25–26, xi.
8. Wheeler, David, Colbert, Barry, and Freeman, R. Edward. "Focusing on Value: Reconciling Corporate Social Responsibility, Sustainability and a

Stakeholder Approach in a Network World," *Journal of General Management*, v. 28, is. 3, 2003: 1–28, pp. 10–11.

9. Tapscott and Ticoll, p. 257.
10. Ibid., pp. 28–29.
11. Philips. "Downloads," www.annualreport2008.philips.com/downloads/index.asp, accessed August 2009.
12. HSBC. "Equator Principles," www.hsbc.com/1/2/sustainability/sustainable-finance/equator-principles, accessed September 2009.
13. Francis Sullivan, e-mail correspondence with Robert Eccles and Michael Krzus, September 10, 2009.
14. Rachael Morgan, e-mail correspondence with Robert Eccles, September 10, 2009.
15. Microsoft. "SilverLight," www.microsoft.com/Silverlight/, accessed September 2009.
16. SAP. "SAP Sustainability Collaboration Forum," https://cw.sdn.sap.com/cw/community/sustainabilityatsap/, accessed September 2009.
17. Scott Bolick, e-mail correspondence with Robert Eccles and Kyle Armbrester, September 28, 2009.
18. Mike Barry, interview with Michael Krzus, July 17, 2009.
19. Tapscott, Don and Williams, Anthony D. *Wikinomics: How Mass Collaboration Changes Everything*. New York: Penguin, 2006, p. 314, 20.
20. Timberland. "Corporate Timeline," www.timberland.com/corp/index.jsp?page=corpTimeline, accessed September 2009.
21. Timberland. "Models of Impact," www.timberland.com/corp/index.jsp?page=csr_transparency_models, accessed September 2009.
22. Beth Holzman, telephone interview with Robert Eccles and Dilyana Karadzhova, September 3, 2009.
23. Timberland, "Models of Impact."
24. The authors would like to thank Eric Cohen of PricewaterhouseCoopers for his contribution to this section and the motto.
25. W3C. "XML Security Working Group," www.w3.org/2008/xmlsec/, accessed September 2009.
26. The authors would like to thank Thomas Roessler at the World Wide Web Consortium for his succinct explanation and editing.
27. Ivan Herman, e-mail correspondence with Robert Eccles, September 22, 2009.
28. Ibid.

Chapter 8

Integrated Reporting for a Sustainable Society

A sustainable society requires rapid and broad adoption of One Report. The greater the number of companies that adopt sustainable strategies and the integrated reporting to support them, and the sooner they do so, the more sustainable our society will be. Rapid and broad adoption of high-quality integrated reporting will require innovation; support from the investment community; the development of standards; legislation and regulation; and support from civil society. In each of these, leadership by individuals, organizations, and nation states will be necessary, and technology should be leveraged as much as possible.

We are not aware of any country that has laws prohibiting integrated reporting; this means that every company is free to start doing so once it feels it is properly prepared. We urge all companies to do so as soon as is feasible. Yes, there are limitations—including some investor indifference, balancing other stakeholders' information needs between One Report and additional reporting, lack of generally accepted standards for nonfinancial information, nonfinancial information systems that need improvement, and internal coordination costs—but integrated reporting can and should be done. Any company that espouses a commitment to CSR and sustainability can and should reinforce this commitment by producing One Report.

This report should be properly *audited* to provide the same level of credibility for One Report that audited financial statements have in the capital markets. Integrated reporting requires integrated auditing. Doing this will bring the same benefit as a rigorous financial audit, ensuring the quality and integrity of a company's internal measurement and control systems. PricewaterhouseCoopers partner Klaas van den Berg remarked:

> [A]n integrated assurance report requires sustainability data which are of the same quality as the financial data. This demands a management approach that applies the same rigor to sustainability data, including monitoring and review controls. Considering the high number of indicators that companies report on in their sustainability reports, it makes sense to prioritize and focus on a limited number of Key Sustainability Indicators that are of real importance to the business. When the auditor can take these Key Sustainability Indicators in scope, providing the same level of assurance as on the financial data, there are no technical obstacles to issuing an integrated assurance report. Although unfeasible at this moment for regulatory reasons, one would expect this to be changed in the near future as integrated assurance on integrated reporting is the only imaginable way forward.[1]

Companies Must Take Responsibility

Encouragingly, there are some experts in the field of nonfinancial reporting who see that companies are starting to face up to their responsibility to make integrated reporting a reality. According to PricewaterhouseCoopers partner and former Chair of the European Sustainability Reporting Association Helle Bank Jorgensen:

> Novozymes was the first company to issue an integrated report, and I have seen growing interest in this approach since then by other companies. Interest on the part of the signatories of

the UN Principles for Responsible Investment (UN PRI) in nonfinancial information and the increasing number of countries around the world that are including nonfinancial information into their financial reporting requirements are powerful forces supporting this trend.[2]

Research by KPMG confirms this trend, although it cautioned that it is still in its early stages and noted that "integration at both the G250 and N100 level remains the exception not the rule." Forty-nine percent of the G250 and 33 percent of the N100 companies had a limited amount of integration by having a CSR section in their annual report. Eight percent of the G250 (9 percent of the N100) had their CSR reporting combined with their annual report, but only 3 percent of both groups had a fully integrated report.[3]

Integrated reporting requires the strong commitment of the CEO. He or she has the ultimate responsibility for the message the company is delivering to all of its stakeholders and for ensuring that it is a coordinated and consistent one. The decision to publish One Report can be made by the CEO, or it can be suggested by someone else in the company and then endorsed by the CEO. Other executives who have key roles to play, both in suggesting this action and in making it happen, are the Chief Operating Officer, the Chief Financial Officer, the head of investor relations, the head of corporate social responsibility (when such a position exists), the Chief Information Officer, and the head of corporate communications.

The board of directors also has a central role to play in the adoption of integrated reporting. The board is responsible for representing the interests of shareholders. The extent to which they are legally obligated to represent the interests of other stakeholders varies by country and over time. Our own view is that, legal requirements aside, directors are morally obligated to take all stakeholders' interests into account and that that they cannot properly represent shareholders without doing so. Professor Rakesh Khurana of the Harvard Business School observed that "while the ethical imperative is important, boards also have a directive toward ensuring that the company is not only meeting its short-term economic obligations, but also retains the capacity to sustain itself over the long run. As a result, it must consider the reputational implications of its decisions, as well as the legitimacy of its actions in the larger context in which it operates."[4] Since a sustainable company strategy depends upon its true commitment to a sustainable society, it is necessary for the board to ensure that all stakeholders are properly heard and, where trade-offs must be made, they are done so in a thoughtful and responsible way. Mervyn King, Chairman of South Africa's King Committee on Corporate Governance, emphasized how important this role can be and the obligation of the board:

> The mindset of boards has moved from thinking in silos of the community in which the corporation carries on business, the financial aspects of the impact of the business, and the environment. I no longer talk of the triple bottom line, but of the context of society, finance, and environment. Governance, strategy, and sustainability have become inseparable. The board of a beverage manufacturer cannot plan strategically long term as a collective good governor without ensuring access to potable water.

And, echoing the philosophy at Ricoh, he added that "People, planet, and profit are inextricably intertwined."[5]

Once the CEO has made the commitment to integrated reporting and gotten the endorsement of the board, someone must be given the responsibility to make it happen. There is no single obvious choice for facilitating the internal coordination process—as is true of any interfunctional initiative. Who plays this role will vary by company. However, and perhaps not obviously at first glance, we believe that the Corporate Communications Officer (CCO) is well-placed to play this role, as was the case at Aracruz. What is common across all the diverse types of information included in One Report is the need to effectively communicate it and to listen to the response it elicits. These are the skills of a good CCO. And since this person often reports to the CEO, he or she is in a good position to know what the company's ultimate spokesperson wants the integrated message to be and to pull together the necessary resources to make it happen. Harris Diamond, CEO of Weber Shandwick, stated, "The head of corporate communications is in a very good position to pull together everybody who is involved in external communications. While it will be a stretch for them to do this for integrated reporting, since they rarely get involved in financial reporting, this person certainly knows what it means to craft an integrated message, and their access to the CEO will give them the clout they need."[6]

Whoever plays the internal integrating role will need to have the necessary resources and support of the CEO. Assuming the necessary systems and Web platform are in place, the required resources will be mostly time and coordination costs. If the appropriate systems are not in place for measuring nonfinancial performance and for being able to integrate financial and nonfinancial information, investments will have to be made. But these are investments that should be made anyway in order to improve internal decision making. Coordination costs can be reduced by a commitment to collaborate across functions and business units. Strong and visible internal support by the CEO will help ensure that this commitment is in place.

In the end, leadership depends upon individual initiative. For this reason, we call on anyone who is reading this book who is in a position to encourage the adoption of One Report by the company they work for or any company for whom they are a stakeholder to do so. In the end, social change happens one individual at a time.

Innovation

The companies discussed in this book that are practicing One Report are certainly innovators. Efforts by companies to innovate will create opportunities for those who supply them with products and services. In some cases they will be what MIT Sloan School Professor Eric von Hippel calls "lead users," which he defined in terms of two characteristics. First, they "face needs that will be general in a marketplace—but face them months or years before the bulk of that marketplace encounters them" and second, they "are positioned to benefit significantly by obtaining a solution to those needs."[7] Identifying lead users is important for "the valuable insights they can offer regarding needs—and, often, prototype solutions—for novel products, processes, and services."[8]

Examples of where lead users in adopting integrated reporting will provide these insights for new products, processes, and services include software for measuring nonfinancial performance and integrating financial and nonfinancial information systems; models, tools, and consulting advice for better understanding the relationship between financial and nonfinancial performance; advice on internal and external communications and stakeholder engagement, including the use of Web 2.0 tools and technologies; and assurance methodologies for providing an integrated audit opinion for an integrated report. Commenting on the early adopters of integrated reporting, von Hippel observed that "while it is too early to tell if integrated reporting will become a trend, should that happen these companies will turn out to be classic lead users. Product and service providers will be able to learn from these customers and develop offerings to help other companies adopt an integrated reporting approach."[9]

Another measure that can speed adoption is that these lead users encourage their product and service providers to practice integrated reporting as well—a type of viral approach to the dissemination of this practice. An interesting example here is the private company Living PlanIT, which is designing, building, and operating research cities around the world, as it believes "that one of the greatest challenges facing our planet is to create a model for sustainable urbanization—to find a way to meet the physical, intellectual, and spiritual needs of our growing populations within urban centers that are ecologically sound."[10] The first of these cities, PlanIT Valley, is being built in northern Portugal, ultimately in partnership with thousands of companies, many of which are in the Fortune 1,000. When introduced to the concept of integrated reporting, CEO Steve Lewis responded that "integrating financial, sustainability, economic, social and technological development performance and forecasts is not an academic exercise but a business imperative. The very essence of Living PlanIT is about sustainability, so I plan to adopt the One Report idea and make it available online for comment, interaction, and analysis. I also plan to make One Report a condition of companies that are to partner with Living PlanIT."[11]

Support from the Investment Community

A common theme in this book is the mixed reaction the investment community is giving to the efforts by companies to practice more integrated reporting. Of course, the growing segment of Socially Responsible

Investment (SRI) funds, which now accounts for about 8 percent of assets under management in the United States[12] and is represented by organizations such as Eurosif and SIF, is likely to support integrated reporting, given their interest in nonfinancial information. As expressed by Lisa Woll, CEO of SIF:

> An integrated report with financial and ESG information side by side has been a priority issue for our members for many years. There is too often a disconnect between corporate investor relations and sustainability departments, which is then reflected in conflicting actions and messages. One Report forces a company to take a hard look on how sustainability issues truly intersect with its day-to-day business practices and long-term planning, and decide upon, communicate and implement a single strategy that eliminates conflicts.[13]

But just as a sustainable society requires sustainable strategies from most of its companies, it requires that a large proportion of assets under management be based on long-term investment strategies that support sustainable development, including by so-called mainstream investors (a distinction we hope will disappear one day), such as those who are signatories to the UN PRI.[14] This is the clear trend in Europe. Matt Christensen, Executive Director of Eurosif, observed:

> . . . in the European market, long-term investment strategies that support sustainable development now represent almost 20% of the total assets under management. The significant growth of Eurosif and other responsible investment initiatives in recent years reflects the mainstreaming of sustainability issues among institutional investors. What is needed now is relevant and consistent ESG data for investors—undoubtedly, a single report approach will become the trend in Europe due to growing demand and the rise of legislation in the Member States within the EU.[15]

The issue of equity investors developing a long-term view is a perennial one. The vicious circle of a focus on short-term earnings by companies and investors alike, and the managing by companies of expectations around them, "the earnings game,"[16] widely regarded as an underlying cause of our periodic financial crises, is a difficult one to break. Some investment strategies, such as those based on technical trading programs or employed by many hedge funds, are inherently short-term in nature, and they contribute important liquidity to the market. However, we believe that fund managers following declared value and growth strategies have an obligation to take a longer-term and more holistic view based on sustainability. As noted by Khurana earlier, this is best for their shareholders if they have a long-term view as well, which certainly is the case for those who have money in pension funds for their retirement. Consistent with this view, the UN Environmental Programme Financial Initiative Asset Management Working Group (UNEP FI AMWG) stated that by "by incorporating ESG considerations into the Statement of Investment Principles or Investment Policy Statement and into the investment management contract, a clear link is established between the fiduciary duties of the pension fund trustees and the asset manager as the duty to act loyally."[17]

We believe that integrated reporting will help asset managers do this, and they should encourage companies in their portfolios to provide it. Some funds may want to be even more proactive than this, such as through shareholder resolutions, an approach that is consistent with the second principle in the UN PRI to be "active owners and incorporate ESG issues into our ownership policies and practices," with shareholder resolutions being given as one example of this.[18] In a study of climate change, environmental disclosure, emissions reduction, and similar shareholder resolutions, Erin M. Reid and Michael W. Toffel have shown that these can be effective in getting companies "to agree to engage in practices consistent with the aims of a social movement."[19]

This chapter is essentially a strategy for making integrated reporting a *social movement*. Stanford Graduate School of Business Professor Hayagreeva "Huggy" Rao defined social movements as "collective endeavors to initiate social change" and noted, "they arise to reshape markets when normal incentives are inadequate and when actors are excluded from conventional channels of redress to address social costs."[20] Financial incentives for both executives and fund managers based on short-term results and the continuous struggle of all stakeholders to get companies to properly engage with them create the exact circumstances for a social movement around One Report.

There are three other things the investment community can do to help support the adoption of One Report. The first is to better integrate nonfinancial information into its analyses and investment decisions, thereby sending a clear signal to companies that integrated reporting has value. Signatories to the UN PRI are already doing this, since the first principle is "We will incorporate ESG issues into investment analysis and decision-making processes."[21] *Lead users* like these create opportunities for their service providers—such as Asset4, Bloomberg, Goldman Sachs, Innovest/Risk Metrics, KLD Analytics, and Trucost—to develop products and services to support them and then the broader investment community. The decisions resulting from this analysis will also be influenced by government policies that affect the use of resources, such as taxes and subsidies. This analysis should always be supplemented by professional judgment for such things as quality of management and robustness of the company's strategy. Second, the asset owners, such as large pension funds, must give the appropriate investment guidelines to their asset managers and establish incentive systems that reward them for long-term rather than short-term performance.

Third, asset owners and asset managers need to practice the same high levels of transparency they are requesting from companies. The International Corporate Governance Network has already issued a *Statement of Principles on Institutional Shareholder Responsibility*, one of which is "transparency and accountability" in areas such as governance and organization.[22]

We think more needs to be done. The investment community—including all of its key members such as brokerage firms, service and data vendors, and even the private partnership international accounting networks—also needs to practice the principles of integrated reporting and publish their own version of One Report in terms of both financial and nonfinancial performance and how the two are related to each other. Gunnar Miller, Head of Equity Research for RCM-Allianz Global Investors, summarized the investment community's responsibility for accelerating the adoption of integration reporting by companies:

> One has to walk the walk as well as talk the talk. Our compensation system is 70% quantitatively based on completely transparent global performance measurement standards, with a three-year trailing element on the individual investment performance scoring so as not to over-reward or penalize short-term performance, and a three-year vest on our long-term incentive plan linked to

> firm profitability targets. Echoing the standards set by our parent company, we feel that we reflect best practice in our external performance reporting. Therefore, we tend to view companies who also take leadership roles in adopting standards of disclosure which exceed local requirements in a more favorable light as investment opportunities. Information overload is a daily occupational hazard for fund managers. The desirable inclusion of nonfinancial elements in corporate reporting threatens to overwhelm us unless companies adopt a more integrated approach. The One Report concept could provide the combination of enhanced information and usability we're all looking for.[23]

Development of Standards

One of the biggest barriers cited by the investment community to incorporating nonfinancial information into their fundamental analysis is the lack of standards. We discussed this topic in some detail in Chapter 4. Here we only want to make two points. First, it would be a mistake to set these standards in isolation from those for financial reporting. Let us be clear. We are not suggesting that standards for nonfinancial information end up as part of U.S. GAAP or IFRS, although some may in time. What we *are* suggesting is that for there to be a paradigm shift to integrated reporting, we also need a paradigm shift in how measurement, reporting, and assurance standards are developed. The unnecessary complexity in financial reporting that is inhibiting transparency and the need for standards on nonfinancial metrics in order to improve transparency cannot be dealt with in isolation from each other. Both must be dealt with together. Not surprisingly, we fully endorse the recommendation of those attending the September 2009 meeting at St. James's Palace to establish an appropriate, sound, timely, and politically accountable process for bringing together those organizations that have responsibility for financial accounting and reporting with those that are widely recognized as leaders in nonfinancial reporting.

Our second point is that a process needs to be developed that will quickly lead to a convergence in standards for nonfinancial information, a process that must move more quickly than the convergence initiative between the FASB and the IASB. The reason for this is that a sustainable society is at risk, particularly in areas around climate change and water (see the section titled "Standards for Water"). Observed Jean-Philippe Desmartin, Head of SRI Research at Oddo Securities, the coming decade will be crucial for the development of these standards:

> Balanced Scorecard, DVFA/EFFAS, GRI, OECD, and SD21000—the number of international nonfinancial reporting initiatives is booming. This is good news to have access to a multiplicity of tools and to see a competition in this still experimental field. Now, let the market work before promoting a necessary standardization we shall see emerging in the period 2015–2020. From an investor point of view, the winning reporting model should and will focus on materiality and help to identify the relevant and consolidated ESG information which have an impact on business models, quality of management and financial statements.[24]

We believe that the best way to achieve this convergence is through leveraging technology in a kind of "open source" way that will bring together various groups working on frameworks and standards for reporting and assurance of nonfinancial information. In the same way that the Internet can be used for dialogue and engagement between a company and its stakeholders, so too can it be used to create a massive collaboration among all stakeholders who believe in the importance of elevating nonfinancial information to the same level as financial information, with standards being an essential part of this. Toward that end it is encouraging that Ernst Ligteringen of the GRI, arguably the most important organization in this domain, expressed the following view:

> While it is encouraging to see that the GRI Guidelines are recognized by many as an emerging global standard for sustainability reporting, we certainly don't think the job is finished and that GRI has all the answers. GRI is set up as an open network of expert stakeholders who want to improve and expand global guidance, through the GRI Reporting Guidance Framework. By extension, GRI is open and eager to collaborate with other groups—including issue-specific reporting framework providers, companies, investors and their specialist associations, government agencies, accounting professionals, and members of civil

society—who share our commitment to more integrated reporting and have critical contributions to make to its progression. The GRI Framework is intended to be a platform that consolidates different issue and user perspectives and that offers overarching guidance to reporting entities regarding legal as well as widely used and respected norms on specific aspects and indicators where these exist.[25]

Standards for Water

One of the short-term implications of climate change is the effect it will have on the availability of water. Already, large parts of the world are facing short- and long-term droughts, and determining ways to properly allocate limited water supplies among the many that need water has become a pressing social concern. Here, the "water footprint" of an individual, business, or community, defined as "the total volume of freshwater that is used to produce the goods and services consumed by the individual or community or produced by the business" has become the foundation concept for managing the Earth's water resources.[26] As with CO_2 and other greenhouse gas (GHG) emissions, there is a need for measurement and reporting standards on water. PricewaterhouseCoopers partner Jon D. Williams commented, "Water is arguably a far bigger issue than climate change, so why is reporting so far behind? That is likely to change, as water disclosure, much like carbon disclosure, grows from infancy to adulthood."[27]

Several organizations are working to develop measurement and reporting standards for water. One is the Water Footprint Network (WFN), a Dutch nonprofit foundation whose members comprise academic institutions, businesses, government agencies, international organizations, and NGOs. The mission of the WFN is to "promote the transition towards sustainable, fair, and efficient use of fresh water resources worldwide." One of the key activities supporting this mission is "developing standards (methods, guidelines, criteria) for water footprint accounting, water footprint impact assessment, and the reduction and offsetting of the negative impacts of water footprints."[28]

The International Organization for Standardization (ISO) is working in this area, as is the Alliance for Water Stewardship, "an independent, international long-term organization" that is developing "a global platform for both the development of a water stewardship system and the permanent organization to house the system" that "will house standards, oversee any certification component that is created, and will administer a branding and marketing system that recognizes and rewards successful water stewards around the world."[29]

Companies are getting actively involved as they realize that water is for the most part no longer a "free good" and its use has economic and broader social implications. Some, like BMW, discussed in Chapter 4, are beginning to report on their increasingly efficient use of this scarce resource. Companies are also recognizing that it is not simply their own use of water but how much and how and from where it is being used in their supply chain. For example, the CEOs of Aluminum Corporation of China, Coca-Cola, H&M (Hennes & Mauritz), Pepsico, SABMiller, and Siemens, among 50 others, have endorsed the CEO Water Mandate, a UN Global Compact–brokered group that is "a unique public-private initiative designed to assist companies in the development, implementation, and disclosure of water sustainability policies and practices."[30]

Despite these efforts, standards for measurement and disclosure are much less well-developed than they are for GHG emissions, and there is no formal body calling for disclosures on water the way some countries are calling for disclosures on CO_2 emissions. In fact, carbon is an exception. For water, like most resources measured in nonfinancial terms, there are a variety of competing initiatives. Ultimately, managing water on a global basis will require a single global standard for measuring and reporting on it.

Legislation and Regulation

The central regulatory question is whether integrated reporting should be mandated by law or regulation. We believe the answer is definitely *yes*, and the sooner the better. Legislation and regulation should be informed by what is being learned in practice by innovative companies that are already producing One Report. The more rapid the dissemination of this innovation on a voluntary basis, the more knowledge we will have about what should be required. This is why it is important for top executives in the world's most important and visible companies to show leadership and start producing One Report, if they are not already doing so. For the full benefit of integrated reporting to be realized, it must be adopted all over the world, by public and private companies alike. Global forums such as the G-20 could help make this happen.

No doubt exactly *when* integrated reporting is mandated will vary by country, and the regulatory bodies that drive the effort will vary as well, with securities regulatory bodies and stock exchanges being obvious possibilities. Steve Lydenberg and Katie Grace analyzed ESG disclosure initiatives in five countries (Brazil, France, Malaysia, South Africa, and Sweden), examining the varying ways government mandates and stock exchange requirements, along with business-led efforts, are now combining to increase the specifics available on ESG to the investment community.[31] "Governments are increasingly viewing ESG disclosure as a means of establishing information-rich and transparent financial markets and, through encouragement of CSR initiatives, of gaining a competitive advantage for their exchanges," according to Lydenberg.[32]

As discussed in Chapter 6, South Africa has already committed to integrated reporting; it will become a listing requirement on the Johannesburg Stock Exchange in June 2010. Other countries could soon follow South Africa's lead. Some could be those that already have the strictest standards around CSR reporting, such as Sweden, where it is required of all state-owned companies using GRI Guidelines on a "comply or explain" basis.[33] It could be in countries where there is a critical mass of companies already doing CSR reporting in a rigorous way. For example, in 2008, 128 companies in Spain produced CSR reports using the GRI Guidelines, the largest number in any country, followed by 100 in the United States, 64 in Brazil, and 56 each in Australia and the United Kingdom.[34] Finally, other early adopters could be developing countries, such as Brazil or China, that want to leapfrog the reporting practices in developed countries. In China, the State-owned Assets Supervision and Administration Commission (SASAC), which supervises the largest State-Owned Enterprises (SOEs) in China, has issued guidelines encouraging these companies to "actively integrate CSR into their business operations" and to "establish CSR reporting systems."[35] Similarly, SASAC could require SOEs to establish integrated reporting systems.

While we believe that legislation and regulation should happen soon, we believe it should be principles-based, on a "comply or explain why not" basis, so that it can be implemented in a way that is most effective in any given industry and for any given company strategy. Unlike more rules-based legislation, or regulation that prescribes very specifically what a company must do—and runs the risk of a "tick-the-box" compliance approach—a principles-based approach requires companies to make a genuine effort to comply in a way that adheres to the spirit rather than simply the letter of the law. Companies that are truly pursuing a sustainable strategy for a sustainable society will obviously do so to the best of their ability. Whether this is accomplished by the blunt instrument of legislation or the potentially more nuanced approach of regulation within existing legislative authority, some of the critical issues that need to be addressed include: (1) just how "integrated reporting" is defined in document and Web-based terms, (2) whether or not to mandate the measurement and reporting standards to be used for nonfinancial information, (3) the definition of what constitutes an integrated audit opinion and whether this must be done by a single assurance provider or can be provided by several working together, (4) what the criteria are to qualify as an assurance provider for an integrated opinion, and (5) whether any legal protections should be provided to the companies producing One Report and the firms providing an assurance opinion on it.

Finally, it should be noted that any mandate for integrated reporting is not a binary act, no more than it can be said that a company is or is not practicing integrated reporting. Integration occurs in degrees. The experience of Denmark is a good example here. In 2001, the government issued a call for companies to publish a voluntary report on their environmental activities with only the broadest of guidelines. In May 2008, the Danish government announced its policy and action plan for CSR and launched 30 specific initiatives to market Denmark as a responsible growth country.[36] On December 16, 2008, "the Danish parliament adopted a bill making it mandatory for about 1,100 of the largest businesses, listed companies and state-owned public limited companies to report on corporate social responsibility (CSR) in their annual reports."[37] However, companies not committed to CSR were simply required to state this position, and companies party to the UN Global Compact or UN PRI needed only refer to their reports for these groups.[38] Reflecting on Denmark's experience and looking into the future, Carsten Ingerslev, Head of the Danish Government Center for CSR, said, "In my point of view, the French have taken a stricter approach to CSR reporting, opting for more detailed regulation. The Danes, the United Kingdom, and the Dutch seem to have a common approach based on a more flexible law. I think there will be EU directives here in the future, possibly for integrated reporting as well, but that will take time, as much as 10 years. In the meantime, all legislation will be at the national level."[39]

Support from Civil Society

Finally, just as accelerating the broad adoption of integrated reporting requires the support of the investment community, it also requires the support of civil society. The UNEP FI AMWG report noted the importance of civil society: "Finally, civil society institutions should collectively bolster their understanding of capital markets such that they can play a full role in ensuring that capital markets are sustainable and delivering responsible ownership."[40] As with a number of terms in this book, *civil society* has many definitions. Here we will simply use this term to refer to organizations other than companies (both public and private, and including institutional investors and money managers) and government agencies.[41] Thus, it includes NGOs, professional associations (such as those of accountants, analysts, corporate communications specialists, and investor relations officers), business associations, organizations supporting better corporate governance, and investor associations.

All of these groups have an important role to play in furthering the adoption of integrated reporting. Their exact role will depend upon their place in civil society. For example, business associations can do studies and hold conferences to help create awareness and knowledge about how to do it. They can also encourage their members to adopt this practice, as the UN Global Compact companies are doing with the GRI Guidelines through a partnership they have with this organization.[42] Investor associations can make the collective view of the investment community known to the business community and relevant regulators and legislators. For example, the signatories to the UN PRI could amend the third principle regarding disclosure of ESG issues to read something like "We will seek appropriate disclosure which integrates financial and ESG performance by the entities in which we invest."[43] NGOs, representing various stakeholder groups, can ensure that their needs are heard by companies, while at the same time encouraging their members and supporters to take the same holistic and integrated view they expect of companies. Finally, all of these groups should practice integrated reporting themselves, with the meaning defined by their particular context.

Robert K. Massie, one of the founders of the GRI, expressed his view on the important role civil society has to play in creating a sustainable society:

> We all know that we live in a magnificent and intricately intertwined world. The whole of life on Earth is much, much more than the sum of whatever we are able to perceive as individuals. Each person carries this awareness deep inside, and then, because our lives are busy and complex, we often lose sight of it. When we succumb to the temptation to oversimplify, our efforts to frame and measure our actions—magnified by large organizations and out into the society—sometimes lead to painful and unintended consequences.
>
> Every generation has participated in an arduous race between our intellectual creativity, our material progress, and our recognition of the physical and moral impact of our own power and use of resources. Remarkably, history shows that, century by century, as new and diverse groups from civil society have been included, we have actually made progress. This is a cause for hope, for it suggests that the more people who take on this task, the more likely we will be able to innovate in a manner that will benefit both humanity and the special planet on which we all depend. Integrated reporting is only one example of such an innovation, but it is an important one.[44]

Every reader of this book is a member of civil society. We hope he or she cares about it being a sustainable society as well. This requires companies with sustainable strategies. Integrated reporting has an essential role to play in creating and implementing these strategies. Thus, we encourage every reader to take personal responsibility for doing whatever he or she can to make integrated reporting a social movement. It truly is time for One Report, and the sooner the better for all of us.

Notes

1. Klaas van den Berg, e-mail correspondence with Robert Eccles, September 23, 2009.
2. Helle Bank Jorgensen, e-mail correspondence with Robert Eccles, September 20, 2009.
3. KPMG. *International Survey of Corporate Responsibility Reporting 2008*, p. 17. G250 refers to the largest 250 companies in the world from *Fortune* magazine's Global 500 list for 2007, and N100 refers to the top 100 companies by revenues in each of 22 countries.
4. Rakesh Khurana, e-mail correspondence with Robert Eccles, September 28, 2009.
5. Mervyn King, e-mail correspondence with Robert Eccles, September 27, 2009.
6. Harris Diamond, e-mail correspondence with Robert Eccles, September 22, 2009.
7. von Hippel, Eric. "Lead Users: A Source of Novel Product Concepts," *Management Science*, v. 32, is. 7, 1986: 791–805, p. 796.
8. Ibid., p. 803.
9. Eric von Hippel, phone interview with Robert Eccles, September 28, 2009.
10. Living PlanIT. "About Living PlanIt," http://living-planit.com/aboutliving plani.html, accessed September 2009.
11. Steve Lewis, interview with Robert Eccles, September 13, 2009.
12. "Socially Responsible Investing (SRI) is a broad-based approach to investing that now encompasses an estimated $2.71 trillion out of $25.1 trillion in the U.S. investment marketplace today." Social Investment Forum. "Socially Responsible Investing Facts," www.socialinvest.org/resources/sriguide/srifacts.cfm, accessed September 2009.
13. Lisa Woll, e-mail correspondence with Robert Eccles, September 25, 2009.

14. For a list of signatories, see: Principles for Responsible Investment. "Signatories to the Principles for Responsible Investment," www.unpri.org/signatories/, accessed September 2009.
15. Matt Christensen, e-mail correspondence with Robert Eccles, September 28, 2009.
16. See Chapter 4, "The Earnings Game," in: Eccles, Robert G., Herz, Robert H., Keegan, E. Mary, and Phillips, David M. H. *The Value Reporting Revolution: Moving Beyond the Earnings Game*. New York: John Wiley & Sons, 1999.
17. Asset Management Working Group, United Nations Environment Programme Finance Initiative. Fiduciary responsibility: Legal and practical aspects of integrating environmental, social and governance issues into institutional investment, July 2009, p. 27.
18. Principles for Responsible Investment. "The Principles for Responsible Investment," www.unpri.org/principles/, accessed September 2009.
19. Reid, Erin M. and Toffel, Michael W. "Responding to Public and Private Politics: Corporate Disclosure of Climate Change Strategies," *Strategic Management Journal*, v. 30, is. 11, 2009: 1157–1178, p. 1171.
20. Rao, Hayagreeva. *Market Rebels: How Activists Make or Break Radical Innovations*. Princeton: Princeton University Press, 2009, p. 7.
21. "The Principles for Responsible Investment."
22. International Corporate Governance Network. *Statement of Principles on Institutional Shareholder Responsibilities*, 2007. www.icgn.org/files/icgn_main/pdfs/best_practice/inst_share_responsibilities/2007_principles_on_institutional_shareholder_responsibilities.pdf, accessed September 2009.
23. Gunnar Miller, e-mail correspondence with Robert Eccles, September 29, 2009.
24. Jean-Philippe Desmartin, e-mail correspondence with Robert Eccles and Michael Krzus, September 16, 2009.
25. Ernst Ligteringen, e-mail correspondence with Robert Eccles, September 14, 2009.
26. Water Footprint Network. "Introduction," www.waterfootprint.org/?page=files/home, accessed September 2009. The concept of the water footprint was developed by Professor Arjen Y. Hoekstra, Scientific Director of the Water Footprint Network.
27. Jon D. Williams, e-mail correspondence with Robert Eccles, September 20, 2009.
28. Water Footprint Network. "About WFN: Mission," www.waterfootprint.org/?page=files/WFN-mission, accessed September 2009.

29. International Organization for Standardization. "TC 207/SC 5," www.iso.org/iso/iso_technical_committee.html?commid=54854; Alliance for Water Stewardship. "Fact Sheet," 2008, www.allianceforwaterstewardship.org/about_pdfs/About_AWS/AWSFact_Sheet.pdf, both accessed September 2009.

30. United Nations Global Compact. "Environment: CEO Water Mandate," www.unglobalcompact.org/Issues/Environment/CEO_Water_Mandate/, accessed September 2009.

31. Lydenberg, Steve and Grace, Katie. *Innovations in Social and Environmental Disclosure Outside the United States*, Prepared for Domini Social Investments, November 2008.

32. Steve Lydenberg, e-mail correspondence with Robert Eccles, September 21, 2009.

33. Ministry of Enterprise, Energy and Communications. *Guidelines for External Reporting by State-Owned Companies*. www.sweden.gov.se/content/1/c6/09/41/25/56b7ebd4.pdf, accessed September 2009.

34. Global Reporting Initiative. "Number of companies worldwide reporting on their sustainability performance reaches record high, yet still a minority," press release, July 15, 2009, www.globalreporting.org/NewsEventsPress/PressResources/PressRelease_14_July_2006_1000GRIReports.htm, accessed September 2009. This count is based on voluntary submissions by companies to GRI in which certain criteria have been met to qualify the report as being based on their guidelines. Thus, it is a minimum estimate of the number of companies producing CSR reports since not all of them may bring this to the attention of the GRI.

35. Syntao. "CSR Guideline for State-Owned Enterprises (SOE)," www.syntao.com/E_Page_Show.asp?Page_ID=6407, accessed September 2009.

36. The Danish Government. *Action Plan for Corporate Social Responsibility*, May 2008, pp. 7–9. www.eogs.dk/graphics/Samfundsansvar.dk/Dokumenter/Action_plan_CSR.pdf, accessed September 2009.

37. Danish Commerce and Companies Agency. *Reporting on Corporate Social Responsibility: An Introduction for Supervisory Boards*, 2009, p. 5. www.eogs.dk/graphics/publikationer/CSR/Reporting_CSR_L5_UK_05.pdf, accessed September 2009.

38. Danish Commerce and Companies Agency. *About the Danish law: Report on social responsibility for large businesses*, December 2008. www.eogs.dk/graphics/Samfundsansvar.dk/Dokumenter/About%20the%20Danish%20law.pdf, September 2009.

39. Carsten Ingerslev, interview with Michael Krzus and Susan Thyne, September 15, 2009.

40. Asset Management Working Group, United Nations Environment Programme Finance Initiative, p. 11.
41. For an expanded definition of civil society, see: Centre for Civil Society, London School of Economics. "Introduction: About the Centre," www.lse.ac.uk/collections/CCS/introduction/default.htm#generated-subheading6, accessed September 2009.
42. United Nations Global Compact. "UN Global Compact and Global Reporting Initiative Form Strategic Alliance," news release, October 6, 2006, www.unglobalcompact.org/NewsandEvents/news_archives/2006_10_06.html, accessed October 2009.
43. The third principle reads "We will seek appropriate disclosure on ESG issues by the entities in which we invest."
44. Robert K. Massie, e-mail correspondence with Robert Eccles and Michael Krzus, September 28, 2009.

Appendix A

Companies and Organizations with URLs

AccountAbility	www.accountability21.net
Allianz Group	www.allianz.com/en/index.html
American Institute of Certified Public Accountants	www.aicpa.org
Aracruz (now part of Fibria)	www.fibria.com.br
Association of Chartered Certified Accountants	www.accaglobal.com
Bloomberg	www.bloomberg.com
BMW Group	www.bmwgroup.com
Business for Social Responsibility	www.bsr.org
Carbon Disclosure Project	stage.cdproject.net
Ceres	www.ceres.org
Climate Disclosure Standards Board	www.cdsb-global.org
Dow Jones Sustainability Index	www.sustainability-index.com
DVFA	www.effas.com/germany
European Commission	http://ec.europa.eu/index_en.htm
European Sustainable Investment Forum	www.eurosif.org
Federation of European Accountants	www.fee.be
Financial Accounting Standards Board	www.fasb.org
Global Accounting Alliance	www.globalaccountingalliance.com
Global Reporting Initiative	www.globalreporting.org

Goldman Sachs	www2.goldmansachs.com
HSBC	www.hsbc.com
Institute of Chartered Accountants in England and Wales	www.icaew.com
International Accounting Standards Board	www.iasb.org
International Corporate Governance Network	www.icgn.org
International Federation of Accountants	www.ifac.org
Living PlanIT	www.living-planit.com
Marks & Spencer	www.marksandspencer.com
Microsoft	www.microsoft.com/en/us/default.aspx
Natura	www2.natura.net
Novartis	www.novartis.com
Novo Nordisk	www.novonordisk.com
Novozymes	www.novozymes.com/en
OECD	www.oecd.org/home
Philips	www.usa.philips.com
PricewaterhouseCoopers	www.pwc.com
Public Company Accounting Oversight Board	www.pcaobus.org
Ricoh	www.ricoh.com
SAP	www.sap.com
Securities and Exchange Commission	www.sec.gov
Social Investment Forum	www.socialinvest.org
Target	www.target.com
The Prince's Accounting for Sustainability Project	www.accountingforsustainability.org
Timberland	www.timberland.com
U.K. Financial Reporting Council	www.frc.org.uk
UNEP Financial Initiative Asset Management Working Group	www.unepfi.org
UN Global Compact	www.unglobalcompact.org
United Nations Environment Programme	www.unep.org
United Technologies Corporation	www.utc.com
Van Gansewinkel Group	www.vangansewinkel.eu/en/default.aspx
World Business Council for Sustainable Development	www.wbcsd.org
World Economic Forum	www.weforum.org/en/index.htm
World Resources Institute	www.wri.org
World Wide Web Consortium	www.w3.org

Appendix B

Acronyms

A4S	Accounting for Sustainability
AICPA	American Institute of Certified Public Accountants
CDSB	Carbon Disclosure Standards Board
CDP	Carbon Disclosure Project
CSR	corporate social responsibility
DVFA	Society of Investment Professionals in Germany
EH&S	environment, health, and safety
ESG	environmental, social and governance
Eurosif	European Sustainable Investment Forum
FASB	Financial Accounting Standards Board (United States)
FRC	Financial Reporting Council (United Kingdom)
GAA	Global Accounting Alliance
GAAP	Generally Accepted Accounting Principles (United States)
GRI	Global Reporting Initiative
IFAC	International Federation of Accountants
ISA	International Standards of Auditing
IASB	International Accounting Standards Board
ICAEW	Institute of Chartered Accountants in England and Wales

IFRS	International Financial Reporting Standards
IP	intellectual property
IPO	initial public offering
KPI	key performance indicator
MD&A	Management's Discussion and Analysis
NGO	nongovernmental organization
OECD	Organization for Economic Cooperation and Development
PCAOB	Public Company Accounting Oversight Board
PwC	PricewaterhouseCoopers
SCEBR	Special Committee on Enhanced Business Reporting
SEC	Securities and Exchange Commission
SIF	Social Investment Forum
UTC	United Technologies Corporation
XBRL	eXtensible Business Reporting Language
XII	XBRL International, Inc.

Index